Quasi Person

The Week 24 Abortion Watershed

By

Pnina Lifshitz-Aviram

Quasi Person: The Week 24 Abortion Watershed

By Pnina Lifshitz-Aviram

This book first published 2024

Ethics International Press Ltd, UK

British Library Cataloguing in Publication Data

A catalogue record for this book is available from the British Library

Print Book ISBN: 978-1-80441-348-7

eBook ISBN: 978-1-80441-349-4

Dedication

To my beloved children:
Vered, Amir, Alon, Erez

To my beloved grandchildren:

Maya, Adam, Ella, Yoav, Adi, Ofir, Romi, Aviv and Liv

You bring boundless happiness and joy to my life
Taking me on remarkable physical, mental, and emotional journeys.
Each one of you holds a significant place in my heart.
Thank you

I would like to thank my Academic home, Zefat Academic College, for ongoing support in my research and the long conceiving process of this book.

Table of Contents

Chapter 1
Introduction

Abortion (after week 24, induced termination of pregnancy) is a highly charged and controversial issue involving medical, moral, ethical, and religious questions. On one side are those who claim that abortion is an expression of a woman's right over her body; and on the other side are those who see the fetus as a living being entitled to the protection of its life. In practice, different countries restrict abortion in different ways in their legislation. It is known that abortion can affect women who undergo it, both physically and mentally. It is important, therefore, to stimulate public debate about both the theoretical and practical aspects of the issue, so that abortions are properly regulated and supervised.

Since the 1950s, a process of liberalization has been underway in Western countries, which resulted in a decline in abortion-related morbidity and mortality.[1] The *Dobbs* ruling of the US Supreme Court, in 2023, has raised concern that if abortions are restricted, a black market of unsupervised abortions may develop, increasing the number of complications and mortality rates. In most countries, restrictions on abortion depend on the stage of pregnancy.

It is common to divide pregnancy into three trimesters of about three months each. In this book, I divide pregnancy into two periods: the first, up to the viability stage, and the second, from week 24 of pregnancy onward, which is the stage of the viable fetus. The book does not deal with the first period and the dilemmas concerning abortion at this stage. It focuses instead on the rights of the fetus in the second period, the viable stage. I do not dispute the fact that in case of danger to the woman or her health, her life takes precedence over that of the fetus,

---

[1] Pinter at al., "Accessibility and availability of abortion in six European countries," The European Journal of Contraception and Reproductive Health Care, March 2005, 10 (1): pp. 51-58.

and I do not dispute the fact that if there is a concern for the life or health of the fetus, an abortion can be performed in the second period as well.

Since it is not possible to discuss the human rights of the fetus during the viable stage without reviewing the legislation concerning the first period, I provide a brief overview of the situation in the US and Israel. Until the mid-19th century, there were no restrictions on abortion in the US, and they were carried out quite freely. From that time until the 1960s, most states began imposing restrictions on abortion. In 1973, two groundbreaking abortion decisions were handed down by the US Supreme Court: *Roe v. Wade* and *Doe v. Bolton,* which for the first time in American history recognized the constitutional right of a woman to abort her fetus, making abortion legal in all 50 states. Sixteen years later, this right was reinforced by the Supreme Court ruling that a woman seeking to end her pregnancy does not need to first secure the approval of her parents or husband *(Planned Parenthood v. Casey*).

Opponents of abortion in the US did not accept these rulings and waged a legal and political struggle for nearly 50 years, culminating on June 24, 2022, when the Court issued its new ruling in *Dobbs v. Jackson. Dobbs* overruled *Roe v. Wade* and held that the US Constitution did not confer a right to abortion, returning the right to decide to the states. *Dobbs* concerned a Mississippi law banning abortion after the 15th week of pregnancy. The Court, with Justice Samuel Alito writing for the six-justice majority, ruled that the Mississippi law was legal and that *Roe v. Wade* and *Planned Parenthood v. Casey* (upholding abortion as an essential right) were invalid. Four judges concurred with his verdict. Chief Justice, John Roberts, wrote a separate opinion, arguing that the part of the *Roe* ruling that prevents states from banning abortions before the fetus can survive outside the womb should be overturned. He concluded that the Mississippi law was legal, but did not wish to overturn *Roe* in its entirety. Three justices, identified with the liberal element of the Court, dissented from the majority ruling, which upheld laws in 13 states that made abortions illegal.

Dobbs has again ignited intense public and political passions. In its wake, the US and other parts of the world are wracked more than ever by the controversy about the right to abortion and the conflict between the right of women to autonomy and the right, if any, of the fetus to life. For example, opponents of abortion in the US are now seeking to pass a federal law prohibiting abortions in all 50 states and five US permanent territories.

Some believe that the *Dobbs* decision will result in some women being forced to continue their pregnancy against their will, which will affect the US not only ethically but also economically. They argue that providing access to abortions is better for the American economy because it results in more women working outside the home and studying, which is expected to increase their earning potential. One of these was US Secretary of the Treasury, Janet Yellen, in her testimony before the Senate Banking Committee.

Some, like Daphna Hacker, believe that the ruling turns *The Handmaid's Tale* into reality. In her opinion, *Dobbs* is shocking by any basic democratic measure. She criticizes the ruling for allowing states to prevent access to abortion even in the early stages of pregnancies, in the case of pregnancies of minors and those resulting from rape or incest, and pregnancies that endanger the life of the woman. I disagree with Hacker. *Dobbs* did not turn the US into the Republic of Gilead nor does it hold that the fetus has more rights than the woman. Rather, it permits state legislatures to limit the range of abortion choices that until now were understood to be a constitutionally protected right.

Assessing the ruling strictly from the economic perspective, as Yellen does, is fundamentally mistaken. In my opinion, it is a shame that the opportunity to legislate rules that emphasize the moral or even human rights of the fetus has not been used to discuss the issue of abortion more broadly and substantively. There is normative value in the life of the fetus, especially at the stage when it can live outside the womb, even if it falls short of human life.

This book uses the language of rights and argues that the viable fetus should be granted human or quasi-human rights that under given circumstances can take precedence over those of the mother (for example, the women's right to smoke or use drugs while carrying the fetus). When the life and health of the fetus are examined from the point of view of rights, the fetus, or someone on its behalf, can demand compensation for neglect in the way it was treated. This position has broad implications. What happens if the woman fails to conduct genetic testing early and a defect is detected later, at the viable stage? Where lies the woman's responsibility and what are the rights of the fetus? Technological changes that affect the survivability of fetuses should be reflected in legal changes that affect their rights. The book seeks to define the status of the viable fetus, which is below that of a living person but it should not be nil. Granting the fetus some form of legal status would make it possible to weigh it along with other factors in deciding whether or not to abort. The solution presented in the book is not acceptable to those who hold a firm opinion that the woman has absolute rights to autonomy and self-definition during all stages of pregnancy. The book argues that the state has a responsibility also toward the viable fetus and that abortion of the viable fetus should be preventable even if the fetus has no concrete legal status but it does have rights. If abortion is perceived as a violation of the right of the fetus to be born, it justifies the intervention of the state. In other words, despite the woman's right to autonomy over her body, the right of the fetus to be born and to be born healthy should prevail over the woman's right to bodily autonomy. The book does not accept a woman's right to such sweeping autonomy during the period when the fetus can survive outside the womb. It argues that a woman has the right to perform an abortion up to week 24, an argument that remains valid even if the fetus has a moral right to live and its life has normative value. But even a fetus that is formed as a result of violence, such as incest or rape, has the right to be born and to live if it can survive outside the womb. If necessary, regulatory solutions should be devised by the welfare authorities for infants born as a result of these types of relations.

* * *

The cry of our ancestress Rachel, "Give me children, else I die," (Genesis 30:1), mentioned by my colleague Justice Tal in his opinion, the silent cry of Hannah "speaking in her heart, only her lips moved, but her voice was not heard" (I Samuel 1:13) and praying "for this child" (I Samuel 1: 27) and countless other cases in our literature and that of other nations powerfully express the force of the yearning for a child, one probably unrivaled in its intensity. This yearning reflects the will of humans to continue their personal physical and spiritual existence, and that of their family and people, through their descendants. It reflects the aspiration of humanity to realize each individual's potential and even fulfill dreams that have not yet been realized. It encompasses each individual's love for his descendants, those who have been born and those as yet unborn; a love of "would that I had died in your stead, (II Samuel 19: 1)," a love even stronger than one's instinct to preserve one's own life.[2,3]

These are the words of Justice Y. Turkel in the Israeli case of *Nahmani v. Nahmani* nearly twenty years ago. Is the primal yearning for a child indeed a pure and simple desire, regardless of sex, height, appearance,

---

[2] CFH 2401/95 Nahmani v. Nahmani, Israel Law Reports [1995–6] 1, 84–85 http://ww3.lawschool.comell.edu/AvonResources/RuthNahmaniv.DanielNahmani.pdf. For a discussion of this landmark verdict in the context of abortion, *see, for example*, Noga Morag-Levine, *Imported Problem Definitions, Legal Culture and the Local Dynamics of Israeli Abortion Politics*, 5(2–3) ISRAEL AFFAIRS 226 (1998); Daphne Barak-Erez & Ron Shapira, *The Delusion of Symmetric Rights*, 19(2) OXFORD JOURNAL OF LEGAL STUDIES 297 (1999); Dalia Dorner, *Human Reproduction: Reflections on the Nachmani Case*, 35 TEX. INT'L L. J. 1 (2000).

[3] I use the term "destruction" deliberately because I ascribe a great deal of significance to terminating pregnancies. I assume that conservatives who are against terminating pregnancies would support the use of this term whereas those favoring termination at any stage would reject its use, at least when referring to the first trimester. I think that when dealing with the stage of viability, when the fetus could technically live outside the womb, those with liberal attitudes may agree that the expression "fetal destruction" is not far off the mark. For an overview of the relation between this notion and the stage of viability, *see* Patrick T. Conley & Robert J. McKenna, *The Supreme Court on Abortion A Dissenting Opinion*, 19 CATH. LAW. 19 (1973); Jeffrey A. Parness, *Crimes Against the Unborn: Protecting and Respecting the Potentiality of Human Life*, 22 HARV. J. LEGIS. 97 (1985); Nancy K. Rhoden, *Trimesters and Technology: Revamping* Roe v. Wade, 95 YALE L.J. 639 (1985–86).

or fitness? Or is there today, instead, a desire for a healthy, "perfect" child? What lies behind the term "perfect" or "healthy"? Do the rights of a viable fetus, whatever its flaws, have a proper value and deserve legal protection by society and the law at a time when the fetus can be treated by medicine as a patient? Or is it rather respect for the woman, her freedom, and her autonomy to choose the child she brings into the world who represents her personal values that require social and legal protection?

I assume that a pregnancy exists, planned or unplanned, and that the woman has decided to end it and destroy the viable fetus. The discussion takes into account that the reasons for the woman's decision involve not only the fetus, its state of health, genetic profile, sex, or facial features, but also factors relating to the woman herself: her desires, convenience, financial state, mental state, and more. This book is not about the right of the woman to terminate a pregnancy that came about against her will as a result of a violent act, such as incest or rape. In cases like these, the pregnancy is terminated in the first or second trimester. The debate concerns more than the rights of the woman and the fetus — I want to stimulate a discussion about ethics, philosophy, and the law. Whose rights should be more strongly defended in any society, those of the woman or those of the fetus? When and under what conditions should this life in the making be protected? Does the fetus have a natural right to life? Should a balance be struck between the rights?

The law does not exist in a vacuum. To be effective, it must be based on the foundations of the values and traditions of society. The issue of abortion is acute yet enduring and complex, and it needs to be addressed comprehensively, especially now, when it will be raised continually in the US at both state and federal levels.

If a person's identity (that is, genetic attributes) is established at the moment of conception and if human beings are the sum of their genetic characteristics, a fetus is human at the moment of conception, and *a fortiori* a live being.[4] If human identity begins to form only during the developmental stage when it can exist outside the womb as a "viable fetus,"[5] it is viability that grants it the right to life. Finally, if the fetus is a human being with rights only from the moment of birth, it cannot be said to have any rights during pregnancy. But if a human identity forms when the brain starts becoming active, i.e., in the sixth week after conception, I submit that the fetus is human even before becoming a viable fetus.

Could the courts adopt the attitude that the viable fetus has full rights? Could it be claimed that the rights of a viable fetus are equivalent to those of a living child? Is there a chance that the legal system would determine that in certain cases, taking all questions surrounding a pregnancy into consideration (including the rights of the woman and her best interests), they would consider the rights and best interests of the viable fetus? Is it appropriate to make an analogy between a child and a viable fetus? It seems unlikely that the system will go so far as to give preference to the rights of "beginning life" or even that of a viable fetus over human rights.[6]

---

[4] Catholics are traditionally opposed to abortion at any stage of pregnancy, from the moment of conception, because they maintain that a human being is created at that moment. *See, e.g.*, John T. Jr. Noonan, *Abortion and the Catholic Church: A Summary History*, 12 NAT. L.F. 85 (1967); Rishona Fleishman, *The Battle against Reproductive Rights: The Impact of the Catholic Church on Abortion Law in Both International and Domestic Areas*, 14 EMORY INT'L L. REV. 277 (2000); TIMOTHY BYRNES & MARY C. SEGERS, THE CATHOLIC CHURCH AND THE POLITICS OF ABORTION: A VIEW FROM THE STATES (1991).

[5] For the correlation between the definition of a viable fetus and the woman's right to abort it, *see* Stephen G. Gilles, *Does the Right to Elective Abortion Include the Right to Ensure the Death of the Fetus*, 49 U. RICH. L. REV. 1009 (2014–15); DOROTHY E. MCBRIDE & JENNIFER L. KEYS, ABORTION IN THE UNITED STATES: A REFERENCE HANDBOOK (2d ed. 2018); Lawrence Nelson, *Provider Conscientious Refusal of Abortion, Obstetrical Emergencies, and Criminal Homicide Law*, 18(7) AMERICAN JOURNAL OF BIOETHICS 43 (2018).

[6] For a discussion of the correlation between the "beginning of life" and human rights, *see* Rhonda Copelon et al., *Human Rights Begin at Birth: International Law and the Claim of Fetal Rights*, 13(26) REPRODUCTIVE HEALTH MATTERS 120 (2005); Kathleen Chambers & Paul Buka, *The Beginning of Life to Adulthood: Human Rights*, in PATIENTS' RIGHTS, LAW AND ETHICS FOR NURSES: A PRACTICAL GUIDE 49 (Paul Buka ed., 2d ed. 2014); Catarina

Today, until the seventh week, pregnancy can be terminated by taking a pill. Terminations from the eighth to the twenty-fourth week are carried out by dilatation and curettage. This is not the case when terminating the pregnancy of a viable fetus beyond the twenty-fourth week. At this stage, because the fetus can survive *ex utero,* the procedure, commonly referred to as inducing childbirth,[7] is also known as feticide.

In this book, I discuss only the acute dilemma of whether a viable fetus has a right to be born healthy at the stage of viability, in light of the latest technological developments.[8] Among the scholarship I discuss is the important work of the legal scholar, Judith Thomson, an abortion advocate, who contends that even stipulating that the fetus has a moral status similar to that of a person in no way infringes on a woman's right to terminate a pregnancy. Thomson additionally asserts that the right to life does not include the prerogative to ensure life[9] because it is unreasonable to conclude that the right to life always prevails. This highly respected and well-reasoned argument begins with a metaphorical scenario of pregnancy:

Delaunay, *The Beginning of Human Life at the Laboratory: The Challenges of a Technological Future for Human Reproduction,* 40 TECHNOLOGY IN SOCIETY 14 (2015).

[7] For the connection between the definitions of feticide and childbirth, *see* Dennis J. Horan & Thomas J. Marzen, *The Moral Interest of the State in Abortion Funding: A Comment on Beal, Maher & (and) Poelker,* 22 ST. LOUIS U. L.J. 566 (1979); John A. Robertson, *Procreative Liberty and the Control of Conception, Pregnancy, and Childbirth,* 69(3) VIRGINIA L. REV. 405 (1983); Nancy K. Rhoden, *The New Neonatal Dilemma: Live Births from Late Abortions,* 72 GEO. L. J. 1451 (1984).

[8] My credo is based on authoritative cases such as *Roe v. Wade,* 410 U.S. 113 (1973), where the US Supreme Court allowed abortions to be performed in the first trimester, limited abortions in the second trimester, and prohibited them entirely during the third trimester. *See also* Donald H. Regan, *Rewriting* Roe v. Wade, 77(7) MICHIGAN L. REV. 1569 (1979); WHAT *ROE V. WADE* SHOULD HAVE SAID: THE NATION'S TOP LEGAL EXPERTS REWRITE AMERICA'S MOST CONTROVERSIAL DECISION (JACK M. BALKIN ED., 2005); N. E. H. HULL & PETER CHARLES HOFFER, *ROE V. WADE*: THE ABORTION RIGHTS CONTROVERSY IN AMERICAN (2010).

[9] Judith J. Thomson, RIGHTS, RESTITUTION, AND RISK: ESSAYS IN MORAL THEORY vii–x (1986); Judith J. Thomson, *A Defense of Abortion,* 1 Phil. & Pub. Aff. 47 (1971); THE ETHICS OF ABORTION 30 (Robert M. Baird & Stuart E. Rosenbaum eds., 1989).

> You wake up in the morning and find yourself back to back in bed with an unconscious violinist. A famous unconscious violinist. He has been found to have a fatal kidney ailment, and the Society of Music Lovers has canvassed all the available medical records and found that you alone have the right blood type to help. They have therefore kidnapped you, and last night the violinist's circulatory system was plugged into yours, so that your kidney can be used to extract poisons from his blood as well as your own. The director of the hospital now tells you "Look, we're sorry the Society of Music Lovers did this to you—we would never have permitted it if we had known. But still, they did it, and the violinist now is plugged into you. To unplug you would be to kill him. But never mind, it's only for nine months. By then he will have recovered from his ailment, and can safely be unplugged from you. Is it morally incumbent on you to accede to this situation?

Even if there is an element of reality in this description, there remains the question of what should be the paramount factor when making a decision about the rights of a viable fetus and its best interests. Is it possible to establish that its best interests involve terminating the process of its development, so it won't be born with a defect?

Does it have a right to be born even if it will suffer from an impairment or a defect? Should the severity of the impairment or defect be considered when deciding to terminate a pregnancy? Can it be determined that it is in the best interests of the fetus not to be born to a woman who does not want it, either because of its looks or any other reason? Should the thread of its future life be severed because of the rights of others? Thomson claims that even conceding that the fetus has a right to live, and that the termination renders this right null and void, does not always mean that a life-stopping act is necessarily prohibited at a moral level. She maintains that the moral status of the fetus does not affect the morality of a decision to terminate or not to terminate a pregnancy, as in the above case of the violinist.[10] This view may be justifiable when the pregnancy is the result of rape or incest, but not otherwise. Thomson maintains that just as the act of unplugging the man from the violinist may seem moral to the majority of people because the violinist was attached to him without his consent, a woman's decision to detach from the fetus is equally moral. Thomson's comparison between the man in her story and a woman whose pregnancy was forced upon her may have validity. But in the case when a pregnancy was not the result of the use of force, the analogy is not valid, and Thomson's conclusion cannot be supported. Lawmakers must balance the competing rights of the mother and fetus. A pregnant woman is a person with legal capacity. She carries the fetus in her womb, where it breathes, is nourished, and develops. At times, the woman deliberately became pregnant and wanted the child and at other times she became pregnant by chance and did not want it.[11] Following Thomson's line of reasoning, given the woman's legal capacity and her rights as a human being recognized by law, the lawmaker should allow her to terminate a pregnancy whenever she likes and for any reason.

The viable fetus faces the pregnant woman and her rights with barely a legal leg to stand on.[12] Until the *Dobbs* decision, the fetus was not considered at all. Even after Dobbs it has no legal rights but is seen as

---

[10] For a discussion of her perception, *see, for example*, Keith J. Pavlischek, *Abortion Logic and Paternal Responsibilities: One More Look at Judith Thomson's "A Defense of Abortion,"* 7(4) PUBLIC AFFAIRS QUARTERLY 341 (1993); David Boonin-Vail, *A Defense of "A Defense of Abortion": On the Responsibility Objection to Thomson's Argument*, 107(2) ETHICS 286 (1997); Eric Wiland, *Unconscious Violinists and the Use of Analogies in Moral Argument*, 22 JOURNAL OF MEDICAL ETHICS 466 (2000).

[11] For the possible correlation between having sex and taking responsibility for the resulting pregnancy and birth, *see* Holly Smith, *Intercourse and Moral Responsibility for the Fetus*, in ABORTION AND THE STATUS OF THE FETUS 229 (William B. Bonderson et al. eds., 1983); Harry S. Silverstein, *On a Woman's "Responsibility" for the Fetus*, 13(1) SOCIAL THEORY AND PRACTICE 103 (1987); Alec Walen, *Consensual Sex without Assuming the Risk of Carrying an Unwanted Fetus: Another Foundation for the Right to an Abortion*, 63 BROOK. L. REV. 1051 (1997).

[12] For the generally problematic status of the fetus, *see, e.g.*, Bonderson et al., *supra* note 10; Gary B. Gertler, *Brain Birth: A Proposal for Defining When a Fetus Is Entitled to Human Life Status*, 59 S. CAL. L. REV. 1061 (1986); BONNIE STEINBOCK, LIFE BEFORE BIRTH: THE MORAL AND LEGAL STATUS OF EMBRYOS AND FETUSES (2011).

existing physically but minimally, entirely dependent on the woman. Following *Dobbs*, each state can consider whether and at what point a fetus has rights. Some consider_the fetus "hardly a person" inside a person; others consider it as "the beginnings of a person" inside a person.[13] By contrast, I maintain that the definition of the status of the fetus reflects the context in which the person defining this status perceives what is being defined. For example, I define the fetus at the viable stage as a person with moral or even human rights. I believe that even those who take a feminist viewpoint, according to which the woman's right to terminate a pregnancy is intrinsic to her rights as an autonomous person, would agree that, at the very least, a viable fetus is a "life beginning." I hope that defining the viable fetus as a "human beginning" with its own rights can be the beam that lights up the depths of our understanding of both ethics and the law. I argue that the viable fetus should receive the status of "almost" a person with the rights of a human being in the process of formation.

Diverse jurisdictions have chosen different ways to balance the rights of the woman against those of the fetus. Before the *Roe v. Wade* decision, some preferred the "life beginning" definition of the fetus and did not allow women to terminate the pregnancy at any stage; others gave preference to the autonomy of the woman over her body and her right to self-determination, allowing her to terminate the pregnancy at any stage, including the viable stage;[14] others yet chose a middle ground that takes the age of the fetus into consideration, its ability to survive outside the womb, and its state of maturity at the time the decision is made to terminate the pregnancy. Now, with *Roe v. Wade* no longer the

---

[13] For strong disagreement, *see* Jeffrey A. Parness, *Crimes Against the Unborn: Protecting and Respecting the Potentiality of Human Life*, 22 HARV. J. LEGIS. 97 (1985); John A. Robertson, *In the Beginning: The Legal Status of Early Embryos*, 76(3) VIRGINIA L. REV. 437 (1990); Jed Rubenfeld, *On the Legal Status of the Proposition That "Life Begins at Conception,"* 43(3) STAN. L. REV. 599 (1991).

[14] This is better known as the "pro-life" vs. the "pro-choice" debate. *See, for example,* RUTH COLKER, ABORTION AND DIALOGUE: PRO-CHOICE, PRO-LIFE, AND AMERICAN LAW (1992); KATHY RUDY, BEYOND PRO-LIFE AND PRO-CHOICE: MORAL DIVERSITY IN THE ABORTION DEBATE (1997); RANDY ALCORN, PROLIFE ANSWERS TO PRO-CHOICE ARGUMENTS (2009).

law, each state can make these complex decisions again, and intense discussions will be held at the state and national levels. In this book, often resorting to the example of Israel, I show why all jurisdictions should choose the middle ground where a balancing test between the rights of the woman and of the beginning life is applied to any woman who wants to terminate a pregnancy.

The high rate of pregnancy terminations should set off alarm bells. We are living in an era of advanced technology, including scientific developments in the field of the human genome and other techniques that enable cloning,[15] stem-cell removal, IVF, identification of fetal defects, choice of the sex of the fetus, evaluation of the state of its health, genetic testing for fetal health and the physical characteristics of an embryo before it has been implanted in a mother's womb. Various types of genetic testing are available throughout the duration of pregnancy. Because of the ease of access to these technological advances and the vast amount of information available at the click of a mouse, many legal, social, ethical, and moral dilemmas about this issue are more palpable than ever. The development of technology that enables access to abundant information about the fetus and the viable fetus in the course of pregnancy gives women increasing information that may prompt them to exercise their right to autonomy and terminate the pregnancy. This represents a threat to the rights of the viable fetus and raises the real and imminent danger that it will result in racial and other profiling.[16]

---

[15] For the recent discussion of this cutting-edge biomedical innovation, *see* Henry T. Greely, *Human Reproduction in the Twenty-First Century*, 1(2) JOURNAL OF POSTHUMAN STUDIES 205 (2017); Arthur L. Caplan, *Monkey See, Humans Won't Do—The Misguided Reaction to the First Cloning of Primates*, EMBO REPORTS (2018), http://embor.embopress.org/content/early/2018/02/21/embr.201845912.full; Shai Lavi, *Cloning International Law: The Science and Science Fiction of Human Cloning and Stem-Cell Patenting*, 14(1) LAW, CULTURE AND THE HUMANITIES 83 (2018).

[16] For a discussion of this concern in relation to abortion, *see* Rene Bowser, *Racial Profiling in Health Care: An Institutional Analysis of Medical Treatment Disparities*, 7 MICH. J. RACE & L. 79 (2001–02); Albert W. Alschuler, *Racial Profiling and the Constitution*, 2002 U. CHI. LEGAL F. 163 (2002); Norma I. Gavin et al., *Racial and Ethnic Disparities in the Use*

Society may decide that only a certain type of person has a right to be born: one with a certain height, weight, appearance, and IQ. Modern society may adopt eugenics based on a combination of prenatal tests, and the growing perception that only a perfect baby is a "good baby," so that the fetus that does not correspond to certain parameters must be eliminated. There is a danger that society may begin to encourage the births of "perfect" humans,[17] not necessarily of simply healthy ones.

At the same time, the ideals that support the absolute right to give birth to a child, whatever its defects, without taking into consideration the financial aspect and the costs of maintaining it, are unrealistic.[18] Whose responsibility is it to raise a child that is dumb, deaf, lame, or suffering from mental defects? Is it the parents' or ours as a society?

In this book, I discuss the moral, philosophical, ethical, and legal reasons why I believe that a viable fetus has the right to develop into a human being, even if the woman[19] believes otherwise. I maintain that in such cases, the state should intervene and prevent the destruction of a fetus that is unwanted because it is not "perfect," because of a low probability of defects, or simply out of convenience. Legislatures should enact laws that respect the potential life of a fetus and offer it

---

of Pregnancy-Related Health Care Among Medicaid Pregnant Women, 8(3) MATERNAL AND CHILD HEALTH JOURNAL 113 (2004).

[17] *See, for example*, Ruth F. Chadwick, *The Perfect Baby: Introduction*, in Ethics, Reproduction AND Genetic Control 93 (Ruth Chadwick Ed., 1993); GLENN MCGEE, THE PERFECT BABY: PARENTHOOD IN THE NEW WORLD OF CLONING AND GENETICS (2000); Larissa Remennick, *The Quest for the Perfect Baby: Why Do Israeli Women Seek Prenatal Genetic Testing?*, 28(1) SOCIOLOGY OF HEALTH & ILLNESS 21 (2006).

[18] For a special attempt to determine an ethical limit to the maximum number of children that a poor single-parent family should produce, see the hotly debated discussion following the bizarre case of the octomom, Nadya Suleman. *See, for example*, Jennifer M. Collins, *Eight Is Enough*, 103 NW. U. L. REV. COLLOQUY 501 (2009); Kimberly D. Krawiec, *Why We Should Ignore the "Octomom,"* 104 NW. U. L. REV. COLLOQUY 120 (2009); Debora L. Spar, *As You Like It: Exploring the Limits of Parental Choice in Assisted Reproduction*, 27 LAW & INEQ. 481 (2009).

[19] In this book, I use the term "woman" and not "mother" because "mother" implies an emotional connection between the woman and the fetus. I do not consider a woman who decides to terminate a pregnancy in the viable state as a person with an emotional connection to the fetus inside her.

protection. The courts should recognize a claim of damages of a fetus against the woman, either post-partum or by means of a trustee, if it was damaged or aborted for reasons that were not in its best interests.

The parents and the child are separate entities whose rights and best interests do not always coincide. A viable fetus is almost a person inside a person, and consequently, two separate living entities are involved in this decision. One entity should not be allowed to harm another. Even if the fetus is not defined as a person,[20] it should not mean that it lacks rights. The law recognizes the fact that a person in a coma is not "hardly a person" and therefore should not be forcibly removed from life-support devices.[21] Neither are people suffering from Alzheimer's disease "hardly a person," and it is unthinkable to hasten their death. Society cannot decide when there is no longer a point to the life of someone who might be "hardly a person" and assist in that person's death.

Today, society promotes the empowerment of individual rights, respect for autonomy, self-determination, and freedom. Critics of the book may argue that the thesis proposed contradicts the progressive concepts regarding human rights, feminism, and autonomy. I am not opposed to respecting the rights of the woman as a person, but I insist on respecting the rights of the other person inside her, the viable fetus.

---

[20] *See, e.g.*, Leonard Glantz, *Is the Fetus a Person? A Lawyer's View*, in ABORTION AND THE STATUS OF THE FETUS 107 (William B. Bonderson et al. eds., 1983); Jean Reith Schroedel, *Is the Fetus a Person?: A Comparison of Policies Across the Fifty States* (2000); Clifford Longley, *Is the Fetus a Person?*, 25(2) Conscience 45 (2004).

[21] For a discussion of this complicated and sensitive issue, *see* David M. Schultz, *Procedures and Limitations for Removal of Life-Sustaining Treatment from Incompetent Patients*, 34 ST. LOUIS U. L.J. 277 (1989–90); George J. Annas, *The Right to Die in America: Sloganeering from Quinlan and Cruzan to Quill and Kevorkian*, 34 DUQ. L. REV. 875 (1995–96); Lois Shepherd, *In Respect of People Living in a Permanent Vegetative State—And Allowing Them to Die*, 16 HEALTH MATRIX 631 (2006).

Some consider parenthood to be a value.[22] Others are of the opinion that the right to be a parent emanates from free will,[23] with no legal obligations, either in the relationships between the state and its citizens or in the relationships between the partners themselves. Others yet consider that the right to be a parent is one whose interpretation should be narrowed to limit it under certain circumstances.[24] A perception that

---

[22] In the sociological scholarly literature, we find a variety of academic opinions as to how exactly parenthood should be defined—whether it is a responsibility, entitlement, benefit, or enrichment. Nevertheless, it seems that the conceptualization of parenthood as an entitlement and right, on one hand, and a responsibility, on the other, is gaining more and more support.

[23] This is the essence of intentional parenthood. For the landmark literature that supports this latest conception of legal parentage, *see* John L. Hill, *What Does It Mean to Be a "Parent"? The Claims of Biology as the Basis for Parental Rights*, 66 N.Y.U.L. REV. 353, 413–20 (1991); Alexa E. King, *Solomon Revisited: Assigning Parenthood in the Context of Collaborative Reproduction*, 5 UCLA WOMEN'S L.J. 329, 367–99 (1995); Perri Koll, *The Use of the Intent Doctrine to Expand the Rights of Intended Homosexual Male Parents in Surrogacy Custody Disputes*, 18 CARDOZO J.L. & GENDER 199, 223–24 (2011); Jesse M. Nix, *"You Only Donated Sperm": Using Intent to Uphold Paternity Agreements*, 11 J. L. & FAM. STUD. 487, 494 (2009); Jason Oller, *Can I Get That in Writing?: Established and Emerging Protections of Paternity Rights* [In re K.M.H., 169 P.3d 1025 (Kan. 2007)], 48 WASHBURN L.J. 209, 220–23, 235–37 (2008); Dara E. Purvis, *Intended Parents and the Problem of Perspective*, 24 YALE J.L. & FEMINISM 210, 227–53 (2012); Marjorie Maguire Shultz, *Reproductive Technology and Intent Based Parenthood: An Opportunity for Gender Neutrality*, 1990 WIS. L. REV. 297, 321–98 (1990); Andrea E. Stumpf, *Redefining Mother: A Legal Matrix for New Reproductive Technologies*, 96 YALE L.J. 187, 192–208 (1986); Katherine M. Swift, *Parenting Agreements, The Potential Power of Contract, and the Limits of Family Law*, 34 FLA. ST. U.L. REV. 913, 930–57 (2007); Deborah H. Wald, *The Parentage Puzzle: The Interplay Between Genetics, Procreative Intent, and Parental Conduct in Determining Legal Parentage*, 15 AM. U.J. GENDER SOC. POL'Y & L. 379, 388–89 (2007); Catherine Villareale, *The Case of Two Biological Intended Mothers: Illustrating the Need to Statutorily Define Maternity in Maryland*, 42 U. BALT. L. REV. 365 (2013); Mary Patricia Byrn & Erica Holzer, *Codifying the Intent Test*, 41 WM. MITCHELL L. REV. 130 (2015); Heather Kolinsky, *The Intended Parent: The Power and Problems Inherent in Designating and Determining Intent in the Context of Parental Rights*, 119 PENN ST. L. REV. 801 (2015); Melanie B. Jacobs, *Parental Parity: Intentional Parenthood's Promise*, 64 BUFF. L. REV. 465 (2016) and more extensively YEHEZKEL MARGALIT, DETERMINING LEGAL PARENTAGE—BETWEEN FAMILY LAW AND CONTRACT LAW (2018).

[24] Daniel Statman, *The Right to Parenthood: An Argument for a Narrow Interpretation*, 10 ETHICAL PERSPECTIVES 224, 229 (2003). For a discussion of this unique opinion, *see* Sarah Chan & Muireann Quigley, *Frozen Embryos, Genetic Information and Reproductive Rights*, 21(8) BIOETHICS 439 (2007); Rhona Schuz, *The Developing Right to Parenthood in Israeli Law*, 2013 INT'L SURV. FAM. L. 197, 201 n.25 (2013).

parenthood represents a value gives rise to a perception that if a right to be a parent exists, there should also be a right *not* to be a parent.[25]

In *Nahmani v. Nahmani,* Justice Goldberg of the Israel Supreme Court stated that the basis of the right to prevent parenthood is rooted in the autonomy of personal wishes, i.e., respecting the desire of the individual to exercise control over his life and his obligations.[26,27] Justice Dorner stated that the right of the woman to terminate a pregnancy derives from the autonomy she has over her body and her right to privacy,[28] and Justice Strassberg-Cohen determined as follows:

> The right not to be a parent is also a liberty. It is the right of the individual to control and plan his life [. . .] The protected value in non-parenthood is liberty, privacy, free will, self-realization, and the right to make intimate decisions without interference. These are protected basic values of supreme importance, from which the liberty not to be coerced into parenthood is derived. Regarding free will as a liberty leads to the conclusion that every person is free to choose and decide whether or not to be a parent. The State may not impose parenthood on a person, either directly or through the courts. Consequently, I do not accept the position of those who consider the right not to be a parent as a right of less value than the right to be a parent.[29]

Even if we accept the view that along with the right to be a parent exists a right not to be a parent, a distinction should be made between the existence of that right before conception and after it. After conception,

---

[25] Glenn Cohen, *The Constitution and the Rights Not to Procreate,* 60 STAN. L. REV. 1135 (2008); Glenn Cohen, *The Right Not to Be a Genetic Parent?* 81 S. CAL. L. REV. 1115 (2008); Christopher Bruno, *A Right to Decide Not to Be a Legal Father:* Gonzales v. Carhart *and the Acceptance of Emotional Harm as a Constitutionally Protected Interest,* 77 GEO. WASH. L. REV. 141 (2008). Accepting these viewpoints could lead to the conclusion that preventing parenthood is also a free choice and therefore the woman is at liberty to decide whether she prefers not to become a mother.

[26] Nahmani v. Nahmani, *supra* note 1, at 66–79.

[27] *Id.* at 52–66.

[28] *Id.*

[29] *Id.* at 13.

and arguably more so after 24 weeks of pregnancy, we are no longer dealing only with the woman's liberty and her rights, but also with the rights of another entity, the fetus. When the woman exercises her liberty to the fullest extent, the result can be the destruction of the fetus.

The focus of this book is not the right to be a parent or the choice to prevent parenthood, because this decision is the concern of the individual and not that of a liberal, modern state, at least as long as it is not required to cover the costs of exercising that right. The decision to become a parent or to refrain from doing so is an autonomous, internal family decision, and the law should not intervene unless there are serious reasons to do so. This book addresses a different issue: *the right not to be a parent at the stage of viability of the fetus*. It discusses the issues that must be acknowledged in balancing the right of the woman to terminate the possibility of parenthood with the right of the fetus to be born, and to be born as healthy as possible. When deciding whether to force parenthood on someone who does not want it, at a stage where termination is still an option, it is important to consider several aspects, among others, the woman's right over her body, the right of the father-to-be and especially the best interests of the future child who will be born to a woman who does not want it.

In *Davis v. Davis,* the US Supreme Court determined that the essence of the right to privacy is, at the very least, non-intervention in the decision to enter parenthood:

> If the right to privacy means anything, it is the right of the individual, married or single, to be free from unwarranted governmental intrusion into matters so fundamentally affecting a person as the decision whether to bear or beget a child.[30]

---

[30] Davis v. Davis, 588 SW 2d 604, 842 (1992). For a discussion of this statement, *see* Thomas B. Stoddard, Bowers v. Hardwick: *Precedent by Personal Predilection*, 54(2) U. CHI. L. REV. 648, 653–54 (1987); Dorothy E. Roberts, *Punishing Drug Addicts Who Have Babies: Women of Color, Equality, and the Right of Privacy*, 104(7) HARV. L. REV. 1419, 1466

In a similar vein, in *Skinner v. Oklahoma,* the Supreme Court ruled that marriage and procreation are "one of the basic rights of man."[31]

But this is not the topic of the present book. Choosing parenthood or non-parenthood is a matter of religious belief, culture, and the woman's decision. I ask only whether there should be increased regulation in terminating a pregnancy, or would it represent an intervention in the very core of the human "sanctum." I believe that the state should intervene in the decision of the woman only if it is a matter of life and death for the fetus.

Admittedly, the decision to terminate a pregnancy is one of the most intimate and fateful in a person's life. But when the life of another potential person is involved, who is in the late stages of development in the womb, the state should intervene by prohibiting the termination of pregnancy at the viable stage. Recognition of the right of the viable fetus is a value sufficiently important to justify intervention by the state. Such recognition is essential for balancing the various values arising from the question of terminating a pregnancy: that of human dignity and the woman's autonomy vis-à-vis that of the potential life of the fetus at the viable stage.[32]

Today, prenatal screening[33] makes it possible to identify many syndromes from which a fetus is suffering, or may be suffering. In the

---

(1991); Katherine M. Franke, *The Domesticated Liberty of* Lawrence v. Texas, 104 COLUM. L. REV. 1399, 1404 n.22 (2004).

[31] Skinner v. Oklahoma, 316 U.S. 355, 541 (1942). *See, for example,* James B. O'Hara & T. Howland Sanes, *Eugenic Sterilization,* 45 GEO. L. J. 20 (1956–57); Wesley D. H. Teo, *Abortion: The Husband's Constitutional Rights,* 85(4) ETHICS 337 (1975); Martha L. A. Fineman, *Masking Dependency: The Political Role of Family Rhetoric,* 81 VA. L. REV. 2181, 2189 n.21 (1995).

[32] For the interaction between human rights, women's autonomy, and abortion, *see* Kristen Boon, *Rape and Forced Pregnancy Under the ICC Statute: Human Dignity, Autonomy, and Consent,* 32 COLUM. HUM. RTS. L. REV. 625 (2000–01); Jennifer Denbow, *Abortion: When Choice and Autonomy Conflict,* 20 BERKELEY J. GENDER L. & JUST. 216 (2005); Christopher McCrudden, *Human Dignity and Judicial Interpretation of Human Rights,* 19(4) EUROPEAN JOURNAL OF INTERNATIONAL LAW 655 (2008).

[33] For a discussion of the far-reaching effect of parental screening on the rate of abortions, *see* R. R. Faden et al., *Prenatal Screening and Pregnant Women's Attitudes*

future, additional methods will be able to discover more defects and imperfections. The question is whether it is justified to require that every potential genetic defect be found, and whether society has the right, or maybe the obligation, to limit permission to terminate pregnancy because of deficiencies of varying severity. The claim that the viable fetus has a legal status and its own rights changes the termination of its life into the murder of an "almost" live human being. The issue of terminating a pregnancy is related also to that of the destruction of other helpless human beings, such as people suffering from dementia or in a permanently comatose state.

The appropriate legal model should recognize the rights of the viable fetus even if it suffers from deficiencies that do not seriously undermine its quality of life or lifestyle. These procedures should be recognized by the state, even at the expense of restricting the autonomy of the woman. This book presents the medical, ethical, philosophical, historical, and legal arguments supporting this point of view and suggests practical approaches to balancing the rights of women and fetuses and protecting the fetus's right to life.

Toward the Abortion of Defective Fetuses, 77(3) AMERICAN JOURNAL OF PUBLIC HEALTH 288 (1987); Paivi Santalahti et al., *Women's Decision-Making in Prenatal Screening*, 46(8) SOCIAL SCIENCE & MEDICINE 1067 (1998); Susan Markens et al., *"Because of the Risks": How US Pregnant Women Account for Refusing Prenatal Screening*, 49(3) SOCIAL SCIENCE & MEDICINE 359 (1999).

Chapter 2
Women's Right to Self-Determination and Autonomy

Recognition of a woman's right to make decisions about her life and her body, including the right to terminate a pregnancy, even of a viable fetus, is based on recognizing her autonomy over her own body. Practically all human beings assume they have such rights. The doctrine of informed consent is based less on a liberal interpretation than on an autonomous one,[1] whereby the woman has an unconditional right over her body, even during pregnancy, when she carries potential life inside her.

Emmanuel Kant, one of the fathers of deontological thinking, and the Enlightenment philosopher, Jean-Jacques Rousseau,[2] maintained that

---

[1] Autonomous interpretation, like Kantianism, considers an autonomous to be subject to rational principles. An irrational act is not an autonomous one, therefore a paternalistic intervention in the case of an irrational decision does not interfere with the patient's autonomy, indeed, it is the realization of such autonomy. Liberal interpretation considers "autonomy" to include also a person's right to act irrationally. For the interaction between autonomy and Kantianism, *see* Thomas E. Hill, *The Kantian Conception of Autonomy*, in THE INNER CITADEL: ESSAYS ON INDIVIDUAL AUTONOMY 91 (John Philip Christman ed., 1989); Robert S. Taylor, *Kantian Personal Autonomy*, 33(5) POLITICAL THEORY 602 (2005); REATH ANDREWS, AGENCY AND AUTONOMY IN KANT'S MORAL THEORY (2006).

[2] JEAN JACQUES ROUSSEAU, AN INQUIRY INTO THE NATURE OF THE SOCIAL CONTRACT, OR, PRINCIPLES OF POLITICAL RIGHT (translated from French, 1791), was discussed recently by Michael Sonenscher, *Jean-Jacques Rousseau and the Foundations of Modern Political Thought*, 14(2) MODERN INTELLECTUAL HISTORY 311 (2017); Gal Michal, *The Social Contract at the Basis of Competition Law*, in COMPETITION POLICY: BETWEEN EQUITY AND EFFICIENCY (I. Lianos & D. Gerard eds., 2018), https://ssrn.com/abstract=3014354; CHRISTOPHER BERTRAM, THE ROUTLEDGE GUIDEBOOK TO ROUSSEAU'S THE SOCIAL CONTRACT (2018). *See also* IMMANUEL KANT, CRITIQUE OF PURE REASON (1899). For the most recent discussion of this landmark research, *see* Allen Wood, *The Final Form of Kant's Practical Philosophy*, in IMMANUEL KANT (Arthur Ripstein ed., 2017); Stephen Howard, *Review of Immanuel Kant: The Very Idea of a Critique of Pure Reason by J. Colin McQuillan*, 50(3) CONTINENTAL PHILOSOPHY REVIEW 403 (2017); YIRMIYAHU YOVEL,

every autonomous person conducts himself according to a program shared by all others in society. By contrast, John Stuart Mill[3] and other liberal philosophers have argued that autonomous people act according to their free will, expressing the unique nature of humans as opposed to other living beings. Whatever differences in their thought, Kant, Rousseau, and Mill all believed that the right of an autonomous person was not absolute, and that an autonomous right could on occasion yield to a superior restrictive paternalistic one. Applying a more relativistic approach of this type, it could be argued that the right of a woman to autonomy over her own body is not an absolute one, especially as the viable fetus is dependent on the "accommodation" she provides for it. Paternalistic legislation may impose certain behaviors on the woman during the course of her pregnancy or prevent her from engaging in some activities.

Kant would also ask the question: What is the duty of society to the mother vs. the viable fetus? Society has conflicting values on this matter. There are legitimate values reflecting a woman's right to control her body. Women believe that it is they, not societal morality or religious institutions, who ought to decide what happens to their bodies. But in today's technological age, with the survival prospects of the fetus always improving, the rights of the unborn, viable fetus to become a live human being are gaining support.

There are times when treatment to prevent serious risk to a fetus is required in addition to the primary treatment given to the pregnant woman. In such cases, the law in the vast majority of jurisdictions

---

KANT'S PHILOSOPHICAL REVOLUTION: A SHORT GUIDE TO THE CRITIQUE OF PURE REASON (2018).

[3] JOHN STUART MILL: ON LIBERTY (1955). For recent discussion of this seminal author and book, *see* Sharon Stanley, *John Stuart Mill, Children's Liberty, and the Unraveling of Autonomy*, 79(1) REVIEW OF POLITICS 49 (2017); JOHN STUART MILL: AUTOBIOGRAPHY (MARK PHILIP ED., 2018); Anshuman A. Mondal, *On Liberty on Listening: John Stuart Mill and the Limits of Liberal Responsiveness*, in ETHICAL RESPONSIVENESS AND THE POLITICS OF DIFFERENCE 41 (Tanja Dreher & Anshuman Mondal eds., 2018).

requires women to give informed consent to any additional treatment.[4] From this follows the doctrine that a woman may decide that no further treatment of the fetus is needed, in which case, no such treatment is provided. In most countries, this reinforces the notion that a woman has rights over her body even when the fetus faces an emergency. The law often mandates providing information to women so that they may exercise their right to decide what treatment to receive. A woman's consent to receive medical treatment[5] means that she consents of her own free will, having understood her medical state.[6] The woman must also be cognitively and intellectually fit.[7]

Thus, any consent to terminate a pregnancy that does not comply with the legal requirements of informed consent is not considered legal. The woman's consent must not be obtained fraudulently, therefore nondisclosure of a fact related to her condition is the equivalent of fraud. For example, if a physician thinks that a woman has an erroneous opinion about a medical treatment she is about to undergo, the physician must advise her of such error, and failure to do so is considered fraud. Would the physician's silence in itself create an intentional misrepresentation?[8] This would be the case only if the

---

[4] For a discussion of this doctrine, *see* RUTH R. FADEN & TOM L. BEAUCHAMP, A HISTORY AND THEORY OF INFORMED CONSENT (1986); William J. Morton, *The Doctrine of Informed Consent*, 6 MED. L. 117 (1987); Sharon N. Perley, *From Control over One's Body to Control over One's Body Parts: Extending the Doctrine of Informed Consent*, 67 N.Y.U. L. REV. 335 (1992).

[5] For a discussion of this point regarding adult and minor women, *see,* respectively, Linda S. Martell, *Leyson v. Steuermann: Is There Plain Error in Hawaii's Doctrine of Informed Consent*, 8 U. HAW. L. REV. 569, 569 (1986); and Harriet F. Pilpel & Ruth J. Zuckerman, *Abortion and the Rights of Minors,* 23 CASE W. RES. L. REV. 779, 799–800 (1972).

[6] The signature required by law on a consent form is merely a formality and proof of consent. The consent required by law is an inner consent, genuine, freely granted from a coherent position based on medical information. This component also includes the satisfactory ability of the woman to understand the essence of the medical treatment, its expected benefits, and its inherent risks.

[7] Some claim that consent to an illegal procedure by a physician is invalid, and therefore the physician who performed an illegal procedure based on such consent is liable as if no consent were given.

[8] JOSEPH CHITTY, CHITTY ON CONTRACTS paras. 127–267 (31st ed. 2014).

physician had an obligation to disclose, and remaining silent created a misrepresentation; no weight can be given to consent based on incorrect information.[9]

According to the Israeli Patients' Rights Law,[10] consent may be given in writing, orally, or by a patient's conduct. Regarding particularly difficult treatments included as an addendum to the Patients' Rights Law, it is stipulated that consent may be given in writing only, after having received an explanation of the treatment, and an abbreviated version of the explanation must be recorded.[11] Thus, in itself, a signature on a treatment consent form does not constitute informed consent. Before signing the consent, the woman must be given the full information and a proper explanation about the nature of the treatment and its inherent risks. If she has received a full explanation about treatment, understood it, and verbally expressed willingness to receive

[9] Consider the example of a physician who is about to perform surgery on a patient knowing that the patient will become sexually dysfunctional. The physician also knows that if the patient were aware of this information, he would not agree to the operation. The physician decides not to disclose this information to the patient and receives the patient's consent. This is consent obtained under intentional misrepresentation. When a deception has caused a deliberate error in the patient's comprehension, this error renders consent null and void.

[10] Patients' Rights Law § 14(a), 1996.

[11] *Id.* § 14(b). Before the enactment of this law, apart from the formal consent on a signed form, the requirement for informed consent was rooted in a legal construct. It was common to say that consent to medical treatment was a declaration of a wish aimed to achieve a legal outcome, and therefore the Israeli terms of Contract Law (General Law) 1973 were applicable. Under section 61(b) of this law, the patient's signature on the consent form was merely proof of the patient's consent to a medical procedure (*see* Karp v. Cooley, 349 F. Supp., 827 (1972)) and therefore was rebuttable. If it was proven that this consent was not informed, it could be contended that at the time of signing, the patient had not decided to agree owing to a lack of information, and therefore formal consent was rendered null and void. Similarly, in cases where there were defects in forming a contract—if the patient signed the consent form in error, was misled, or forced to do so—the consent could be rendered invalid. For a discussion of this landmark verdict, *see* Joseph Gary Trichter & Peter W. Lewis, *Informed Consent: The Three Tests and a Modest Proposal for the Reality of the Patient as an Individual*, 21 S. TEX. L.J. 155, 156 n.3, 159 (1980); Eve R. Green Koopersmith, *Informed Consent: The Problem of Causation*, 3 MED. & L. 231, 233 (1984); George J. Annas, *Death and the Magic Machine: Informed Consent to the Artificial Heart*, 9 W. NEW ENG. L. REV. 89, 95 n.19 (1987).

the treatment but has not signed a formal consent form,[12] her consent is valid even without her written signature. This is true except for six types of special treatments listed in the addendum to the Patients' Rights Law, for which written consent cannot be waived.[13]

Can the state enact a law that contradicts the doctrine of informed consent[14] and force treatment for the benefit of the viable fetus on the woman? Can the state prevent her from terminating a pregnancy? Can the state obligate her to undergo a Cesarean section (C-section) to save a viable fetus?

The Elements of Informed Consent

The expression "informed consent" relates to the legal obligation of a physician to provide patients with all information relevant to their decision and receive their consent before any medical procedure is carried out on their body. To obtain informed consent, the physician must first diagnose the medical problem and provide general information and specific details of the treatment method.[15] At this stage,

---

[12] According to the Patients' Rights Law § 14(a).

[13] By contrast, common law and English law did not require written consent, although in practice, the patients were given a form to sign. The practice arose because physicians thought that something in writing was proof and would prevent the patient from filing a statement of claim after treatment. This thinking is essentially erroneous because in and of itself, the writing does not prevent patients from filing a claim if consent was uninformed. *See* Hernandez v. United States, 465 F. Supp. 1071–73 (1979), indicating that the position of the common law and that of US judicial decisions do not differ on this issue. For a discussion of this ruling, *see* Abraham P. Ordover, *Surprise—That Damaging Turncoat Witness Is Still with Us: An Analysis of Federal Rules of Evidence* 607, 801 (d)(1)(A) and 403, 5 HOFSTRA L. REV. 65, 72 n.40 (1976); Karen A. Ruzic, *Military Justice and the Supreme Court's Outdated Standard of Deference:* Weiss v. United States, 70 CHI.-KENT L. REV. 265, 276 n.104 (1994); Erron W. Smith, Apprendi v. New Jersey*: The United States Supreme Court Restricts Judicial Sentencing Discretion and Raises Troubling Constitutional Questions Concerning Sentencing Statutes and Reforms Nationwide,* 54 ARK. L. REV. 649, 695 n.265 (2001).

[14] Patients' Rights Law § 13.

[15] Ladonna L. Griffith, *Consent: Informed Consent—Patient's Right to Comprehend,* 27 HOWARD L.J. 975, 975–93 (1984); Alan Meisel & Loren H. Roth, *Towards an Informed Discussion of Informed Consent: A Review and Critique of Empirical Studies,* 25 ARIZONA L. REV. 265, 265–346 (1983). For discussion of the latter article, *see* Janet Dolgin, *The Legal*

the proposed treatment[16] should be discussed: the description of the treatment should include alternatives, results, ramifications,[17] any inherent risks (death or bodily harm),[18] problems that may arise during convalescence, and any other information that physicians supply in similar circumstances.[19]

As part of informed consent, in the case of a pregnant woman, it is also necessary to examine her competence and ability to comprehend the information she has received. If the woman is of unsound mind (owing to madness, mental deficiency, drugs, or inebriation), her consent to medical treatment or the lack thereof is invalid. Still, it is not the extreme cases, but the situations that occur daily that raise the challenge to ensure that a woman has reached her decisions independently, based on the information provided by the physician who had not exerted any

---

Development of the Informed Consent Doctrine: Past and Present, 19(1) CAMBRIDGE QUARTERLY OF HEALTHCARE ETHICS 97, n.49 (2010); Christopher Robertson, *Should Patient Responsibility for Costs Change the Physician-Patient Relationship?*, 50 WAKE FOREST L. REV. 363, 374 n.64 (2015); Camilla Louise Scanlan, *The Legal and Ethical Limits of Consent in High-Risk Medical Interventions: An Empirical Study* 124 n.441, 141 n.490 (2015) (Ph.D. thesis, University of Sydney).

[16] Hartwell v. Pittman, 428 So. 2nd 1049 (1983) (physician required to inform a high-risk patient of material risks of non-emergency surgery for a noncritical ailment). For a recent discussion of this case, *see* Griffith, *supra* note 16, at 976 n.3; JAMES WALKER SMITH, HOSPITAL LIABILITY 10–21 n.58 (2018).

[17] Holland v. Sisters of Saint Joseph of Peace, 523 P. 2nd, 211 (1974). This ruling dealt with the issue of a cancer patient who had undergone radiotherapy after having given consent. His consent was considered invalid because he had not been offered alternatives to radiation, such as a surgical procedure or chemotherapy. For an academic discussion of this ruling, *see* Walter Probert, *Nibbling at the Problems of Medical Malpractice*, 28 U. FLA. L. REV. 56, 60 n.28 (1975); Prentiss E. Feagles et al., *An Analysis of State Legislative Responses to the Medical Malpractice Crisis*, 1975 DUKE LAW JOURNAL 1417 (1976); Jon F. Merz, *An Empirical Analysis of the Medical Informed Consent Doctrine: Search for a Standard of Disclosure*, 2 RISK 27, 60 n.73 (1991).

[18] *See* Cobbs v. Grant, 8 Cal, 3rd 299, 502 P. 2nd 1 (1972), in which it was determined that nondisclosure of inherent risks invalidates the patient's consent. For a discussion of this often-cited verdict, *see* Timothy W. Kenna, *The Patient-Physician Relationship: Present Law and Trends for the Future Implied in* Cobbs v. Grant, 8 U.S.F. L. REV. 320 (1973); Alan J. Weisbard, *Informed Consent: The Law's Uneasy Compromise with Ethical Theory*, 65 NEB. L. REV. 749, 750, 756, 762 n.31 (1986); Lawrence O. Gostin, *Informed Consent, Cultural Sensitivity, and Respect for Persons*, 274(10) JAMA 844 (1995).

[19] Holland v. Sisters of Saint Joseph of Peace.

pressure on her. These elements are mandatory; if any of them is missing, the woman's consent is considered invalid, that is, not informed consent.

The informed consent requirement existed in Israel even before the enactment of the Patient's Rights Act, in 1996. The term "informed consent" has two components: "inform" and "consent."[20] For the patient to be informed, she must receive proper information about her medical state and that of the fetus, the nature of the recommended treatment, the inherent risks, and the available alternatives.[21] What type of information and how much of it should be given to the woman to enable her consent to be truly informed. Neither case law nor scholarship has yet provided a definitive answer to this question.[22] The conceptual foundation of the obligation to disclose requires that the woman be a partner in every decision made regarding her treatment,[23] and that the decision not be coerced. The current Israeli tests of the extent of disclosure required from the physician include the

[20] *See* PRESIDENT'S COMMISSION FOR THE STUDY OF ETHICAL PROBLEMS IN MEDICINE AND BIOMEDICAL AND BEHAVIORAL RESEARCH, SPLICING LIFE: THE SOCIAL AND ETHICAL ISSUES OF GENETIC ENGINEERING WITH HUMAN BEINGS, vol. 3, 7 (1982), https://bioethics.georgetown.edu/archives/Presidents-Commission-for-Study-of-Ethical-Problems-in-Medicine-and-in-Biomedical-and-Behavioral-Research-Original-Archive-Finding-Aid.pdf.

[21] Patients' Rights Law § 13(b).

[22] In this context, the term "reasonable" refers to both the amount of conveyed information and the reasonable nature of the information to be conveyed (see *supra* note 1).

[23] As determined by the Israeli Supreme Court in the *Berman* case. *See* CA 434/94 Berman v. Mor, IsrSc 51(4), 205, 213 (1997) ("the paternalistic approach, which maintains that the physician fulfilled his obligation to the patient regarding conveying information if he acts according to the accepted medical practice was nevertheless overruled. In our judgment, the standard of disclosure that can be found in the American judiciary and accepted in Canada and Australia reflects the needs of the patient who is required to consent to the medical treatment"). For a discussion of this verdict, *see* CA 5604/94 Osama Hemed and Ibrahim Hemed v. The State of Israel, IsrSc 58(2) 498 (2004), http://www.hamoked.org/files/2015/5510 eng.pdf; Sagit Mor, *The Dialectics of Wrongful Life and Wrongful Birth Claims in Israel: A Disability Critique*, 63 STUDIES IN LAW, POLITICS, AND SOCIETY 113 (2014), law.haifa.ac.il/images/Publications/Sagit_Mor_-_The_Dialectics_of_WL_and_WB_-_Print.pdf.

"reasonable physician" test,[24] the "good medical practice" test,[25] and the "reasonable patient" test, all of which are used to establish what medical information should be expected by a reasonable patient before consenting to the treatment.

Debates in US courts on the issue of informed consent to receive or refuse medical treatment have been based on customary medical practice standards, the Constitution,[26] or the right of freedom of religion.[27] It is no longer necessary to resort to these sources, as there is now a fundamental assumption that informed consent is a basic human right deriving from the right to self-determination,[28] as set forth in the leading Supreme Court ruling on this issue in *Canterbury v. Spence*.[29] The Canadian Supreme Court accepted the reasonable patient test in the

---

[24] A paternalistic test that checks what information a reasonable physician conveys to the patient. For an academic survey of this test, *see* Robert Schwartz & Andrew Grubb, *Why Britain Can't Afford Informed Consent*, 15(4) HASTINGS CENTER REPORT 19 (1985); Carole B. Pinnock, *PSA Testing in General Practice: Can We Do More Now?*, 180 MEDICAL JOURNAL OF AUSTRALIA 379, 379 (2004), https://www.mja.com.au/system/ffles/issues/180 08 190404/pin10813 fm.pdf; Rob Heywood et al., *Informed Consent in Hospital Practice: Health Professionals' Perspectives and Legal Reflections*, 18(2) MEDICAL LAW REVIEW 152, nn. 46–47, 50 (2010).

[25] PHYSICIANS, PATIENTS AND THE LAW 47, 65 (CLARE DYER ED., 1992).

[26] Especially in light of the ruling in *Roe v. Wade*, 410 U.S. 113 (1973). For a discussion of this landmark verdict, *see supra* Chapter 1, p. 7, n. 8 and the references cited there.

[27] In some cases, the right of patients not to consent to medical treatment was recognized by virtue of religious beliefs. *See, for example*, In re Estate of Brooks, 205 N.E.2d 435 (1965).

[28] On this matter, see also the following sources: A. D. Nieuw, *Informed Consent*, 12 MED. LAW 125 (1993); Margaret A. Somerville, *Labels versus contents: Variance Between Philosophy, Psychiatry and Law in the Concepts Governing Decision Making*, 39 MCGILL L.J. 179 (1994); EDWARDS RICHARDS & KATHARINE RATHBUN, LAW AND THE PHYSICIANS: A PRACTICAL GUIDE §§ 145 (1993); GEORGE POZGAR, LEGAL ASPECTS OF HEALTH CARE ADMINISTRATION 301 (1993).

[29] Canterbury v. Spence, 464 F.2D 772 (1927), which based the obligation of disclosure required by the physician on the trust between physician and patient. For an academic discussion of this ruling, *see* Thomas A. Knapp & Richard L. Huff, *Emerging Trends in the Physician's Duty to Disclose: An Update of* Canterbury v. Spence, 3(1) JOURNAL OF LEGAL MEDICINE 31 (1975); Editorials, *Consent for Transfusion: A Duty of Care*, 315(7105) BMJ 380, 380 (1997); *Influence of the Law on Risk and Informed Consent*, 327 BMJ 731, 732 (2003).

case of *Arndt v. Smith* and rejected the medical practice test.[30] In the case of *Rogers v. Whitaker*,[31] the Australian High Court determined that the law must recognize the physician's obligation to warn the patient about possible risks in accordance with the specific needs of the patient, including the patient's level of understanding, language, state of health, and more. Samuels[32] maintained that the physician's general obligation to disclose information derived from both the physician's professionalism and the patient's interests. The extent of the disclosure should be further broadened to include information about the medical state of the fetus when the pregnant woman seeks to undergo a medical procedure involving a viable fetus or decides to refrain from one.

This matter was debated, among others, in the Israeli case of *Kohari v. State of Israel*,[33] in which it was determined that the woman must be provided with an explanation about the fundamental risks that a typical

---

[30] Arndt v. Smith, 126 D.L.R. (4th) 705 (1995), in the opinion of Justice Lambert; Arndt v. Smith, 148, D.L.R. (4th) 48 (1997). *See* the following discussions of this verdict: Mitchell McInnes, *Failure to Warn in Medical Negligence—A Cautionary Note from Canada:* Arndt v. Smith, 6(2) TORTS LAW JOURNAL 135 (1998); Erin Nelson & Timothy Caulfield, *You Can't Get There from Here: A Case Comment on* Arndt v. Smith, 32 U. BRIT. COLUM. L. REV. 353 (1998); Vaughan Black, *The Rise and Fall of Plaintiff-Friendly Causation*, 53 ALTA. L. REV. 1013, 1014 n.5 (2016).

[31] Rogers v. Whitaker, 175, C.L.R 479, 490 (1992). This case was extensively discussed in scholarly literature. *See, for example*, Don Chalmers & Robert Schwartz, *Rogers v. Whitaker and Informed Consent in Australia: A Fair Dinkum Duty of Disclosure*, 1(2) MED. L. REV. 139 (1993); R. C. Pincus, *Has Informed Consent Finally Arrived in Australia? A Comment on the Law Following the Decision of the High Court of Australia in* Rogers v. Whitaker, 159(1) MEDICAL JOURNAL OF AUSTRALIA 25 (1993); I. H. Kerridge & K. R. Mitchell, *Missing the Point: Rogers v Whitaker and the Ethical Ideal of Informed and Shared Decision Making*, 1 J. L. & MED. 237(1994).

[32] A. Samuels, *What the Physician Must Tell the Patient*, 22 MED. SCI. LAW 41 (1982). This research was discussed by Alan G. Fraser, *Do Patients Want to Be Informed? A Study of Consent for Cardiac Catheterization*, 52(4) BR. HEART J. 468, 470 (1984); Kathryn M. Taylor & Merrijoy Kelner, *Informed Consent: The Physicians' Perspective*, 24(2) SOCIAL SCIENCE & MEDICINE 135 (1987); Frances H. Miller, *Informed Consent for the Man on the Clapham Omnibus: An English Cure for the American Disease*, 9 W. NEW ENG. L. REV. 169, 172 n.18 (1987).

[33] CA 323/89 Kohari. v. State of Israel, IsrSc 45(2), 142 (1991), discussed by Baruch Bar-Alon, *A Digest of Selected Judgments of the Supreme Court of Israel*, 28(4) ISRAEL L. REV. 685 nn.32–33 (1994); Oren Asma & Nili Tabak, *Professional Standards Expected of Nurses from an Israeli Legal Perspective*, MED. & L. 53, 59 nn.25–26 (2017).

patient would consider important when deciding to agree to medical treatment. The good medical practice test, as well as the reasonable patient criteria, require the physician to disclose any information reasonable patients would need to enable them to decide about agreeing to the proposed medical treatment. These criteria address the basic human right to autonomy. In the matter under discussion, the issue is the reasonable woman test. The physician must act with utmost loyalty toward patients, implying that the physician must tell the woman what she should expect to undergo. This approach suggests that for a woman to give informed consent to medical treatment for the benefit of the viable fetus she is carrying, subjective factors must be considered, such as the woman's age, character, personality, mental and medical history, and the nature of the treatment being proposed.

The amount of information the physician is obligated to give the pregnant woman is determined based on an objective test: the physician must find out every piece of information necessary for a reasonable woman to decide whether or not to consent to the treatment offered, and whether it is treatment for her benefit alone or for that of the viable fetus, including in the case of a C-section. This test was used in Israel for the first time in *Noam Raibi v. Dr. Kurt Weige.*[34] When the treatment is innovative, the woman must be informed of this fact.

All the above-mentioned information within the framework of the doctrine of informed consent is intended to address only the health of the patient, the pregnant woman. When initially considered, the concept did not include the provision of information referring to a viable fetus. Tests in the course of pregnancy and the expectation to give birth to a "normal" fetus broadened the requirement to supply information regarding its health. Is there a legal requirement to provide the woman with information about the fetus within the framework of

---

[34] CA 3108/91 Noam Raibi v. Dr. Kurt Weige, IsrSC 47(2) 497, 509 (1993), discussed by Haim Povarsky, 7 JEWISH L. REP. 1, 30 (1994); Jonathan Davies, *Legal and Forensic Medicine in Israel, in* THE LEGAL AND FORENSIC MEDICINE ENCYCLOPEDIA 475 (2013); Limor Malul, *The Role of the Israeli Courts in Formulating the Physician–Patient Relationship*, 33 MED. & L. 61, 73 n.57 (2014).

the doctrine of informed consent, as defined in the Israeli Patients' Rights Law?[35] The answer to this question is relevant both when discussing the "rights" of a viable fetus during the pregnancy and when discussing the possible conflict between the "rights" of a viable fetus to "receive information and treatment" (provided through another actor—the woman—whose wishes are not necessarily aligned with the needs of the fetus, but who has to nevertheless provide consent to treatment).

A derivative of the woman's right over her body is her freedom to prevent medical action being taken on her body without consent.[36] This is the case when the action is intended purely for the benefit of the viable fetus she is carrying, both during pregnancy and in the event of a C-section.[37]

---

[35] For an overview of this law, *see* Michael L. Gross, *Autonomy and Paternalism in Communitarian Society: Patient Rights in Israel*, 29(4) HASTINGS CENTER REPORT 13 (1999); Gil Siegal et al., *Physicians' Attitudes Towards Patients' Rights Legislation*, 20 MED. LAW 63 (2001); Gila Yakov et al., *Nurses' Perceptions of Ethical Issues Related to Patients' Rights Law*, 17(4) NURSING ETHICS 501 (2010).

[36] *See* Roger B. Dworkin, *Medical Law and Ethics in the Post-Autonomy Age*, 68 IND. L. J. 727, 733 (1993) ("It is a physical concept rather than an intellectual one. If you touch me or eavesdrop on me, you have injured my autonomy by invading my space. If you actually do something to change my body, you have injured my autonomy by changing the very constitution of what I am"). For a discussion of this research, *see* Jacqueline M. Nolan-Haley, *Court Mediation and the Search for Justice through Law*, 74 WASH. U. L. Q. 47, 88 n.200 (1996); Mark A. Hall, *A Theory of Economic Informed Consent*, 31 GA. L. REV. 511, 515 n.10 (1997); Lars Noah, *Informed Consent and the Elusive Dichotomy between Standard and Experimental Therapy*, 28 AM. J.L. & MED. 361, 365 n.14 (2002).

[37] Consent expressing the autonomy of free will is an important tool in private law. *See* Danuta Mendelson, *Historical Evolution and Modern Implications of Concepts of Consent to, and Refusal of, Medical Treatment in the Law of Trespass*, 17 J. LEG. MED. 1 (1996) and the following consequential articles: Adam A. Milani, *Better Off Dead than Disabled: Should Courts Recognize a Wrongful Living Cause of Action When Physicians Fail to Honor Patients' Advance Directives?*, 54 WASH. & LEE L. REV. 149, 156 n.42 (1997); Joan H. Krause, *Reconceptualizing Informed Consent in an Era of Health Care Cost Containment*, 85 IOWA L. REV. 261, 267 n.9, 275 n.40 (1999); William Grizzle et al., *Recommended Policies for Uses of Human Tissue in Research, Education, and Quality Control*, 123 ARCH. PATHOL. LAB. MED. 296, 300 n.18 (1999).

From this perspective, it can be concluded that the woman has a right to prevent medical treatment for the viable fetus, even if it is likely to improve its health or save its life. Is this situation acceptable, even when the woman is about to give birth and refuses a C-section? In most countries, a woman can refuse a C-section, and physicians will not operate on her against her will, even if her refusal leads to the death of the viable fetus and even if she is in her 38th week of pregnancy.

Does the fact that a woman admitted herself to the delivery room, having contractions, imply consent to a surgical procedure? Should this procedure be done without her consent? Should it be carried out even if her life or health are not at risk? Is it possible to infer from her conduct that her implied consent has been given to any life-saving medical procedure for her or the viable fetus, including a C-section? Referring to implied consent, it can be assumed that anyone entering a hospital of one's own free will agrees to non-invasive standard medical treatment, for example, having one's blood pressure taken. But whenever a non--routine treatment is considered, informed consent must be obtained. An example of the difference between general consent and special consent appears on the Israeli informed consent form for amniocentesis[38] and on forms for other procedures. The informed consent form for amniocentesis contains an explanation of the nature of the test and the risks involved. The amniocentesis consent form includes the patient's declaration that she has received full explanatory details. The name of the person providing the explanation must be specified, and the declaration must be signed by the woman.[39] The Israeli Patients' Rights Law allows urgent medical treatment to be provided in emergencies even in the absence of informed consent.[40] The law additionally allows informed consent to be given verbally in case of any of the special treatments enumerated in the addendum to this law.[41]

---

[38] People's Health Regulations (Amniocentesis) 1980.

[39] Noam Raibi v. Dr. Kurt Weige, *supra* note 35, according to Justice Shamgar.

[40] Patients' Rights Law § 15(3).

[41] *Id.* § 14(d).

This means that in the present legal situation, treatment may be administered even without the woman's informed consent if she is unable, physically or mentally, to provide such consent.[42] If her life is in immediate danger and she refuses treatment, the physician or the qualified professional is allowed to treat her even against her will.[43] The law does not deal directly with emergencies but it allows the ethics committee to provide substitute consent for the patient. The law could conceivably be expanded to apply to situations when the fetus is in mortal danger if not removed from the womb by C-section.

In the Israeli *Kaira* case, the court ruled that the physician is allowed to infer that a woman has consented to treatment based on her returning for follow-up treatment.[44] Can it be inferred from this that a woman in the advanced stages of labor consents to any treatment of the fetus to save its life? Israeli case law does not recognize a patient's consent by implication when it is not a follow-up treatment but a deviation from the original treatment to which the patient provided consent, unless during the treatment to which the patient had consented the need arises for additional treatment that could not have been reasonably expected.

This jurisprudence, accepted in Israel and influenced by US law, is based on the assumption that the patient was physically or mentally unable to provide *de facto* consent to the additional treatment.[45] In

---

[42] *Id.*, § 15(1).

[43] *Id.* § 15(2). It is possible, according to Israeli law, Section 15(1) of the Patient's Rights Law, to provide medical treatment without informed consent if the patient is physically or mentally unable to give such consent. Section 15(2) of the same law also states that if a patient who is in serious danger opposes treatment, the therapist may provide treatment even against the patient's will. This section of the law does not specifically deal with an emergency but allows the Ethics Committee to grant substitute consent in place of the patient.

[44] C.C: (T.A.) 1425/57 Kaira v. The Attorney General, P.M. 73 (1959). Discussed by Zeev Weil & Dana Gruber, *The Doctrine of Two Schools of Thought—A Shield or a Sword*, 19 MED. & L. 663, 687 n.126 (2000).

[45] Millard v. Nagle, 587 A. 2D 10 (1991). For an academic discussion of this ruling, *see* Grant H. Morris, *Dissing Disclosure: Just What the Physician Ordered*, 44 ARIZ. L. REV. 313, 335 n.120 (2002); Thaddeus Mason Pope, *Clinicians May Not Administer Life-Sustaining Treatment without Consent: Civil, Criminal, and Disciplinary Sanctions*, 9 J. HEALTH & BIOMEDICAL L. 213, 262 n.319 (2013); Thaddeus Mason Pope, *Certified Patient Decision*

general, the physician's obligation to disclose is extensive. This is the case in situations where an operation or treatment is not intended to prevent immediate danger and the treatment can be delayed without causing the situation to deteriorate. If a patient has consented to an anticipated medical treatment, but in the course of it the need for a further, non-urgent procedure arises, and delaying it would not place the patient's life and health at risk, the additional treatment should not be carried out. The patients' autonomy grants them the right to make this decision.[46]

Where implied consent is involved, it is vital to identify how such consent is obtained in similar cases, at the same and other medical institutions. Usually, no objections are raised about implied consent when complex, nonstandard treatment is concerned, as opposed to conventional treatment. Informed consent is not required from a patient if in the course of treatment to which consent has been given the need arises for further treatment that could not have been foreseen.[47]

Meisel and Roth[48] presented the results of research carried out by Boreham and Gibson on providing explanatory details by physicians to their patients in private clinics.[49] They concluded that physicians are not in the habit of explaining alternative methods of treatment and their risks and chances unless they are asked specifically, and even less so

---

Aids: Solving Persistent Problems with Informed Consent Law, 45(1) JOURNAL OF LAW, MEDICINE & ETHICS 12 n.32 (2017).

[46] CA 253/85 Kupat Holim Clalit v. Amiel (1987), https://www.nevo.co.il/psika html/elyon/NOPADI- NX-9-066-L.htm, discussed by Bar-Alon, *supra* note 34, at 697 n.30, ruled that a surgeon who decided in the process of an operation to change course in a way that increased the risks should have interrupted the operation to consider an alternative treatment and even to warn the patient about the risks of the secondary plan. In a similar case, Justice Beinisch ruled that as long as the operation or treatment was not intended to avoid immediate danger, and as long as it was possible to delay treatment without worsening the situation so that the patient could receive information and give informed consent, the physician's obligation for disclosure was greater.

[47] *Supra* note 35, at 506.

[48] Meisel & Roth, *supra* note 16, at 274, 277, 323.

[49] See Boreham & Gibson, *The Informative Process in Private Medical Consultations: A Preliminary Investigation*, 12 SOC. SC. & MED. 409 (1978).

during patients' subsequent visits to their clinics. The same concept is applied in the US.

The *Murray* case examined a situation where a woman arrived at the hospital to give birth and the physician had to perform a C-section. During the procedure, the physician discovered some tumors on the patient's uterine walls and estimated that future pregnancies and births in this situation might endanger the woman's life, therefore he decided to tie her fallopian tubes during the course of the C-section to prevent future pregnancies. The court decided that the physician was not entitled to take such a step without the woman's consent.[50]

Recognition of a woman's right to have an abortion even at the stage when the fetus is viable stems from a broader right of the woman to make decisions concerning her life and body. Given this right, a liberal interpretation of the doctrine of informed consent would consider a woman's right to make a decision about her body absolute, even when she is pregnant, that is, even when potential life is concerned and when the fetus can live outside the womb. Yet, even liberal philosophers who support the notion of individual autonomy, such as Emmanuel Kant, Jean-Jacques Rousseau, and John Stuart Mill, believed that the right to autonomy is not absolute and can be subject to other rights. Thus, I conclude the woman's right to autonomy over her body is not absolute, especially when the fetus can survive outside the womb.

In sum, this chapter sought to extend the doctrine of informed consent by a pregnant woman to medical treatments that affect the fetus she is carrying. In both American and Israeli law, the extent of the information that the physician must provide to the patient to obtain legally valid informed consent is determined by an objective test. The doctrine of

---

[50] *See* Murray v. McMurchy [1949] 2 DLR 442 (Sup. Ct BC), discussed by Brian Bromberger, *Patient Participation in Medical Decision-Making: Are the Courts the Answer?*, 6 U.N.S.W.L.J. 1 (1983) *passim*; Editorial, *Consent and the Anaesthetist*, 43 ANAESTHESIA 265, n.4 (1987); M.A. Branthwaite, *Consent and the Incompetent Adult—The Legal Perspective*, 10(3) CLINICAL INTENSIVE CARE 77 (1999), https://www.tandfonline.com/action/showCitFormats?doi=10.3109%2Ftcic.10.3.77.79.

informed consent concerns the health of the patient, in this case, the pregnant woman; it does not concern the health of the fetus even in the viable phase. The concept of informed consent did not foresee a preoccupation with fetal health in the viable phase. I argue that pregnancy tests and the resulting expectation of giving birth to a healthy fetus have expanded the obligation of disclosure within the doctrine of informed consent. This argument is relevant also to the discourse of women's health, but for the sake of this discussion, it concerns especially the health of the fetus. I argue that during pregnancy, before giving informed consent to a medical procedure, women should be provided information about the health of the fetus and the possible consequences of the proposed treatment for the viable fetus. The corollary of this argument is that the viable fetus is a patient who should enjoy rights already in the womb.

Chapter 3
The Fetus

1. Development of the Fetus

1.1 Developmental stages of the fetus as described in ancient times

A fetus is a living being in the womb of mammals, which was created as a result of fertilization of an ovum by sperm; after its birth, a fetus is referred to as a "neonate." In antiquity, scholars described the stages of fetal development from the moment of fertilization until the moment of birth based on their knowledge at the time.[1] Pythagoras thought that the sperm incubates in the heat of the womb and the formation of a fetus results from this incubation, composed of three parts: a human part, an animal part, and a vegetal part. The brain creates the human part of the fetus, the heart creates the animal part, and the umbilicus the vegetal part. By contrast, in an essay on fetal formation, Aristotle claimed that the development of the fetus is gradual, and the development begins with the heart.

At the time, it was believed that the fetus was a complete, albeit miniature, being from the moment of fertilization. Galenus, writing about 100 years after Aristotle, maintained that fetal development begins in the liver, moves to the heart, and only then is the brain created. He described the blood-filled fetal organs (such as the liver) as emanating from the woman and the sperm-filled fetal organs (such as the brain) as emanating from the man.[2] Pliny described fetal

---

[1] All data are from AVRAHAM STEINBERG, ENCYCLOPEDIA OF JEWISH MEDICAL ETHICS: A COMPILATION OF JEWISH MEDICAL LAW ON ALL TOPICS OF MEDICAL INTEREST vol. 1, s.v. 'fetus' (Fred Rosner trans., 2003).

[2] *See* the parallel description of the Babylonian Talmud *Niddah* 31a: "The child's bones, sinews, nails, the brain in his head and the white in his eye"—are formed, and his mother supplies "the semen of the red substance out of which are formed the child's skin, flesh, hair, blood and the black of his eye." Discussed by YEHEZKEL MARGALIT, THE JEWISH FAMILY—BETWEEN FAMILY LAW AND CONTRACT LAW 155 n.92 (2017) and

development as beginning in the heart, whereas Alcmaeon claimed that it begins in the head. Until the Middle Ages, no further descriptions emerged. Leonardo da Vinci was the first to visually represent the offspring in its mother's womb in the way we know it today. Only in the 17th century, with the invention of the microscope, was a significant advance made in understanding the stages of creation and development of the fetus. Graff discovered the follicles in the ovary that release the ova, and Leeuwenhoek discovered sperm cells.

1.2 Developmental stages of the fetus as recognized in modern times

In the 19th century, the modern perception of the stages of pregnancy as a continuous process from the moment of fertilization to the moment of birth was already developing. Today, it is common to distinguish two main stages of fetal development. The first (embryonic) stage begins at the moment of fertilization and ends after eight weeks of pregnancy.[3]

---

in *Towards Establishing Parenthood by Agreement in Jewish Law*, 26(2) AMERICAN UNIVERSITY JOURNAL OF GENDER, SOCIAL POLICY & THE LAW 647, 671 n.90 (2018).

[3] During the fertilization process, two mature germ cells meet in the fallopian tube: the male sperm and the female ovum. The two cells become one zygote. The zygote divides into two cells, and then each cell divides itself again and again (two cells become four, four become eight, and so on) until a morula is formed (*morus* in Latin is a mulberry tree), after which a blastocyst—a mass of cells some of which will be differentiated to form the fetus and others the placenta. As the ovum is dividing, it begins to move down through the fallopian tube to insert itself into the womb. Within five to seven days after fertilization, the blastocyst reaches the womb and is absorbed by the uterine mucosa. At this stage takes place the process of differentiation of the blastocyst cells to form the fetus and its supporting elements (placenta, amniotic sac, etc.). At the end of the second week of formation, the fetus has the shape of a head and tail and the cells differentiate into tissues that comprise the fetus's heart, brain, urinary and digestive systems, etc. This stage is characterized by rapid development, both in structure and in pre-fetal functioning. In the fourth week of fertilization, the back of the fetus begins to curve, its heart starts to develop in a functional form as well as the central nervous system, kidneys, and urinary tract. The fifth week sees the budding of the tongue, the eyes, ears, lungs, heart, and limbs. The development of the heart, the nervous system, and the renal system continues; the fetus measures about 8 millimeters. In the sixth week, the teeth, nose, intestines, spleen, and reproductive system begin to develop. The fetus already has a head and neck, and its ears and eyes begin to bud. It now measures 13 millimeters. In the seventh week, the skeletal muscles and fingers begin to grow, the back and head start to move, and the reproductive

At the end of this stage, the skeleton starts to form, and sex gland activity affects the specific development related to the sex of the fetus. By then, the fetus weighs about 1 gram and is about 30 millimeters long. The second (fetal) stage[4] lasts from the end of the eighth week to birth.[5] It seems that from the 23rd week onward, the fetus is able to hear the mother's voice and other external noises, and its lungs are almost completely formed. In the 32nd week, the fetus is almost completely formed, with eyes open. From this week on, the fetus takes up most of the womb space and its movements are limited. At the end of the 35th week, the average weight of a fetus is 2.5 kg, and in the 36th week, its head starts to move down into the birth canal.

There may be deviations from this general developmental process but they are rare. In this book, I differentiate between a fetus in the developmental stage (up to 24 weeks) and the viable stage (after 24 weeks), which I refer to as a "viable fetus."

In the past,[6] pregnancy could be discovered only when the woman missed a menstrual period, or even later, only when the fetus began to

---

system continues to develop. The tiny fetus now measures about 17 millimeters. In the eighth week, enamel begins to form on the teeth, soft muscles develop, and limbs start to grow on the sides of the fetus.

[4] For the medical, ethical, and legal differences between these two stages, *see* Carson Strong, *The Moral Status of Preembryos, Embryos, Fetuses, and Infants*, 22(5) JOURNAL OF MEDICINE AND PHILOSOPHY: A FORUM FOR BIOETHICS AND PHILOSOPHY OF MEDICINE 457 (1997); ROBERT P. GEORGE & CHRISTOPHER TOLLEFSEN, EMBRYO: A DEFENSE OF HUMAN LIFE (2008); BONNIE STEINBOCK, LIFE BEFORE BIRTH: THE MORAL AND LEGAL STATUS OF EMBRYOS AND FETUSES (2011).

[5] Steinberg, *supra* note 1. This stage of fetal development is typified mainly by functional development: nails, bone marrow, external sexual signs with clear differentiation between the testicles and the ovaries, increasing movements and reactions to outside stimuli (for example, an increase in heartbeat during amniocentesis). At this stage, the fetal muscles begin to work; the fetus can move its arms and legs, and also open and close its hands; the spine and ribs harden and its nails are formed. In the 12th week, it is already possible to identify the sex of the fetus on an ultrasound image. The nervous system is not yet complete and the eyes are shut. The fetus is already active, kicking, and turning over, and by the 20th week, its average weight is between 200 and 250 grams and the woman can already feel its movements.

[6] Only some 150 years ago.

move.[7] Today, a pregnancy can be discovered at a much earlier stage of development using technologies such as ultrasound.

The developmental stages of the fetus present existential questions with ethical, moral, cultural, and religious aspects. One such pertinent question, perhaps the central one, is the following: Do developments in medical technology provide sufficient information to establish whether a viable fetus is a person or almost a person, and therefore entitled to certain rights? Rimon-Zarfati asked Israeli students this question[8] and found that the students distinguished between the early gestational stage and the later one in which the fetus is a person. The students did not define the term "person," but we can infer from their statements that on some level, the viable fetus has rights.

Today, medical technology can be used to track the fetus at almost all stages of development in the womb for medical reasons. In the 1970s and 1980s, prenatal tests were aimed at diagnosing defects of the fetus, including the number of chromosomes it had (e.g., to diagnose Down's syndrome), cleft palate, and hydrocephalus. Today, prenatal tests extend to diagnosing minor fetal defects, such as short stature, deafness,

---

[7] These movements are known as "quickening." For the correlation between these movements and the legality of the abortion of the viable fetus, *see* Robert H. Blank, *Judicial Decision Making and Biological Fact:* Roe v. Wade *and the Unresolved Question of Fetal Viability*, 37(4) POLITICAL RESEARCH QUARTERLY 584 (1984); Randy Beck, *The Essential Holding of Casey: Rethinking Viability*, 75 UMKC L. REV. 713 (2007); Randy Beck, Gonzales, Casey, *and the Viability* Rule, 103 NW. U. L. REV. 249 (2009).

[8] Nitzan Rimon-Zarfaty, Aviad E. Raz, & Yael Hashiloni-Dolev, *When Does a Fetus Become a Person? An Israeli Viewpoint*, 37 JOURNAL OF FAMILY AND REPRODUCTIVE HEALTHCARE 216 (2011). For a discussion of this research, *see* Carlos Y. Valenzuela, *The Ontogenetic Origin of Human Beings in the Scientific–Ethics Perspective and Its Implications on Abortion*, 4 J. CLIN. RES. BIOETH. 148, n.42 (2013), https://pdfs.semanticscholar.org/9aec/f4ce09c828424c98b433a5238e2265afd0e0.pdf; Aviad Raz et al., *Donation of Surplus Frozen Pre-Embryos to Research Israel: Underlying Motivations*, 5 ISRAEL JOURNAL OF HEALTH POLICY RESEARCH 25 n.15 (2016), https://ijhpr.biomedcentral.com/track/pdf/10.1186/s 13584-016-0085-4; Yael Hashiloni-Dolev & Silke Schicktanz, *A Cross-Cultural Analysis of Posthumous Reproduction: The Significance of the Gender and Margins-of-Life Perspectives*, 4 REPRODUCTIVE BIOMEDICINE & SOCIETY ONLINE 21 (2017), https://www.sciencedirect.com/science/article/pii/S2405661817300126.

or asymmetrical limbs. Test results are presented to the women to determine whether to terminate the pregnancy. Some, upon learning that the fetus has a serious defect, do so because they are not prepared to give birth to such a child; others decide to terminate even when the defect is minimal.[9]

2. Historical Review

2.1 Status of the fetus in antiquity

This section examines how different ancient cultures and religions related to the termination of pregnancy (abortions) and whether these attitudes influenced modern legislation. During the ancient times, there was an extremely strict approach toward terminating pregnancy. The origin of this attitude is not clear. The prohibition may have derived from the fear of interfering with the natural process of the pregnancy[10] or from a desire to preserve the future life of the fetus.[11] Whatever the reason, there was great ambivalence regarding the termination of pregnancy,[12] and each culture had its reasons for it.

In India, Buddhists forbade the termination of pregnancy for religious reasons.[13] The ancient Indian law books[14] considered termination of pregnancy to be murder, and thus forbade the Brahmins from carrying

---

[9] For a discussion of the phenomenon of aborting every fetus that is "not perfect," *see* GLENN MCGEE, THE PERFECT BABY: A PRAGMATIC APPROACH TO GENETICS (1997); Larissa Remennick, *The Quest for the Perfect Baby: Why Do Israeli Women Seek Prenatal Genetic Testing?*, 28(1) SOCIOLOGY OF HEALTH & ILLNESS 21 (2006); Ruth Kannai, *"Maybe It Would Be Better If You Spoke to My Mother?"—Genetic Counseling and Personal Experience*, 80(2) PATIENT EDUCATION AND COUNSELING 260 (2010).

[10] The techniques used in the past to terminate pregnancy were primitive and dangerous.

[11] Legislation at the time demonstrated an ambivalent approach to the status of the fetus. Until the second half of the 20th century, there were few examples of the absence of conscientious objection to killing the fetus.

[12] Halperin, *supra* note 14.

[13] According to the perception that the souls of extinct fetuses are considered bad and dangerous.

[14] The Aryas and the "Manava Dharma-Shastra." *See, e.g.*, Ms. Shiney Vashisht, *Manusmriti: Exploring Gender Justice in Ancient Hindu Legal Framework*, in FEMINISM AND LITERATURE TEXT AND CONTEXT 150 (2015).

it out; anyone who disobeyed was severely punished. The ancient Persians also prohibited termination of pregnancy on religious grounds. In ancient Assyria, the Code of the Assura[15] imposed the death sentence on women who killed their fetuses. The bodies of such women were not allowed to be buried. In ancient Greece, termination of pregnancy was considered a crime, and women who carried it out were sentenced to death.[16]

In ancient Egypt, termination of pregnancy was considered a serious crime, but the severity of the punishment is unclear. Infanticide was openly tolerated in ancient Egypt, and the Pharoah's royal command, "every newborn male child should be thrown in the river,"[17] was not exceptional or extreme.

Pythagorean philosophers of the 4th century BCE considered the fetus a living being from the moment of fertilization, and therefore forbade harming it. Some regard this claim as the basis for the Hippocratic oath, which explicitly prohibits providing any assistance in terminating a

---

[15] Code of the Assura, c. 1975 BCE. *See* Ancient History Sourcebook, https://sourcebooks.fordham.edu/ancient/1075assyriancode.asp. For a discussion of the approach of Assyrian law to the dilemma of abortion, *see* Tom C. Clark, *Religion, Morality, and Abortion: A Constitutional Appraisal*, 2 LOY. U. L. A. L. REV. 1, 4 (1969); H. Wayne House, *Miscarriage or Premature Birth: Additional Thoughts on Exodus 21:22–25*, 41(1) WESTMINSTER THEOLOGICAL JOURNAL 108, 115–17 (1978), http://faculty.gordon.edu/hu/bi/ted hildebrandt/otesources/02-exodus/Text/Articles/House-Exod21-WTJ.pdf; Daniel B. Sinclair, *The Legal Basis for the Prohibition on Abortion in Jewish Law*, 15 ISR. L. REV. 109, 111 (1980)

[16] The termination of pregnancy in ancient Greece was described by Ovid, Seneca, Juvenal, and other prominent philosophers as a crime on one hand and as an accepted phenomenon on the other. Pregnancies were terminated on a vast scale, not only because of social constraints but also because of the women's desire to preserve their figure from the changes caused by pregnancy and giving birth. Plato claimed that the fetus is a living being because it moves and is nourished in its mother's womb. By contrast, the Aryas of India, much like the Greek and Roman Stoics, claimed that it is not a living being but rather one of the mother's internal organs because it does not breathe until after it is born, and the fact that it lives inside the mother does not give it independent status.

[17] Exodus 1:22.

pregnancy.[18] Platonic and Stoic philosophers differed, claiming that the fetus was a human being only from the moment of birth, therefore did not oppose the termination of pregnancy at any stage. Plato stated that every woman over the age of 40 should be forced to terminate her pregnancy, but Aristotle—who, as noted, claimed that life begins from the moment the woman feels the fetal movements in her womb—was prepared to accept termination of pregnancy for social reasons[19] on condition that the procedure was carried out before the first kick of the fetus.

Ancient Roman law was in favor of the absolute right of the father over family members, including complete ownership of his children after their birth, whereas the fetus was considered part of the woman's body.[20] The accepted perception until the 2nd century BCE was that killing a fetus was a legal act, and termination of pregnancy was not forbidden by the Roman emperors.[21] Ovid[22] was critical of "women who puncture and prick themselves with an instrument or who give a

---

[18] From the Hippocratic oath (4th century BCE): "I will never give to a woman a drug or instrument to perform an abortion." *See, e.g.*, James S. Murray, *The Alleged Prohibition of Abortion in the Hippocratic Oath*, 35(3) ECHOS DU MONDE CLASSIQUE: CLASSICAL VIEWS 293 (1991); Ben A. Rich, *Postmodern Medicine: Deconstructing the Hippocratic Oath*, 65 U. COLO. L. REV. 77, 87–119 (1993); Thomas Rutten & Leonie von Reppert-Bismarck, *Receptions of the Hippocratic Oath in the Renaissance: The Prohibition of Abortion as a Case Study in Reception*, 51(4) JOURNAL OF THE HISTORY OF MEDICINE AND ALLIED SCIENCES 456 (1996).

[19] Such as families with many children. For a discussion of Aristotle's perception of abortion, *see, e.g.*, Anthony Nathan Cabot, *History of Abortion Law*, 1980 ARIZ. ST. L.J. 73, 77–86 (1980); Patrick Gray, *Abortion, Infanticide, and the Social Rhetoric of the Apocalypse of Peter*, 9(3) JOURNAL OF EARLY CHRISTIAN STUDIES 313 (2001); Carrie-Ann Biondi, *Aristotle's Moral Expert: The Phronimos*, in ETHICS EXPERTISE: PHILOSOPHY AND MEDICINE 87 (Lisa Rasmussen ed., 2005).

[20] *Pars viscerum matris*. For a legal discussion of this dictum, *see* B. Frey, *Injuries to Infants en Ventre sa Mere*, 12 ST. LOUIS L. REV. 85, 91 (1927); Robert M. Byrn, *The Abortion Question: A Nonsectarian Approach*, 11 CATH. LAW. 316, 317 (1965); David A. Gordon, *The Unborn Plaintiff*, 63 MICH. L. REV. 579, 582 (1965).

[21] Although many abortions like these ended in infection and death.

[22] 23 BCE-17 AD. For his significant influence on the abortion dilemma, *see* Sheila K. Dickison, *Abortion in Antiquity*, 6(1) ARETHUSA 159 (1973); W.J. Watts, *Ovid, the Law and Roman Society on Abortion*, 16 ACTA CLASSICA 89 (1973); M.K. Gamel, *Non sine caede: Abortion Politics and Poetics in Ovid's Amores*, 16 HELIOS 183 (1989).

deadly drug to their children before they are born," and condemned women who terminated their pregnancy themselves, something even wild animals do not do.

Therefore, the fetus appears to have had no rights in antiquity, and destroying it was forbidden not necessarily because of opposition to terminating its life, but rather out of fear of its ghost. In the majority of Western countries, most measures requiring severe punishment for those involved in terminating pregnancies were omitted from legislation,[23] although the prohibition itself remained in force for many years almost everywhere in the world.

Despite objections on the part of religious institutions, and the fact that the right to terminate pregnancy remains in public dispute, the feminist movement succeeded in changing the law in many countries, and some criminal prohibitions against terminating pregnancies have been repealed. The goal of feminism is to improve the condition of women worldwide. Feminists of the mid-20th century demanded the liberation of women from their stereotypical role and a reexamination of powerful conventions, to secure women's control over fertility and the right to terminate an unwanted pregnancy. Thus, feminism has changed the female experience of pregnancy, allowing "conditional pregnancy." In the wake of these ideological shifts, the law has been changed in the past generation in many countries, including the US, the Netherlands, and Israel. Since the 1970s, a woman's right to be in control of her fertility, whether preventing pregnancy or terminating it, has become the focal point of feminist struggle in most countries in the world.

2.2 The Jewish approach

Judaism relates to the life of a fetus as God's property and maintains that life is given to a person on loan. During pregnancy, the woman is responsible for the life of the fetus. Because only God has the right to harm the life of a person, the woman cannot terminate a pregnancy at

[23] The death penalty was repealed in Prussia in 1837.

will. Therefore, Jewish law forbids the termination of a pregnancy at any stage, even without giving legal rights to the fetus. In general, Jewish law does not consider termination of a pregnancy to be murder,[24,25] although it is forbidden to do so without serious justification because this would harm something that Jewish law deems to be a live being. As a living being, the fetus has the right not to be harmed during pregnancy, and if someone harms the fetus while it is in the womb, they must pay damages either to the fetus itself or to the woman.[26]

Despite the absolute prohibition on terminating a pregnancy, there are diverse approaches to abortion in Judaism. In the book of Genesis,[27] it is written that according to the Noahide laws, aborting a helpless fetus is considered murder. The Torah distinguishes between an injury that causes the death of the woman, which is considered murder and is punished by death, and the fetus dying as a result of a fight, which is

---

[24] *See generally* DAVID M. FELDMAN, BIRTH CONTROL AND JEWISH LAW: MARITAL RELATIONS, CONTRACEPTION, AND ABORTION AS SET FORTH IN THE CLASSIC TEXTS OF JEWISH LAW (1968); DAVID M. FELDMAN, MARITAL RELATIONS, CONCEPTION AND ABORTION IN JEWISH LAW (1978); DANIEL SCHIFF, ABORTION IN JUDAISM (2002).

[25] Although some consider this possible, *see* Mordechai Halperin, *Termination of Pregnancy: Legal, Moral and Jewish Aspects*, 6(2) JEWISH MEDICAL ETHICS AND HALACHA 41 (2008). Halperin maintained that when the fetus is harmed by being in the woman's womb, it is the fetus who is the prosecutor:

The main obligation is to the fetus itself, and the father is entitled to monetary compensation under the law of inheritance, but only if the fetus dies. But if it is harmed—the obligation is to the fetus itself. And if the fetus dies inside the mother, the father inherits its right [. . .] thus whoever harms a fetus pays the fetus itself. According to Maimonides, only when the fetus is killed no money should be paid [.] But if the damage is to the fetus, it is judged according to the law concerning a person who harms his friend, and the payment belongs to the fetus.

[26] Raphael Weinberger, *Claim for Damages of the Fetus*, 8–9 MAGAL 103, 114 (1992) (Heb.). Weinberger argued that the fetus has no right to make a claim and that only the woman can make a claim because it is her body that has been damaged: "It is possible that its claim will be rejected until the day when it comes into the world and has its own mind, but the court could provide it with a custodian, or pass a special bylaw enabling it to claim damages even before it is born."

[27] Genesis 9:5.

not considered manslaughter, and the offender must only pay damages.[28]

For the first 40 days after conception, Jewish law considers the fetus "only water," therefore terminating a pregnancy before the 41st day of fertilization is less problematic than doing so later. In multifetal pregnancies, it is permissible to reduce the number of fetuses to ensure the survival of the remaining ones. The status of the fetus increases as it becomes more viable, in the second and third trimesters of the pregnancy.

If the fetus endangers the woman's life, the latter can be saved at the expense of the former.[29] Maimonides established the point of balance between saving the woman's life and saving that of the fetus. Subsequently, rabbinical scholars have taught that if a woman encounters difficulties in giving birth, the fetus may be cut. But if its head has already appeared, it cannot be harmed, because one soul cannot be saved at the expense of another, and that is the nature of the world.[30]

In our generation, some rabbinical authorities allow the termination of a pregnancy if there is a likelihood that continuing it might endanger the woman's life. Other authorities permit termination if there is a danger that continuing the pregnancy might cause severe physical or psychological harm to the fetus. The renowned 20th-century Jewish philosopher, Yeshayahu Leibowitz,[31] stated that there was no difference, scientifically or philosophically, between a fetus and a baby

---

[28] Exodus 21:22–23.

[29] Tosefta with the commentary *Hasdei David*, Tractate *Ohalot* 87b. For a general discussion of the Tosefta, *see* Paul Mandel, *The Tosefta*, *in* THE CAMBRIDGE HISTORY OF JUDAISM vol. 4: THE LATE ROMAN–RABBINIC PERIOD 316 (Louis Finkelstein et al. eds., 1984). But, *compare* this commentary with what is cited by Daniel B. Sinclair, *in The Legal Basis for the Prohibition on Abortion in Jewish Law*, 15 ISR. L. REV. 109, 113 n.24 (1980).

[30] Maimonides, supra note 14, 1, 9, 2.

[31] Yeshayahu Leibowitz, *Medicine and the Values of Life*, in PROCEEDING OF THE CATHEDRA OF THE MEDICINE HISTORY 1, 2, 12 (1977) (Heb.).

that has been born. He argued that human life develops on a continuum that starts with fertilization, proceeds with pregnancy, and after birth, continues at least to adolescence.

There is no definitive borderline in life apart from the moment of fertilization and that of death. Therefore, he finds it unacceptable that society should deviate from the norm of not harming a living being. Leibowitz's philosophical approach to this matter is similar to that of Catholicism. This position is shared also by Alessandra Piontelli, who observed fetuses in the wombs of their mothers using three-dimensional ultrasound scans, following up on their development after birth to the age of four.[32] Her central finding was that there was a remarkable continuity of behavior before and after birth, and that after birth many small children showed signs of being affected by prenatal experiences.[33]

Jewish law does not consider terminating a pregnancy as the murder of a person, but does prohibit carrying it out without proper justification[34] and makes a distinction between doing it during the first or the other two trimesters.[35] Different theoretical opinions exist regarding the fetal status in the various stages of pregnancy, but in general, the Jewish approach is less rigid than that of Catholicism. Until the mid-19th century, neither Jewish nor Christian religion offered protection to the

---

[32] ALESSANDRA PIONTELLI, FROM FETUS TO CHILD: AN OBSERVATIONAL AND PSYCHOANALYTICAL STUDY (2003). For a discussion of this book, *see* JOAN RAPHAEL-LEFF, PREGNANCY: THE INSIDE STORY (2001); KAY MILTON, LOVING NATURE: TOWARDS AN ECOLOGY OF EMOTION (2002); DEBORAH MARKS, DISABILITY: CONTROVERSIAL DEBATES AND PSYCHOSOCIAL PERSPECTIVES (2014).

[33] Alessandra Piontelli, *From Fetus to Child: An Observational and Psychoanalytic Study* (Routledge, 1992).

[34] The very use of the term "proper justification" indicates that discretion is used. The terminology allows for an interpretation according to which if the fetus endangers the woman's life the pregnancy can be terminated.

[35] For more on this issue, *see* Yehiel M. Bar-Ilan, *Za'ar Gufa Kodem: Induced Abortion in Halakhah and Israeli Law*, in THE RIGHT TO LIFE WITH NO MALFORMATION 81 (Jonathan Davies & Avraham Sahar eds., 2007) (Heb.), discussed by Daphne Barak-Erez, *Reproductive Rights in a Jewish and Democratic State*, in CONSTITUTIONAL SECULARISM IN AN AGE OF RELIGIOUS REVIVAL 232 n.19 (Michel Rosenfeld & Susanna Mancini eds., 2014).

fetus from the moment of fertilization through the 40th week, when the "soul" comes into being (also known as ensoulment). At about this time, Christianity changed its approach and began to consider the beginning of fetal life at the moment of fertilization.[36] The position of Israeli law today is related to the distinction Judaism makes between the rights of a fetus and the rights of a neonate. In Israeli law, the fetus lacks legal rights until it is born, which is different from the position of other Western societies and is more similar to that of Christianity and Islam.

2.3 The Catholic approach

Christian literature dealt extensively with the termination of pregnancy.[37] As early as 305 AD, authorities administered cruel punishments to women who terminated their pregnancy, although later the restrictions became less severe.[38] Regarding the actual beginning of life, Thomas Aquinas wrote[39] that the consciousness and movement of the fetus show evidence that life exists, and therefore, like Aristotle, he supported the approach that life begins when the woman feels "the first kick." Other theologians accepted Aristotle's view, according to which the soul develops in three stages: a soul of "developing energies" during fertilization, a soul of a minimal life system at a later stage, and finally, a complete human soul.[40] Even in the 21st century, Pope John Paul II wrote in an Apostolic Letter: "Human lives are holy because they

---

[36] Shai Levi, *The Paradox of Jewish Bioethics in Israel: The Cast of Reproductive Technologies*, in RELIGION IN BIOTEHISCHEN DISKURSE. INTERDISZPLINARE, INTERNATIONALE UND INTERRELIGIOSE PERSPEKTIVEN 81–102 (2010). For a recent discussion of this research, *see* Eimi Lev, *Prenatal Googling: Online Information Seeking by Israeli Women During Pregnancy*, 3(2) INTERNATIONAL REVIEW OF SOCIAL RESEARCH 69, 70, 72, 80 (2013); Shirin G. Naef, *Modern Reproductive Technologies in the Light of Traditional Ontologies: An Anthropological Reflection on Assisted Reproduction in Iran, in* SELBSTGESTALTUNG DES MENSCHEN DURCH BIOTECHNIKEN 157, 171 (Narr Francke Attempto et al. eds., 2015); Hashiloni-Dolev & Schicktanz, *supra* note 8. *See also more generally* BIOETHICS AND BIOPOLITICS IN ISRAEL: SOCIO-LEGAL, POLITICAL, AND EMPIRICAL ANALYSIS (Hagai Boas et al., 2018).

[37] Steinberg, *supra* note 1.

[38] *See* Halperin, *supra* note 14.

[39] 13th-century Christian philosopher and theologian.

[40] Popes Innocent III and Gregory IX supported this approach in the 13th century.

reflect God's work and His creation, they are fixed in their connection to Him and it is for this purpose that Man was created. God is the Master of life from beginning to end."[41] In other writings of Pope John Paul II, he stated that an ultrasound test during pregnancy was legitimate because it was intended to prevent harm to the lives of the fetus and the woman.

Over the years, following the Samaritan Torah, the Septuagint, and the interpretation of Philo of Alexandria, the Christian approach underwent significant changes. Christianity reached a compromise that distinguished between the stages of fetal development regarding the termination of pregnancy. This approach derived from the belief that in male fetuses, the creation of the soul is complete by the 40th day after fertilization, when the fetus develops a complete external human form; in female fetuses, the process is complete later, by the 80th day after fertilization. Establishing the time when the soul is created led to relating differently to the termination of pregnancy at the early or later stages, and at the viable stage. All significant changes were rescinded in 1588, when Sixtus V reinstated all the previous punishments regarding the termination of pregnancy at any stage of fetal development. Any termination of pregnancy was considered murder. This principle was also ratified in the punitive laws published by Pius V in 1862, as well as in the last canonical law that was adopted in 1918.

Catholicism was bitterly opposed to the termination of pregnancy at any stage because adherents of the religion considered the fetus a living being with full human rights from the very moment of fertilization. In the 20th century, Catholic physicians were adamant that termination of pregnancy should be avoided even if the life of the woman was at stake:

---

[41] *See* also the prolific writing of Pope John Paul II regarding this issue. For a discussion of his legacy, *see, e.g.*, JAMES J. MCCARTNEY, UNBORN PERSONS: POPE JOHN PAUL II AND THE ABORTION DEBATE (1987); Michele Dillon, *Cultural Differences in the Abortion Discourse of the Catholic Church: Evidence from Four Countries*, 57(1) SOCIOLOGY OF RELIGION 25 (1996); Kenneth Mulligan, *Pope John Paul II and Catholic Opinion Toward the Death Penalty and Abortion*, 87(3) SOCIAL SCIENCE QUARTERLY 739 (2006).

according to them, two deaths were preferable to one murder.[42] Fetal reduction in case of multiple pregnancies, when the chances of all fetuses surviving are very low, is still rejected by traditional Catholicism, which equates it with throwing several people off a sinking ship to save the others. This approach influenced lawmakers in Western countries, especially regarding the termination of a pregnancy at the viable stage.

The general trend in the Catholic religion is to oppose termination of pregnancy, even if occasionally they distinguish between the initial and later stages of pregnancy.[43] The Catholic Church maintains that the fetus has rights from the moment of fertilization. Today, most modern legal systems hold that the right to life manifests itself from the moment the fetus is capable of existing independently from the womb, which is usually identified as the 24th week of pregnancy. In recent years, however, a growing number of different groups have adopted a more traditional Catholic answer to the question of when life begins.[44] The struggle in the US against termination of pregnancy is gaining ground, and those in favor of abortion fight against various pro-life organizations.

2.4 The Islamic approach

In Islam, the termination of pregnancy is controversial. Similarly to Catholics, scholars of the Malaki stream, the Shi'ite, the Abachi, and the Thahari posit that the fetus already has a soul at the moment of fertilization. Therefore, terminating a pregnancy at any stage is

[42] ALPHONSUS BONNAR, THE CATHOLIC DOCTOR (9th ed. 1948). For a discussion of this book, *see, e.g.*, ROSS A. ARMSTRONG, PRIMARY AND SECONDARY PRECEPTS IN THOMISTIC NATURAL LAW TEACHING 186 (2012); NICHOLAS P. CAFARDI, VOTING AND HOLINESS: CATHOLIC PERSPECTIVES ON POLITICAL PARTICIPATION (2012).

[43] Halperin, *supra* note 14.

[44] For the far-reaching influence of the stringent Catholic perspective on both US and international law, *see* John T. Jr. Noonan, *Abortion and the Catholic Church: A Summary History*, 12 NAT. L.F. 85 (1967); TIMOTHY BYRNES & MARY C. SEGERS, THE CATHOLIC CHURCH AND THE POLITICS OF ABORTION: A VIEW FROM THE STATES (1991); Rishona Fleishman, *The Battle against Reproductive Rights: The Impact of the Catholic Church on Abortion Law in Both International and Domestic Areas*, 14 EMORY INT'L L. REV. 277 (2000).

tantamount to murder. Scholars of the Hanbal stream permit the termination of pregnancy in the first 40 days. Scholars of the Hanafi and Zaidi schools permit terminating pregnancy in the first 120 days. Within the Sha'afi school, some scholars permit terminating pregnancy in the first 80 days, others allow it to be performed until the 120th day, and others forbid it outright. Most adjudicators on this issue consistently return to the rationale of endangering the life of the woman: if continuing the pregnancy endangers the woman, saving her life is preferable to saving the life of the potential human being.[45]

Islamic law did not ignore the human rights discourse. The Koran does not adamantly oppose termination of pregnancy, and the Organization of Muslim Countries[46] maintains this discourse.[47] in several Muslim countries, presenting differing attitudes and declarations on the issue. According to Egyptian law,[48] before agreeing to terminate a pregnancy, it should be determined whether or not the fetus is a human being. Egyptian law[49] forbids terminating pregnancy unless it poses a danger

---

[45] For an overview of the position of Islam on the abortion debate, *see, e.g.*, Leila Hessini, *Abortion and Islam: Policies and Practice in the Middle East and North Africa*, 15(29) REPRODUCTIVE HEALTH MATTERS 75 (2007); Kiarash Aramesh, *Abortion: An Islamic Ethical View*, 6 (Suppl. 5) IRAN J. ALLERGY ASTHMA IMMUNOL. 29 (2007), http://citeseerx.ist.psu.edu/viewdoc/download?doi=10.1.1.835.7088&rep=rep1&type=pdf; Yassar Abdullah Alamri, *Islam and Abortion*, 43(1) JOURNAL OF THE ISLAMIC MEDICAL ASSOCIATION OF NORTH AMERICA 39 (2011).

[46] These declarations lack legal validity but do indicate the current attitude toward the termination of pregnancy, deriving from the discourse on human rights.

[47] A Muslim declaration regarding human rights was recognized on September 19, 1981, and can be found in SHAHEEN ALI, GENDER AND HUMAN RIGHTS IN ISLAM AND INTERNATIONAL LAW: EQUAL BEFORE ALLAH, UNEQUAL BEFORE MAN? 287–97 (2000); Islamabad Declaration on the Role of Muslim Women Parliamentarians in the Promotion of Peace, Progress and Development of Islamic Societies, accepted on August 1–3, 1995. For an overview of this declaration, *see* Shaheen Sar Da R Ali, *Women's Rights, CEDAW and International Human Rights Debates: Toward Empowerment?*, in RETHINKING EMPOWERMENT: GENDER AND DEVELOPMENT IN A GLOBAL/LOCAL WORLD (Jane L. Parpart et al eds., 2002); KATRINA RIDDELL, ISLAM AND THE SECURITISATION OF POPULATION POLICIES: MUSLIM STATES AND SUSTAINABILITY (2009); *1st World Muslim Women Summit & Exhibition (WISE 2016): Conference Report*, 24(2) INTELLECTUAL DISCOURSE 333, 336 (2016).

[48] § 2(A).

[49] Criminal Code (1937), § 61.

to the woman's life.[50] Although similar to the Jewish approach, Egyptian law confers rights on a newborn only at the time of birth. According to Tunisian law, as of 1973, termination of pregnancy at the woman's request is permitted only in the first trimester, but in the following months, it is permitted if the fetus's life is at stake or if the woman's mental health is in danger. The original Kuwaiti law of 1981 included severe punitive measures for terminating pregnancy even in the first trimester unless the procedure was intended to save the woman's life, or the fetus was likely to be born with a defect. The consent of both parents is required.[51]

3. The Right to Life

3.1 The right to life and its definitions

This book addresses the termination of pregnancy at the viability stage, when the fetus is capable of surviving outside the womb, even if it requires artificial means to do so. At this stage, a great similarity can be seen between a viable fetus and a live baby. It is this similarity that leads me to the conclusion that guides me throughout the book—that a parallel should be drawn between the ethical status of the two. If the ethical status of the fetus is established from the stage of birth it would be difficult, although not impossible, to endorse a thesis that claims that killing a fetus at the viable stage is tantamount to murder. If the ethical status of the fetus is established at the viability stage, from the time of its ability to live independently outside the womb, it is more justifiable to endorse its ethical status and its right to life.

---

[50] Cairo Declaration, § 7(A).

[51] This is different from other existing legal systems, including Israeli law, where the father has no status in the matter. In 1984, it was also established in Kuwait that the committee for termination of pregnancy must confirm the request and that all committee members must be Muslim. For an overview of the different current perspectives of the various Muslim jurisdictions, *see, e.g.*, Vardit Rispler Chaim, *The Right Not to Be Born: Abortion of the Disadvantaged Fetus in Contemporary Fatwas*, 89(2) MUSLIM WORLD 130 (1999); Oren Asman, *Abortion in Islamic Countries—Legal and Religious Aspects*, 23 MED. & L. 73 (2004); Leila Hessini, *Islam and Abortion: The Diversity of Discourses and Practices*, 39(3) IDS BULLETIN 18 (2009).

Some differentiate between the biological and ethical development of a human being, and it would be difficult to persuade them that when it comes to the status of a viable fetus, biological and ethical development should be equivalent. They would probably argue that not every biological human creature is entitled to human rights, even if able to live outside the womb. Below I examine when the biological "creature" can be considered to have a right to life or ethical rights that should not be infringed. This is a person's most basic right, and it deserves protection in legal systems worldwide.

John Locke[52] included the right to life among the "natural" rights of every person as a person *per se* purely because of the individual's nature and human dignity. Locke claimed that this right cannot be restricted by state control. He assumed that there exists a sort of social covenant according to which the state is organized solely for achieving, securing, and promoting the interests of every individual, which includes the life and integrity of the body. Locke's treatise formed part of the basis of the American Declaration of Independence of 1778 and of the French Declaration of the Rights of Man and of the Citizen of 1789. But the positivist school of thought did not see this in the same light in the 19th century, however. René Cassin[53] maintained that the source of human rights is religion and that a declaration of human rights is merely a rewrite of the Ten Commandments. Despite the disagreements between the positivists and those in favor of natural law, all member states of the

---

[52] JOHN LOCKE, THE SECOND TREATISE OF CIVIL GOVERNMENT (1689) was the main thinker among the liberal philosophers who spoke about human rights as natural rights. *See* John D. Gorby, *The Right to an Abortion, the Scope of Fourteenth Amendment Personhood, and the Supreme Court's Birth Requirement*, 4 S. ILL. U. L.J. 1, 6 (1979); Michael W. McConnell, *God Is Dead and We Have Killed Him: Freedom of Religion in the Post-Modern Age*, 1993 BYU L. REV. 163 (1993) *passim*; Catharine A. MacKinnon, *Crimes of War, Crimes of Peace*, 4 UCLA WOMEN'S L.J. 59, 72 n.37 (1993).

[53] A jurist who was head of the United Nations committee for the formulation of the UDHR, adopted by the organization in 1948. For his unique contribution, *see, e.g.*, Kenneth Cmiel, *The Recent History of Human Rights*, 109(1) AMERICAN HISTORICAL REVIEW 117 (2004); Daniel Cere, *Human Rights and the Family*, 22(1) ACADEMIC QUESTIONS 63 (2009); Tania Penovic, *Reviewed Work: Human Rights and the Unborn Child by Rita Joseph*, 33(1) HUMAN RIGHTS QUARTERLY 229 (2011).

United Nations accepted the Universal Declaration of Human Rights (UDHR) in 1948, the main right being, in my opinion, the right to life.

Some authors noted that the theoretical and practical importance of human rights from a historical perspective is that they are the vital foundation for a life of justice in society.[54] Since the end of World War II, there has been a rise in the status of human rights internationally, above and beyond legislation in every individual country. International treaties address the defense of human rights, for example, the Convention on the Prevention and Punishment of the Crime of Genocide (1948);[55] the Convention on the Political Rights of Women (1953); the International Convention on the Elimination of All Forms of Racial Discrimination (1966); the International Covenant on Economic, Social and Cultural Rights (1966); and UN Declaration on the Elimination of All Forms of Intolerance and of Discrimination Based on Religion or Belief (1981).[56] Developing socialist countries [not clear what countries you're referring to] caring for weaker communities—those suffering from hunger, poverty, sickness, unemployment, and lack of education—have exerted international pressure and brought about a sea change in economic, social, and cultural rights. [ref?] Wieacker compiled a list of personal rights that are accepted today in most

---

[54] Ruth Gavison & Hagai Schneider, HUMAN RIGHTS AND THE CITIZEN IN ISRAEL: READINGS 1:26 (Tali Ben-Gal et al. eds, 1991) (Heb.).

[55] Discussed by Harry M. Rhea, *The Nuremberg Effect on Contemporary International Criminal Justice*, 21(4) CRIMINAL JUSTICE STUDIES 361 (2008), https://www.tandfonline.com/doi/full/10.1080/14786010802554246?scroll=top&needAccess=true; Kristin E. Henderson, *Missing Link: The Rehabilitation of Child Soldiers* 86 (2015) (unpublished thesis, California State University, Chico).

[56] For this substantial treaty, *see* Donna J. Sullivan, *Advancing the Freedom of Religion or Belief Through the UN Declaration on the Elimination of Religious Intolerance and Discrimination*, 82(3) AMERICAN JOURNAL OF INTERNATIONAL LAW 487 (1988); Ruth Lapidoth, *Freedom of Religion and of Conscience in Israel*, 47 CATH. U.L. REV. 441, 442 n.2 (1997–98); PAUL M. TAYLOR, FREEDOM OF RELIGION: UN AND EUROPEAN HUMAN RIGHTS LAW AND PRACTICE 391 (2005).

Western countries.[57] These rights were confirmed in European accords and most non-European countries, by adopting international treaties.[58]

Included in this list of rights, among others, are human dignity, fair procedures for protection against arbitrary government actions, equality before the law,[59] and the responsibility of society for the social and economic conditions of its members. In most modern constitutions, there is a special section that enumerates protected individual rights. Until World War I, most of the laws included special sections to protect the "classic" individual liberties, with basic social rights having been added later. Today, the right to life is guaranteed both in state legislation and international treaties. Some countries have yet to include in their legislation a provision about human rights, but these are in the minority, and in the last few years, they have also begun to protect these rights. Different countries have different models for social rights that receive constitutional protection. For example, in the US, an effective system of judicial constitutional scrutiny of the protection of rights has been in place, although, as *Dobbs* shows, these can be subject to review.[60]

The right to life is not mentioned explicitly in the US Constitution, but the Fifth Amendment determines that denial of life is subject to the due process of law, and the Fourteenth Amendment places this obligation

---

[57] Franz Wieacker, *Foundations of European Legal Culture*, 38 AM. J. COMP. L. 1, 29 (1990) (a European legal historian). For a discussion of this often-cited article, *see* Reiner Schulze, *European Legal History—A New Field of Research in Germany*, 13(3) JOURNAL OF LEGAL HISTORY 270, 287 (1992); FRANCIS SNYDER, THE UNFINISHED CONSTITUTION OF THE EUROPEAN UNION: PRINCIPLES, PROCESSES AND CULTURE 20 n.69 (2003), opj.ces.uc.pt/portugues/novidds/comunica/FrancisSnyder.pdf; Rafal Manko, *The Culture of Private Law in Central Europe After Enlargement: A Polish Perspective*, 11(5) EUROPEAN LAW JOURNAL 527 (2005).

[58] Wieacker, *supra* note 66, notes correctly that if ratified international treaties and adopted standards are not implemented in practice, but remain mere "lip service," many countries, especially in the third world, cannot provide a decent existence for their citizens.

[59] For this basic human right, see, e.g., *Equality before the Law*, 8 VA. L. REG. n.s. 481 (1922–23); David M. Byrne, *Equality before the Law*, 2 DUBLIN U.L. REV. 40 (1970); AUSTRALIA LAW REFORM COMMISSION, EQUALITY BEFORE THE LAW (1993).

[60] Mary Ann Glendon, *Rights in Twentieth-Century Constitutions*, 59 U. CHI. REV. L. 519, 521 (1992).

on the states, too. At the same time, the US Supreme Court held that the term "human" that appears in the Fourteenth Amendment does not include "fetus," so where the fetus is concerned, the obligation to observe due process before termination of pregnancy ("taking its life") does not exist. Justice Blackmun ruled explicitly: "In short, the unborn have never been recognized in the law as persons in the whole sense."[61] Many of the questions concerning the US Constitution arise largely from the fact that when the Constitution and the American Bill of Rights were adopted, the idea of a social welfare state was not yet conceptualized.[62] In 1973, in most US states, there were still strict laws regarding anything related to the termination of pregnancy.

In the landmark *Roe v. Wade* case, the Court ruled on a minimum test for constitutionalizing laws regarding the termination of pregnancy, holding that the legislator cannot intervene in a woman's desire to terminate her pregnancy in the first trimester. In the second trimester, however, the state, with the mediation of the legislator, can restrict women's rights and prevent the termination of pregnancy for health reasons. The Court held that in the third trimester, the fetus is already at the viability stage and can survive outside the womb, therefore the state may prohibit termination of pregnancy under certain circumstances. Although these tests are no longer the law of the land in the US, following *Dobbs*, they will be addressed in each state as abortion laws are being re-examined.

In the US, protected rights in society were granted before social rights, but in Europe and most other liberal-democratic countries, the opposite was true. In Germany and France, for example, the foundations of a

---

[61] *See Roe v. Wade*, 410 U.S. 113 (1973) (in this case, the "quickening" test, used to determine the development of the fetus, was ruled out and the "viability" test was recognized instead). This significant statement has been discussed in numerous articles, among others, John H. Ely, *The Wages of Crying Wolf: A Comment on* Roe v. Wade, 82 YALE L.J. 920 (1972–73); Richard A. Epstein, *Substantive Due Process by Any Other Name: The Abortion Cases*, SUPREME COURT REV. 159 (1973); David Kader, *The Law of Tortious Prenatal Death Since* Roe v. Wade, 45 MO. L. REV. 639 (1980).

[62] Furthermore, some three-quarters of the 160 constitutions in force today worldwide have been adopted since 1965. *See Roe v. Wade*, at 520.

welfare state were laid before regimes based on constitutional rights came into being. Thus, the right to life was recognized in the English legal system, although not constitutionally, and only in 1998 did the UK ratify the European Convention on Human Rights, thereby protecting generally accepted human rights.[63]

In contrast to US case law, the British model has no constitutional judicial review but legally[64] it is forbidden to cause the death of a viable fetus, subject to the specified restrictions.[65] The law in the UK contains a presumption according to which a fetus is considered viable from 28 weeks onward, although today it is recognized that it can be viable from 24 weeks and is likely to survive with a reasonable quality of life from 25 weeks. As a result, in 1990, UK law was amended to reflect the presumption that the fetus is viable from the 24th week onward.[66]

In Canada, there was a basis for a welfare state even before regimes based on constitutional rights came into being. The term "human" in Section 7 of the Canadian Charter protects the right to life. The Charter decrees, among others, that this right can be denied only according to the basic principles of justice:[67] "Everyone has the right to life, liberty

---

[63] AUSTEN G. GOWERS, JOHN TINGLE, & TOM LOUISE, HEALTH CARE LAW: THE IMPACT OF THE HUMAN RIGHTS ACT 1998 (2001). For a discussion of this book, *see* JONAS WADSTROM & ROBERT GASTON, LIVING DONOR KIDNEY TRANSPLANTATION: CURRENT PRACTICES, EMERGING TRENDS AND EVOLVING CHALLENGES 164 (2005); ELIZABETH WICKS, HUMAN RIGHTS AND HEALTHCARE 277 (2007); Austen Garwood-Gowers, *Time to Address the Problem of Post-Mortem Procurement of Organs for Transplantation Occurring without Proper Pre-Mortem Consent*, 20 EUR. J. HEALTH L. 383, 386 n.10 (2013).

[64] Infant Life (Preservation) Act, 1929, 19 Goe, c. 34

[65] Human Fertilization and Embryology Act, 1990 c. 37

[66] Abortion Act, 1967, c. 87.

[67] Canadian Charter of Rights and Freedom, § 7. For a discussion of this article and the dilemma of abortion, *see, e.g.*, SHEILAH L. MARTIN, WOMEN'S REPRODUCTIVE HEALTH, THE CANADIAN CHARTER OF RIGHTS AND FREEDOMS AND THE CANADA HEALTH ACT (1989); Joanne Barker, *Gender, Sovereignty, and the Discourse of Rights in Native Women's Activism*, 7(1) MERIDIANS 127 (2006); Federico Fabbrini, *The European Court of Human Rights, the EU Charter of Fundamental Rights, and the Right to Abortion:* Roe v. Wade *on the Other Side of the Atlantic*, 18 COLUM. J. EUR. L. 1, 25 n.216 (2011).

and protection of the person and the right not to be deprived thereof except in accordance with the principles of fundamental justice."

The first section of the New Zealand human rights law, similar to the Canadian Charter, is devoted to the right to life. The law forbids denying life unless it is in accordance with the law and the principles of basic justice.[68] The Australian Constitution from 2001 rules that everyone has the right to life.[69] The Irish Constitution[70] establishes that the state will respect the right to life and protect it from unjust attacks. The right to life was the focus of a lengthy discussion on the subject of the legal nature of termination of pregnancy, which led to an amendment in the Irish Constitution;[71] a referendum in 1983 brought about an addendum balancing fetal and women's rights, allowing abortion in the first 12 weeks of pregnancy, and later only if the pregnancy endangers a women's health or life.

In Germany, according to Section 2 of the Basic Law, every human being has the right to life.[72] In *G. v. Board Uchta'la*,[73] the court ruled definitively that the right to life includes the right to be born and the right to live. After World War II, the constitutional court of Germany ruled that the life of a human being begins from the 14th day after implantation. Until the Abortion Law in 1974, termination of pregnancy was considered a criminal offense unless it had been given legal

---

[68] New Zealand Bill of Rights Act, Pt. 1.

[69] GEORGE WILLIAM, HUMAN RIGHTS UNDER THE AUSTRALIAN CONSTITUTION (2002). *See also*, George Williams, *Race and the Australian Constitution: From Federation to Reconciliation*, 38 OSGOODE HALL L.J. 643, 747 n.18 (2000); Elizabeth Handsley, *Reviewed Work: Human Rights under the Australian Constitution by George Williams*, 73(2) AUSTRALIAN QUARTERLY 34 (2001); David Clark, *Human Rights under the Australian Constitution*, 37 U.N.S.W.L.J. 231 (2014).

[70] Ireland Const. arts. 40, 3(2).

[71] *Id*. amend. VIII.

[72] Basic Law of the Federal Republic of Germany, 1949, § 2. For a general discussion of the German regulation of various human rights, *see* SABINE MICHALOWSKI & LORNA WOODS GERMAN CONSTITUTIONAL LAW THE PROTECTION OF CIVIL LIBERTIES (1999); Ernst Benda, *The Protection of Human Dignity (Article 1 of the Basic Law)*, 53 S.M.U. L. REV. 443 (2000); Matthias Mahlmann, *The Basic Law at 60—Human Dignity and the Culture of Republicanism*, 11 GERMAN L.J. 9 (2010).

[73] G. v. Board Uchta'la IR 32, 69 [1980].

ratification. The law of 1974 ruled that termination of pregnancy after the 13th week was a criminal offense, and that before the 13th week, pregnancy could be legally terminated if carried out by a physician with the woman's consent, and if it was justified to prevent endangering the life or health of the woman, or if the fetus had a serious genetic defect.

Pressure from the Catholic Church and various organizations of the handicapped led to an amendment to German law in 1995 canceling provisions that permitted terminating a pregnancy for a medical reason that related to the fetus.[74] In the viable stage, the restriction on terminating a pregnancy for reason of the woman's physical or mental health was removed, therefore pregnancy can be terminated at the viable stage for these reasons.[75]

Sections 38-40 of the Polish Constitution hold that the Republic of Poland has an obligation to legally protect the life of every person.[76] In Russia, the Constitution grants the right to life to everyone.[77] The Latvian Constitution states that every person's right to life is protected

---

[74] For this critical amendment, see, e.g., Eva Maleck-Lewy, *Between Self-determination and State Supervision: Women and the Abortion Law in Post-Unification Germany*, 2(1) SOCIAL POLITICS: INTERNATIONAL STUDIES IN GENDER, STATE & SOCIETY 62 (1995); Gerald L. Neuman, *Casey in the Mirror: Abortion, Abuse and the Right to Protection in the United States and Germany*, 43 AM. J. COMP. L. 273 (1995); Nanette Funk, *Abortion Counselling and the 1995 German Abortion Law*, 12 CONN. J. INT'L L. 33 (1996).

[75] GERMAN NATIONAL ETHICS COUNCIL, GENETIC DIAGNOSIS BEFORE AND DURING PREGNANCY: OPINION, NATIONALER ETHIKRAT (2003) available at http://www.ethikrat.Org/files/.Opinion genetic- diagnosis-before-and-during-pregnancy.pdf. For a discussion of the conclusion of this Council, *see* e.g., THE JANUS FACE OF PRENATAL DIAGNOSTICS: A EUROPEAN STUDY BRIDGING ETHICS, PSYCHOANALYSIS, AND MEDICINE 41, 271 (Eve-Marie Engels et al. eds., 2008); Marianne Leuzinger-Bohleber, *Ethical Dilemmas Due to Prenatal and Genetic Diagnostics. An Interdisciplinary, European Study (EDIG, 20052008), in* ETHICAL DILEMMAS IN PRENATAL DIAGNOSIS (Tamara Fischmann & Elisabeth Hildt eds., (2011); Kathrin Braun, *From Ethical Exceptionalism to Ethical Exceptions: The Rule and exception Model and the Changing Meaning of Ethics in German Bioregulation*, 17(3) DEVELOPING WORLD BIOETHICS 146 (2017).

[76] Republic of Poland Const. arts. 38–40.

[77] Federation of Russia Const. art. 20.

by law.[78] Similarly, the constitutions of Romania,[79] Croatia,[80] the Czech Republic,[81] Slovenia,[82] Tanzania,[83] South Africa,[84] Pakistan,[85] India,[86] and Japan[87] protect the right to life.[88]

3.2 Definition of "person" or "human being"

Does life begin at the moment of fertilization or only after birth? Does life begin in the third trimester of the pregnancy or only when the fetus is viable? Does the term "life" describe life vis-à-vis death or a life with significance? Does the term "person" mean a viable fetus, or a fetus at every developmental stage? Is a fetus a living creature and therefore a person? Many legislators did not define the term "person" from the time when life begins but established the time from when obligations

---

[78] Republic of Latvia Const. Chapter VII, art. 93.

[79] Romania Const. Chapter ii, art. 22.

[80] Republic of Croatia Const. art. 21.

[81] Czech Republic Const

[82] Republic of Slovenia Const. art. 18.

[83] United Republic of Tanzania Const. art. 14

[84] Republic of South Africa Const. art. 11. See also Jeremy Sarkin, *The Effect of Constitutional Borrowings on the Drafting of South Africa's Bill of Rights and Interpretation of Human Rights Provisions*, 1 U. PA. J. CONST. L. 176, 183–88 (1998) and *The Drafting of South Africa's Final Constitution from a Human-Rights Perspective*, 47(1) AMERICAN JOURNAL OF COMPARATIVE LAW 67 (1999); Karen A. Trueman & Makgoale Magwentshu, *Abortion in a Progressive Legal Environment: The Need for Vigilance in Protecting and Promoting Access to Safe Abortion Services in South Africa*, 103(3) AMERICAN JOURNAL OF PUBLIC HEALTH 397 (2013).

[85] Islamic Republic of Pakistan Const. art. 9.

[86] India Const.

[87] Japan Const. art. 13.

[88] For example, in Africa, a child is defined by formation and does not exist as a human being before being subjected to physical or ceremonial modifications that initiate him into adult society and accord him the status of an adult. In the Wunda tribe, the infant has no social significance until his teeth begin to appear; he is "water" and not a "person." In the Nuar tribe, an infant becomes a "person" only when he is able to halter cattle and herd goats. A man does not tell anyone he has a son before the child reaches 6 years of age because only then does he become a "person" in his own right. For this reason, there is no mourning for a child who dies under the age of 6. Thus, in Africa, some conditions must be fulfilled for the live creature to become a person, and until then the child is not a human being. According to the literature, by considering infants as not being part of the population of human beings, communities can accept an extremely high rate of infant mortality.

can be handled, and rights granted. The discussion regarding the meaning of life, its beginning, and its importance is ethical, religious, moral, judicial, and social. Answers to these questions can be found based on the time when the viable fetus may be considered to have rights.

There are several approaches to analyzing the term "person:" physical (biological), sociological, and psychological. I examine these approaches with reference to the viable fetus, a potential person whose identity has yet to be formed, whose moral status is unclear, and whose status as a human is in doubt according to society because its humanity is marginal. Following the biological approach, a person should be defined based on one's external form. The opposing argument is that having an external form is not enough: the form of a person can be made up of different materials and still be perceived as a human creature. And what about a person whose human form has been destroyed? Is such an individual not worthy of protection as a person? If an intelligent creature suddenly appears from another planet, with a different external form than the human shape we are familiar with, will it not have the right to protection of life? Would killing it not be considered murder?[89]

The genetic approach maintains that a person is defined based on genetic characteristics.[90] But this definition is flawed. Should the right to life of every human cell be protected, we would reach an absurd point where peeling off some skin from a body is considered murder. The sociological approach claims that a person is a "social animal" because humans reach perfection only when living in a social environment. But other populations exist and function in a social community, including

---

[89] CARL SAGAN, DRAGONS OF EDEN: SPECULATIONS ON THE EVOLUTION OF HUMAN INTELLIGENCE (2012)

[90] For some possible applications of this approach, *see, e.g.*, Lawrence C. Becker, *Human Being: The Boundaries of the Concept*, 4(4) PHILOSOPHY & PUBLIC AFFAIRS 334 (1975); John M Goldenring, *The Brain–Life Theory: Towards a Consistent Biological Definition of Humanness*, 11 JOURNAL OF MEDICAL ETHICS 198 (1985); Thomas A. Magnani, *The Patentability of Human-Animal Chimeras*, 14 BERKELEY TECH. L.J. 443 (1999).

ants or bees. We may define a person based on the individual's intellectual capacity and ability to think and express thoughts.[91] If this is how we define the person, how do we relate to individuals[92] who suffer from brain damage? What about those suffering from Alzheimer's and similar conditions? Even Leibniz,[93] who defined people as intelligent creatures with self-awareness, and Kant, who maintained that the human's unique nature is the result of human intelligence,[94] are unhelpful in defining the term.

Therefore, the conclusion must be that it is not the familiar external form, intelligence, spirit, or social ability that constitutes a person. A person must be any human creature that we can visualize as a physical person. This definition includes every person with a defect or a disability, whether physical or mental, with limited mental capacity, with deformation, and in my opinion, also a viable fetus capable of surviving outside the womb.

In *The Dragons of Eden*,[95] Carl Sagan addressed the question of how humans comprehend human intelligence, and among others, asked:

---

[91] RENE DESCARTES, DISCOURSE ON THE METHOD (2018). For a consequential discussion of his unique attitude, *see, e.g.*, John Cottingham, *Descartes on Mind and Body*, 2(2) COGITO 10 (1988), https://www.pdcnet.org/cogito/content/cogito_1988_0002_0002_0010_0013; Yakare-Oule Jansen, *The Right to Freely Have Sex Beyond Biology: Reproductive Rights and Sexual Self-Determination*, 40 AKRON L. REV. 311, 311 n.1 (2007); Brendan F. Pons, *The Law and Philosophy of Personhood: Where Should South Dakota Abortion Law Go from Here*, 58 S.D. L. REV. 119, 141–42 (2013).

[92] People who are either deaf or dumb, who communicate with others by lip-reading.

[93] GOTTFRIED WILHELM LEIBNIZ, THE MONADOLOGY AND OTHER PHILOSOPHICAL WRITINGS (Robert Latta trans., 2014). For a discussion of his approach, *see, e.g.*, BENSON MATES, THE PHILOSOPHY OF LEIBNIZ: METAPHYSICS AND LANGUAGE (1989); BERTRAND RUSSELL, A CRITICAL EXPOSITION OF THE PHILOSOPHY OF LEIBNIZ (1992); JOHANN G. FICHTE, INTRODUCTIONS TO THE WISSENSCHAFTSLEHRE AND OTHER WRITINGS, 1797–1800 (1994).

[94] For some consequences of his unique attitude, *see* THE MORAL STATUS OF PERSONS: PERSPECTIVES ON BIOETHICS 3 (GERHOLD K. BECKER ED., 2000); D. Scott Bennett, *Chimera and the Continuum of Humanity: Erasing the Line of Constitutional Personhood*, 55 EMORY L.J. 347 (2006); Michael Friedman, *Kant on Geometry and Experience*, *in* MATHEMATIZING SPACE: TRENDS IN THE HISTORY OF SCIENCE (Vincenzo De Risi ed., 2015).

[95] *See* SAGAN, *supra* note 100.

What is "life"? According to Sagan, the better we understand the human brain, the more this will affect social issues such as the definition of death and termination of pregnancy. He noted that according to ethics accepted in Western countries, nonhuman mammals may be killed for a good reason, but human beings may not be killed under similar circumstances. He argued that according to these perceptions, the difference lies in the typical characteristics of the human brain, which are different from those of other mammals. Sagan found the claim of potential life to be a weak one because every human ovum or sperm can become a person under the right circumstances, but according to him, masturbation or involuntary ejaculation is considered normal human behavior and not a reason for being accused of murder.

According to Sagan, only our intelligence can be an essential human characteristic; therefore, he tied the sanctity of human life to the functional development of the cerebral cortex. He argued that complete development of the brain is not necessary to establish that a person is a person, because this takes place many years after birth; but it can be established that the transition to "humanity" takes place when the activity of the fetal cerebral cortex begins, as revealed by medical technology. If this is the case, according to Sagan, a person is eligible for protection when cerebral cortex activity begins. Does this view help confirm a thesis supporting the right of the fetus to live based on the development of its cerebral cortex? Whoever defines a fetus as a creature developing in the woman's womb and as a conglomeration of cells and tissues, even at the viable stage, would disagree with this rationale. Embryologists who deal with the scientific aspects of fetus development, and perinatologists who deal with the clinical aspects of fetuses, find reasons why this developmental definition is not sufficient to establish that life begins in the womb.

Various scholars described the approaches to the different phases of fetal development for identifying the beginning of life, of personhood. According to them, the first moment of the beginning of a person could be the moment of fertilization, when the sperm and the ovum meet, and the unique genetic code is created. Such scholars consider the fetus as a living creature enjoying full human rights from the moment of fertilization.[96] The transition to life may also be taken to be at the end of the first trimester or the beginning of the second trimester of pregnancy.

Sagan argued that during the course of expressing the above ideas through legislation, human chauvinism should be avoided because if intelligent organisms do exist, similar to developed human beings, they should be offered the same protection of life that we offer to the fetus at the viable stage. Because there is quite convincing evidence of intelligence in dolphins, whales, and monkeys, any ethical approach regarding the termination of pregnancy must also include injunctions against killing these animals.

It has not yet been established in any country whether the right to life means the protection of life in general or of significant life of a certain quality. An examination of international conventions and legislation in various countries reveals that most of them protect the right to life but do not define the term "life" and maintain different perceptions regarding when it begins. Is it possible to establish when life begins?[97] Is the value protected by society and legislation life in and of itself? A meaningful life? Life free of physical or mental defects? Does the legislator protect only life that is not dependent on anyone or anything?

---

[96] *See, e.g.*, the Christian approach, described *supra* note 35 and accompanying text. *See also* RONALD DWORKIN, LIFE'S DOMINION (1993); JONATHAN GLOVER, CAUSING DEATH AND SAVING LIVES (1977). For a discussion of the first book, *see* Gerard V. Bradley, *Life's Dominion: A Review Essay*, 69 NOTRE DAME L. REV. 329 (1993); Nancy S. Jecker & Courtney S. Campbell, *Life's Dominion: An Argument about Abortion, Euthanasia, and Individual Freedom*, 3 CAMBRIDGE Q. HEALTHCARE ETHICS 303 (1994); Samuel A. Gunsburg, *Frozen Life's Dominion: Extending Reproductive Autonomy Rights to in Vitro Fertilization*, 65 FORDHAM L. REV. 2205 (1997). For an academic discussion of the latter book, *see* Choo Han Teck, *Termination of Non-Viable Life*, 21 SING. L. REV. 230, 233 n.25, 241 n.69, 252 n.138 (2000–01); Stephen W. Smith, *The Killing of Severely Disabled Newborns: The Spectre Behind the Legalisation of Physician-Assisted Suicide and Euthanasia*, 24 MED. & L. 791, 802 (2005); Meredith Blake, *Whose Life Is It Anyway? A Comment on the* Terri Schiavo *Case*, 10 INT'L TRADE & BUS. L. REV. 69 (2006) *passim*.

[97] Steinberg, *supra* note 1.

The answers to these questions are a critical platform for a discussion on the right to life of a fetus with a defect. If we conclude that a viable fetus meets the conditions of these definitions of a person,[98] it does indeed have the right to life protected by law even if it has a defect that does not detrimentally affect its life or the length thereof. Socrates declared that life itself is not the main thing, rather it is the good life that counts,[99] and the assumption is that a good life is meaningful. By contrast, in the modern era, the right to life is protected as a right unto itself, and the philosophical justification for human life goes unchallenged.[100]

In Israel,[101] there is a similar attitude regarding the right to life because its protection is included in the general protection of human rights.[102]

---

[98] Even if it does not come under the definition of a person, it should be given rights as a *quasi*-person.

[99] *See* the Dialogue Between Plato and Aristotle (PLATO, THE COLLECTED DIALOGUES OF PLATO (1961)), where the classic Socratic perception appears regarding the good life, as Socrates refuses to save his own life and escape from prison after being sentenced to death.

[100] The world of medicine, for example, undertakes to prolong life even in the case of terminal illness, treating unconscious patients and those who suffer from Alzheimer's disease. In these cases, the question whether the patient's life is good or meaningful is not asked, but rather life is valued in itself. This perception supports the argument that the life of a viable fetus with a defect deserves protection.

[101] Yoram Dinstein, *Human Rights: The Quest for Concretization*, 1 ISRAEL YEARBOOK ON HUMAN RIGHTS 13 (1971). Dinstein listed five main groups of human rights in Israel, according to the five recognized categories found in international law: civil, political, economic, social, and cultural. In the past, human rights were defined with regard to the first two groups only: civil and political. Dinstein maintained that civil rights included the right to life, freedom, and security; freedom of thought, religion, and expression; freedom of movement, assembly, and corporation; the right to nationality and the right to due process. For a discussion of his work, *see* Thomas Buergenthal, *International and Regional Human Rights Law and Institutions: Some Examples of Their Interaction*, 12 TEX. INT'L L. J. 321, 324 n.15 (1977); Luis Kutner, *Soviet Jewry and World Habeas Corpus*, 37 OKLA. L. REV. 495, 527 n.86 (1984); Sinai Deutch, *Are Consumer Rights Human Rights?*, 32 OSGOODE HALL L. J. 537, 545 n.31 (1994).

[102] RUTH GAVISON, HUMAN RIGHTS IN ISRAEL 32 (1994) (Heb.). *See also* Shlomo Hasson & David Ley, *Neighborhood Organizations, the Welfare State, and Citizenship Rights*, 33(1) URBAN AFFAIRS REVIEW 28 (1997); Russell A. Stone, *Human Rights within Israel, in* MIDDLE EAST AND NORTH AFRICA (Paul Magnarella ed., 1999); Alek D. Epstein, *The Freedom of Conscience and Sociological Perspectives on Dilemmas of Collective Secular Disobedience: The Case of Israel*, 1(3) J. HUM RTS. 305 (2002).

The Israeli legal system considers the recognition of the value, dignity, and sanctity of a person's life as a core democratic value that includes the values of universal ethics recognizing the value of life. As enshrined in Israel's Basic Law, human dignity is highly influential in all legal fields in the State of Israel. The courts use the valve terminology [not clear what this is] with regard to this law to form the correct legal policy, and the legal system provides them with content. [no clue what this means; who forms the correct legal policy; and to whom does "them" refer?] Therefore, the dignity of a viable fetus may also be said to have a protected value, even if it has disabilities.[103]

3.3 Who (or what) is a viable fetus?

A fetus is a living creature that develops in the woman's womb from the beginning of its formation until birth. Today, fetuses can be created using various techniques of fertility treatment[104] and IVF,[105] and preserved through cryopreservation.[106] I do not discuss here the

---

[103] For a discussion of the interaction between this basic law and the dilemma of abortion, *see, e.g.*, Doron Shultziner, *Human Dignity: Functions and Meanings*, *in* PERSPECTIVES ON HUMAN DIGNITY: A CONVERSATION 73 (Jeff Malpas & Norelle Lickiss eds., 2007); Christoph Mollers, *Democracy and Human Dignity: Limits of a Moralized Conception of Rights in German Constitutional Law*, 42(2) ISRAEL LAW REVIEW 416 (2009); Luis Roberto Barroso, *Here, There, and Everywhere: Human Dignity in Contemporary Law and in the Transnational Discourse*, 35 B. C. INT'L & COMP. L. REV. 331, 340 n.66 (2012).

[104] Israel is the only country in the world that covers the full cost of fertility treatments for single women, married women, lesbians, and others. *See, e.g.*, SUSAN M. KAHN, REPRODUCING JEWS: A CULTURAL ACCOUNT OF ASSISTED CONCEPTION IN ISRAEL (2000); Leslie King, *From Pronatalism to Social Welfare? Extending Family Allowances to Minority Populations in France and Israel*, 17 EUR. J. POPULATION 305 (2001); Larissa Remennick, *Contested Motherhood in the Ethnic State: Voices from an Israeli Postpartum Ward*, 8 ETHNICITIES 199 (2008).

[105] *In vitro* fertilization. For a discussion of the various far-reaching legal ramifications of these procedures, *see* Nicole L. Cucci, *Constitutional Implications of In Vitro Fertilization Procedures*, 72 ST. JOHN'S L. REV. 417 (1998); Olivia Lin, *Rehabilitating Bioethics: Recontextualizing in Vitro Fertilization Outside Contractual Autonomy*, 54 DUKE L.J. 485 (2004); Daphne Barak-Erez, *IVF Battles: Legal Categories and Comparative Tales*, 28 DUKE JOURNAL OF COMPARATIVE & INTERNATIONAL LAW 247 (2018).

[106] Preservation in a frozen state. *See, e.g.*, the vivid academic discussion of the "cryopreserved embryos," in Sara D. Petersen, *Dealing with Cryopreserved Embryos upon Divorce: A Contractual Approach Aimed at Preserving Party Expectations*, 50 UCLA L. REV. 1065 (2003); Susan B. Apel, *Cryopreserved Embryos: A Response to "Forced Parenthood" and*

dilemmas faced by researchers of fetal status when dealing with the fetuses created outside the womb. The questions of whether a status should be applied to a fertilized ovum, and if so, what should that status be; whether the fertilized ovum should be called "fetus" or "pre-fetus;" whether destroying fertilized eggs is the same as killing a fetus—these dilemmas are beyond the scope of this book. I cannot discuss the status of a viable fetus, however, without saying a few words about a "young fetus" (i.e., up to the 24th week). Some maintain that even a young fetus is a potential person and therefore it must not be harmed or destroyed, whereas others claim that there is no moral issue in destroying such a fetus in the first stages after fertilization with the understanding that this is merely a fertilized ovum and not the beginnings of life.

We have seen that views vary between countries,[107] both legally and morally, regarding the young fetus in the first stages after fertilization. A bioethical debate on the status of a viable fetus is simpler, despite the dichotomy between its rights and those of the woman. My starting point is that dealing with a viable fetus is dealing with the status of a sustainable "creature," whose human identity, ethical status, and "interests" (protected by others) are those of a potential person, a human organism with a right to life and the right to be born healthy. The viable fetus can continue to develop outside the womb,[108] therefore it can be said that it is biologically independent and has the ability to realize its potential for life. At the viable stage, the more developed the fetus, the stronger its status, and the woman's right to terminate the pregnancy by destroying it in the womb decreases.[109]

---

the Role of Intent, 39 FAM. L.Q. 663 (2005); Fotini A. Skouvakis, *Defining the Undefined: Using a Best Interests Approach to Decide the Fate of Cryopreserved Preembryos in Pennsylvania*, 109 PENN. ST. L. REV. 885 (2005).

[107] In countries such as Sweden, Denmark, and Spain it is permissible to conduct research on these fetuses, and in others, such as Norway, Switzerland, and France, this is forbidden. In Israel, these fetuses are unprotected by law.

[108] Treatment of premature babies has become much more sophisticated in recent years.

[109] This position has been ratified in the US in *Roe v. Wade*, which ruled that a pregnancy can be terminated in the first trimester; under certain circumstances, it can

Some oppose the termination of pregnancy for reasons that have nothing to do with the status of the fetus, such as the commandment "to be fruitful and multiply,"[110] but I consider the opposition to terminating the pregnancy strictly from the angle of fetal status, without addressing other considerations. David Heyd[111] raised an idea that I am prepared to adopt as an "anti-termination of pregnancy" argument (although this was not his intention):

Nowadays, when developments in medical technology allow us to implant fetuses into another woman's womb, this opens up the way to disconnect between the end of the pregnancy and the death of the fetus. There will be far-reaching ramifications to this possibility also regarding the ethical nature of abortions, at least for those who assume that the fetus has the status of a human being.

He goes on to explain:

Even if the mother has a right over her body, even if the fetus is defined as "a pursuer" (*rodef*)[112]—as an unwanted visitor in her womb, the woman can be prosecuted to prevent her from killing the fetus and transferring it to another "home," in other words, the womb of another woman who is willing to nurture it. Although the womb is the woman's

---

be terminated even in the second trimester, but in the third—the viable stage—it is absolutely forbidden. Thus, the courts recognized the status of the fetus.

[110] DAVID HEYD, ETHICS AND MEDICINE 56 (1989) (Heb.). According to this argument, it is incumbent on us to bring children into the world because of our obligation to God, society, increasing joy in the world, etc. For a discussion of the centrality and importance of this injunction, *see* FELDMAN, *supra* note 13, at 46–50; RICHARD V. GRAZI, BE FRUITFUL AND MULTIPLY: FERTILITY THERAPY AND THE JEWISH TRADITION (1994); Pamela Laufer-Ukeles, *Gestation: Work for Hire or the Essence of Motherhood? A Comparative Legal Analysis*, 9 DUKE J. GENDER L. & POL'Y 91, 120–22 (2002); RONIT IRSHAI, FERTILITY AND JEWISH LAW: FEMINIST PERSPECTIVES ON ORTHODOX RESPONSA LITERATURE 225 (Joel A. Linsider trans., 2012).

[111] Heyd, *supra* note 121, at 59.

[112] For this Jewish notion, *see Justification and Excuse in the Judaic and Common Law: The Exculpation of a Defendant Charged with Homicide*, 52 N.Y.U. L. REV. 599 (1977); Marilyn Finkelman, *Self-Defense and Defense of Others in Jewish Law: The Rodef Defense*, 33 WAYNE L. REV. 1257 (1987); Mark C. Alexander, *Religiously Motivated Murder: The Rabin Assassination and Abortion Clinic Killings*, 39 ARIZ. L. REV. 1161 (1997).

possession as her property, the fetus itself is not her property and she cannot do whatever she wants with it. The ova formed in her ovaries may be her private property, but the moment an ovum is fertilized by the sperm of a man and the developmental process of a separate being begins, the question becomes what will be the fate thereof, and the man and society also have a stake in the matter.

Finally, Heyd concludes that:

> Therefore, the interest of the man and society in the fate of the fetus is weaker than that of the mother, at least as long as the biology of the pregnancy is connected in such a definite way to the woman's body, although we are in the midst of a technological breakthrough that will make a dramatic change even in this matter.[113]

This position may help determine the desirable ethical and legal positions in the case of a viable fetus that can continue to develop outside the womb—even in an "artificial womb," if and when that becomes relevant. In some jurisdictions, as in Israel, where the fetus lacks all rights until it is born and is dependent on the goodwill of the woman who became pregnant with it, this can give rise to absurd situations. For example, a young woman with a mental defect might refuse to undergo an emergency C-section to save the life of the fetus for fear that the newborn will be taken from her by social services after she gives birth. [not sure I understand this example; what does the C-section have to do with social services taking the infant?] If the medical team applies to the court for a warrant to carry out the surgery despite the woman's refusal, the court will not provide the warrant because the aim of the operation is to save the fetus and not the woman, and the

---

[113] See how this conservative stance is represented in BARUCH A. BRODY, ABORTION AND THE SANCTITY OF HUMAN LIFE: A PHILOSOPHICAL VIEW (1975). For a discussion of this book, *see e.g.*, George P. Smith, *Defective Newborns and Government Intermeddling*, 25 MED. SCI. & L. 44, 47 n.32 (1985); Francis J. Beckwith, *Thomson's Equal Reasonableness Argument for Abortion Rights: A Critique*, 49 AM. J. JURIS. 185, 187 n.8 (2004); Margaret Olivia Little, *Abortion and the Margins of Personhood*, 39 RUTGERS L.J. 331, 331 n.1 (2008).

fetus has no rights. The principle suggested by this book is that the fetus does have a status, whatever its ethical content, and whether the status derives from the right to life as a person or from the right to life based on its potential for life.

Current medical technologies make it possible to diagnose the medical condition of the fetus while it is in the womb at almost any stage of pregnancy. If a defect or disability is discovered in the fetus, it is possible to terminate a pregnancy even in the viable phase of the fetus (feticide). The term "disability" is subject to interpretation. It may include minor defects, an unwanted gender, [? I don't think so] or statistical expectations of a genetic or incurable disease. Multiple tests and knowledge inevitably lead to pregnancy terminations even in the viable phase of the fetus. Technology also allows us to obtain pictures of a fetus that differ little from those of a baby outside the womb. Some philosophers see life as a gift to parents and others believe that parenthood is an unconditional acceptance of a person we produce. I believe that parental love should not be conditioned on the qualities of the future child, at least not in the viable stage, after week 24, when it is able to survive outside the womb.

Chapter 4
State Intervention in the Woman's Autonomy

1. Autonomy vs. Paternalism

1.1. Paternalism: Pure vs. impure

To discuss whether the state has the right to force a woman to proceed with a pregnancy or undergo a C-section without her consent,[1] we need to consider the issues of paternalism[2] vs. autonomy.[3] In the legal world, does "paternalism" mean "enforcement of ethics"? Dworkin defined paternalism as the lawmaker's intervention in an individual's liberty, justified only on grounds of an individual's wellbeing. If so, it may be argued that achieving "ultimate wellbeing" would be a legitimate objective for intervention by a paternalistic body in a person's liberty. In our case, paternalism would mean enforcing the continuation of the pregnancy or certain behavior during the course of a woman's pregnancy, and forcing a C-section on her against her will and without her consent, for her wellbeing. We will define a basic presumption of what constitutes the best interest of a woman—physically, psychologically, and socially—for the purposes of giving birth to a

---

[1] On forced C-sections, *see* Monica K. Miller, *Refusal to Undergo a Cesarean Section: A Woman's Right or a Criminal Act?*, 15 HEALTH MATRIX 383 (2005); V. Chandis & T. Williams, *The Patient, the Doctor, the Fetus, and the Court-Compelled Cesarean: Why Courts Should Address the Question Through a Bioethical Lens*, 25 MED. & L. 729 (2006); Theresa Morris et al., *Forced and Coerced Cesarean Sections in the United States*, 16(2) CONTEXTS 24 (2017).

[2] This notion has been discussed in numerous books and articles. *See, e.g.*, Gerald Dworkin, *Paternalism*, 56(1) THE MONIS 64 (1972); JAMES F. CHILDRESS, WHO SHOULD DECIDE? PATERNALISM IN HEALTH CARE (1982); ANTAL SZERLETICS, PATERNALISM (2015).

[3] For this notion in the context of medical ethics, *see, for example*, G.M. Stirrat & R. Gill, *Autonomy in Medical Ethics After O'Neill*, 31 J. MED. ETHICS 127 (2005); ALFRED I. TAUBER, PATIENT AUTONOMY AND THE ETHICS OF RESPONSIBILITY (2005); ANDREW SNEDDON, AUTONOMY (2013).

viable fetus. These factors should provide a sufficiently compelling reason to intervene in her autonomy.

Dworkin based his approach on John Stuart Mill, who maintained that it is impossible to justify one individual telling another that it is in his best interest not to do with his life what he chooses to do.[4] The starting point of Mill's book, *On Liberty*,[5] is that a person may limit or deny another person's freedom of action only (a) for self-defense or (b) to prevent harm to another. An individual's welfare is never sufficient justification for forcing anything on him, whether by society in general or by anyone else. According to this view, there should be no intervention in the freedom of a woman to prevent her from terminating a pregnancy or to force her to undergo a C-section just because society, through the mediation of the state, believes that it would be for her own good. Can the terms "paternalism" and "autonomy" also be so tested when such enforcement is not for the wellbeing of the person being forced (the woman) but rather in the best interest of another (the viable fetus)?

Does the best interest of the viable fetus, a separate entity from the woman, constitute a legitimate justification for intervention in the woman's freedom? Those who consider the viable fetus to be part of the woman's body will definitely accept that restricting the woman's liberty for the good of the viable fetus is a just cause. Those who consider the viable fetus as a separate entity could claim that it is unjustified to restrict the woman's liberty in the best interest of the fetus but could find sufficient justification in such a restriction for the benefit of a third

---

[4] Roger B. Dworkin, *Medical Law and Ethics in the Post-Autonomy Age*, 68 IND. L.J. 727, 733 (1993) ("It is a physical concept rather than an intellectual one. If you touch me or eavesdrop on me, you have injured my autonomy by invading my space. If you actually do something to change my body, you have injured my autonomy by changing the very constitution of what I am"). Discussed by DAVID ORENTLICHER ET AL., BIOETHICS AND PUBLIC HEALTH LAW (2018).

[5] JOHN STUART MILL, ON LIBERTY (1871). For the importance of this seminal book, *see* GERTRUDE HIMMELFARB, ON LIBERTY AND LIBERALISM: THE CASE OF JOHN STUART MILL (1974); JOHN C. REES, JOHN STUART MILL'S ON LIBERTY (1985); JOSEPH HAMBURGER, JOHN STUART MILL ON LIBERTY AND CONTROL (1999).

party, similarly to restricting another person's freedom to smoke in public because it causes harm to others. On these paternalistic grounds, the legislature may determine that a pregnant woman is obligated to maintain a certain weight[6] or to eschew alcohol, drugs, and smoking.

This approach is problematic because it is nearly always possible to find other reasons that do not justify the intervention and that are not paternalistic. For example, it may be argued that a woman who takes advantage of her right to terminate a pregnancy would be healthier mentally, having asserted her autonomy. It is also obvious that there are financial and social reasons, among others, that justify allowing the woman to carry out her wishes for her benefit. It has been argued that in some cases women should be allowed to terminate a pregnancy because it will save public funds, which benefits society as a whole; in this way, a viable fetus that is unwanted or "unfit" (with a handicap or defect) will not become a burden on society.[7] According to the paternalistic perception, it is society that decides what is good for the individual. To address claims that paternalism is the correct way to

---

[6] *See, e.g.*, the new restrictive regulation in the UK for eligibility to have access to IVF, requires among others that the woman lose weight before starting these procedures. *See, for example*, NATIONAL COLLABORATING CENTRE FOR WOMEN'S AND CHILDREN'S HEALTH (UK), FERTILITY: ASSESSMENT AND TREATMENT FOR PEOPLE WITH FERTILITY PROBLEMS (2013), https://www.nice.org.uk/guidance/cg156/evidence/full-guideline-pdf-188539453; VALUE BASED CLINICAL COMMISSIONING POLICIES HAMBLETON, RICHMONDSHIRE AND WHITBY CCG VERSION FOR GB RATIFICATION—25/05/17 (2017), https://www.hambletonrichmondshireandwhitbyccg.nhs.uk/documents/6631319/11909076/Item+10+App endix+1+Clinical+Commissioning+Policy+25.05.17.pdf/696ef478–9a5e-4b90-9dec-afaf672d4318.

[7] For an attempt to determine an ethical limit to the maximum number of children that a poor single-parent family should produce, *see* the hotly debated discussion following the bizarre case of the octomom, Nadya Suleman. *See, for example*, Jennifer M. Collins, *Eight Is Enough*, 103 NW. U.L. REV. COLLOQUY 501 (2009); Kimberly D. Krawiec, *Why We Should Ignore the "Octomom,"* 104 NW. U. L. REV. COLLOQUY 120 (2009); Debora L. Spar, *As You Like It: Exploring the Limits of Parental Choice in Assisted Reproduction*, 27 LAW & INEQ. 481 (2009). Similarly, to save public funds, the federal authorities in the US have been fighting for the last four decades to establish legal parenthood for all newborn children. Scholars differ in opinion on whether this effort has been a success. Some feel that it failed and have even tried to introduce reforms. *See, for example*, *Changing American State and Federal Childcare Laws*, 92 CHI.-KENT L. REV. 3–208 (2017).

protect the viable fetus, I briefly discuss several definitions of paternalism.

The definition of "pure paternalism"[8] has two components: intervention in personal liberty and benefits to a particular person. "Impure paternalism"[9] is intervention in a person's liberty to increase benefits to others, not to the person in question. Dworkin[10] distinguishes between pure and impure paternalism: intervention in the liberty of a person or a group of people is made taking their benefit into consideration. Dworkin's example of impure paternalism is the legal prohibition of cigarette production to prevent detrimental effects on the health of consumers. In this case, damage is caused to the freedom of the cigarette producers' business, and the reason for the damage is to benefit consumers. But the real reason for the legal prohibition is to protect consumers against any harmful effects of an action—smoking cigarettes—they choose to take on their own.

Dworkin wanted to prove that anti-paternalistic claims can be refuted completely. Viewing Mill's arguments as insufficiently corroborated, Dworkin used Herbert Hart's critique of Mill's perception of the human figure. According to Hart, when referring to the average person, Mill meant an adult (in the legal sense), and so he attributed many adult characteristics to the average person. The elements that characterize an adult person include relatively steady ambitions, greater immunity to being influenced by others, knowing what they want and what brings them satisfaction or pleasure, and having a certain ability to achieve these aims. Mill himself was aware that his factual claims were not

[8] For this notion, *see* Robert D. Dinerstein, *Client-Centered Counseling: Reappraisal and Refinement*, 32 ARIZ. L. REV. 501, 513 (1990); Mario J. Rizzo & Douglas Glen Whitman, *Little Brother Is Watching You: New Paternalism on the Slippery Slopes*, 51 ARIZ. L. REV. 685, 720 (2009); Willem H. van Boom & Anthony Ogus, *Introducing, Defining and Balancing Autonomy v. Paternalism*, 3 ERASMUS L. REV. 1, 12 (2010).

[9] *See, e.g.*, John Hospers, *Libertarianism and Legal Paternalism*, 4(3) JOURNAL OF LIBERTARIAN STUDIES 255, 259 (1980); Kalle Grill, *The Normative Core of Paternalism*, 13 RES PUBLICA 441, 453 n.24 (2007); Emma C. Bullock, *A Normatively Neutral Definition of Paternalism*, 65(258) PHILOSOPHICAL QUARTERLY 1 (2015).

[10] *See* Dworkin, *supra* note 4.

always valid in every situation. Consequently, in discussing justifying state intervention, Mill posited two exceptions to the assertion that a person is the best judge of his interests and able to take the steps necessary to promote them: one is when a person is uneducated and the other when a person makes a judgment based on something irrelevant.

These points are valid when dealing with pure paternalism. Dworkin claimed that certain versions of paternalism could be justified on a moral-philosophical level, such as parental paternalism and legal paternalism toward adults suffering from a lack of knowledge, adequate cognitive functioning, or ability to make decisions. Dworkin compared children to disabled adults.[11]

Even Mill, who espoused anti-paternalism, was prepared to consider guiding principles that would justify paternalism in generally agreed-upon legitimate cases. Based on the essence of this idea, idealistic philosophers devised theories of free will. To support the expansion of paternalism, they argued that some people who suffer from various knowledge-related defects lack the ability for rational thought and decision making. Therefore, when we intervene in their freedom we are doing what they would do if they were rational. The question arises: Is pure paternalism[12] justified? Mill referred to utilitarian theory,[13] noting that willingness and the moral value of actions are measured by their probable and reasonable outcome. According to this theory, a result can be considered acceptable if it has two characteristics. The first is that the

---

[11] For the last issue, *see* F. James Hoffmann et al., *Needs of Learning Disabled Adults*, 20(1) JOURNAL OF LEARNING DISABILITIES 43 (1987); JEAN MARTIN & AMANDA WHITE, THE FINANCIAL CIRCUMSTANCES OF DISABLED ADULTS LIVING IN PRIVATE HOUSEHOLDS (1988); JEAN MARTIN ET AL., DISABLED ADULTS: SERVICES, TRANSPORT AND EMPLOYMENT (1989).

[12] For the attitude of Mill toward paternalism, *see* John D. Hodson, *Mill, Paternalism, and Slavery*, 41(1) ANALYSIS 60 (1981); Fred D'Agostino, *Mill, Paternalism and Psychiatry*, 60(4) AUSTRALASIAN JOURNAL OF PHILOSOPHY 319 (1982); L.O. Gostin & K.G. Gostin, *A Broader Liberty: J.S. Mill, Paternalism and the Public's Health*, 123(3) PUBLIC HEALTH 214 (2009).

[13] *See, for example*, JOHN S. MILL, UTILITARIANISM (1910); JOHN S. MILL & JEREMY BENTHAM, UTILITARIANISM AND OTHER ESSAYS (ALAN RYAN ED., 1987); JOHN S. MILL, ON LIBERTY, UTILITARIANISM, AND OTHER ESSAYS (2015).

result causes more good than harm. The second is that the benefits of the action for the people who were the objects of the action, and for everything it affected (also indirectly) are greater than its drawbacks. Combining the two features into one definition of a reasonable outcome leads to the conclusion that according to utilitarianism, a reasonable outcome is one that increases the total amount of pleasure compared with the total amount of pain because the ultimate aim of utilitarianism is to afford as much pleasure as possible to the greatest number of people.

Applying this theory to our case raises the following questions: Can pure paternalism justify intervening in a woman's liberty to protect her or the viable fetus even against her will? Is the suffering involved in forcing a woman to continue with a pregnancy greater than the suffering from curtailing her autonomy (to smoke[14] or imbibe alcohol) or forcing her to have a C-section to save a viable fetus without her consent greater or smaller than the anticipated pleasure from preventing the death of the viable fetus even if it results in a life of pain? After all, paternalistic intervention is purportedly for the benefit of the viable fetus in these cases.

According to Mill's utilitarian position, paternalism is never justified, therefore he attempted to show that the suffering involved in paternalism is always greater than any anticipated pleasure. Mill based this claim, among others, on two factual assumptions about the nature of man and the nature of paternalistic intervention. The first is that every person knows best one's own good and what promotes one's

---

[14] The correlation between preventing smoking during pregnancy and the newborn's welfare is well known in the scholarly literature. *See, e.g.*, Ira M. Bernstein et al., *Maternal Smoking and Its Association with Birth Weight*, 106(5) OBSTETRICS & GYNECOLOGY 986 (2005); CENTERS FOR DISEASE CONTROL AND PREVENTION, PREVENTING SMOKING AND EXPOSURE TO SECONDHAND SMOKE BEFORE, DURING, AND AFTER PREGNANCY (2007), http://www.minneapolismn.gov/www/groups/public/documents/webcontent/wcms1q-073351.pdf; Lisa Wood et al., *Indigenous Women and Smoking During Pregnancy: Knowledge, Cultural Contexts and Barriers to Cessation*, 66(1) SOCIAL SCIENCE & MEDICINE 2378 (2008).

sense of serenity, satisfaction, health, and the like. The second assumption is that every person wants to promote one's own good more than that of others. According to Mill, if a person agrees to become enslaved, this agreement is considered null and void, and nonbinding, both legally and morally, because a person is not at liberty to surrender his liberty: this is the limit of his autonomy.[15] Mill did not consider autonomy to be a moral value but rather a more fundamental one that is conceptually related to that of the individual as an autonomous and rational being. Therefore, relinquishing moral autonomy, which is what happens when a person sells himself into slavery, is morally unacceptable.

Dworkin had a different opinion on the matter. According to him, a person can be completely autonomous in relinquishing his personal autonomy, that is, an individual can make a choice of his own free will, considered justified and in his best interest, to relinquish or limit his personal freedom. It is clear why Mill was opposed to paternalism. As with every intervention in an individual's freedom that is not based on the goal of preventing the individual from causing harm to others, paternalism, by limiting the individual's freedom and denying or preventing his voluntary decisions in matters concerning his life, contradicts the principle of autonomy. Therefore, intervention cannot be morally justified, whatever advantage may accrue to the individual whose freedom has been denied.

Dworkin's and Mill's arguments are valid in the case of pure paternalism, but if in the case of intervention in abortion, paternalism is impure, these arguments hold minimal weight. I maintain that when it comes to a viable fetus, those in favor of paternalism would claim that a rational woman who becomes pregnant intentionally, or as a result of negligence, would not ask to terminate the pregnancy; that a rational

---

[15] For a discussion of the appropriate limits on the freedom of contract, *see* Roscoe Pound, *Liberty of Contract*, 18 YALE L.J. 454, 484 (1908–09); Anthony T. Kronman, *Paternalism and the Law of Contracts*, 92(5) YALE L.J. 763 (1983); MICHAEL J. TREBILCOCK, THE LIMITS OF FREEDOM OF CONTRACT (1993).

woman would want to become a mother to exercise her right to parenthood,[16] to hold her child in her arms, to show her motherly love, etc. Therefore, a state restriction on her autonomy forbidding her to terminate the pregnancy would not represent a restriction on her freedom because it helps her exercise her freedom and follow her true desires.

This approach involves a danger of intervention not only in the life of a pregnant woman but also in that of a patient who refuses medical treatment[17] and of anyone whose autonomous decisions society considers irrational. Therefore, it must be applied with utmost caution. May society's paternalism toward the woman to save the life or ensure the wellbeing of a viable fetus be considered impure paternalism? It is possible to argue that interference with the woman's choice by preventing her from terminating the pregnancy in the viable phase is intended to promote the welfare of the fetus. Thus, the intervention in the woman's choice is intended not to harm the woman's decision making, but to prevent harm to the fetus. It may be called "vague" paternalism. Accepting the thesis that the fetus has the right to be born helps justify interfering with the woman's choice on moral, social, and ethical bases even more so than theories of pure paternalism do. Dworkin claimed that in cases of impure paternalism, the intervention is not intended to prevent harm to the person whose freedom is being compromised but rather to prevent action that would harm the actor or her health. No distinction is made between a viable fetus and a newborn. A viable fetus is one whose life or health is at risk from an

---

[16] For this basic right, *see* Daniel Statman, *The Right to Parenthood*, 10(3–4) ETHICAL PERSPECTIVES 224 (2003); J. Boivin & G. Pennings, *Parenthood Should Be Regarded as a Right*, 90 ARCHIVES OF DISEASE IN CHILDHOOD 784 (2005); Anca Gheaus, *The Right to Parent One's Biological Baby*, 20(4) JOURNAL OF POLITICAL PHILOSOPHY 432 (2012).

[17] For the nexus between paternalism and forced medical treatments, *see* Lisa C. Ikemoto, *Furthering the Inquiry: Race, Class, and Culture in the Forced Medical Treatment of Pregnant Women*, 59 TENN. L. REV. 487 (1992); S. Elizabeth & Wilborn Malloy, *Beyond Misguided Paternalism: Resuscitating the Right to Refuse Medical Treatment*, 33 WAKE FOREST L. REV. 1035 (1998); Matthew McCoy, *Autonomy, Consent, and Medical Paternalism: Legal Issues in Medical Intervention*, 14(6) JOURNAL OF ALTERNATIVE AND COMPLEMENTARY MEDICINE 785 (2008).

action taken by the woman, either to terminate the pregnancy or to withhold consent to undergo a necessary C-section.

The intervention in the woman's autonomy aims to directly advance the interests of another: a viable fetus. This aspect of impure paternalism completely distinguishes it from pure paternalism,[18] both in its moral-philosophical essence and in considerations for justifying the intervention. If one accepts the right of a viable fetus to be born, and that being born healthy is a significant value deserving protection, intervention to save the life of the fetus is easier to justify than non-intervention in the woman's freedom aimed at protecting the woman and at the same time defining her best interest subjectively.

Imposing limits on a woman's autonomy for reasons related to the rights of a viable fetus—whether weak or strong, complete or partial—as an act of impure paternalism is no less morally, socially, and ethically justified than imposing limits as an act of pure paternalism. Having discussed the term "impure paternalism,"

1.2. Paternalistic intervention

Paternalistic intervention can be real or apparent. Whoever makes claims about "apparent paternalistic intervention" assumes that the woman agrees to relinquish her autonomy in areas where she wants the intervention of the legislature, and therefore no paternalism applies, and hence no loss of autonomy. Apparent paternalistic intervention is the one that gives expression to the desires of people whose freedom is theoretically restricted, and these desires can be realized only within coercive legal limits. For example, when the legislature enacts laws setting the maximum number of daily or weekly working hours for employees, it is seeking to protect their health, safety, and quality of life. This legislation is based on the assumption that workers need law

---

[18] For the interaction between "impure paternalism" and "pure paternalism" regarding the right of a woman to terminate her pregnancy, *see* van Boom & Ogus, *supra* note 8, 1; Jessica L. Roberts & Elizabeth Weeks Leonard, *What Is (and Isn't) Healthism*, 50 GA. L. REV. 833 (2016).

enforcement to fully protect their rights and their persons. The legislation is intended to assist workers who request restriction of their autonomy to work as much as they might otherwise seek to do. This intervention is the coercive and normative way society ensures the obedience of all members. Some claim that this type of intervention should not be considered an intervention in autonomy because individuals in society agree to it.

In our case, apparent paternalistic intervention would claim that the woman agrees to relinquish her autonomy in areas where she wants legislative intervention (such as preventing abortion). Therefore, there is no paternalism or resulting loss of autonomy. This can be the justification for society to intervene in a woman's freedom. I examine this question with reference to two schools of thought: utilitarianism and deontology.[19] According to utilitarianism, it is possible to argue for restricting the woman's freedom to make decisions about a viable fetus because the restriction improves or prevents deterioration in the state of health of the viable fetus and grants it life. For the utilitarian paternalist,[20] every woman who did not prevent a pregnancy, is incapable of understanding which decision is in her best interest. She does not understand that her behavior could harm the fetus or cause it to die, preventing her from becoming a mother, therefore a paternalistic decision "for the woman's sake" is preferable.

The same paternalist would say that improving the health of the fetus and preventing its death would increase the general or average number of happiness or decrease the general or average amount of suffering in

[19] For discussion on deontology in the abortion dilemma, *see* Rosalind Hursthouse, *Virtue Theory and Abortion*, 20(3) PHILOSOPHY & PUBLIC AFFAIRS 223 (1991); Katherine A. Knopoff, *Can a Pregnant Woman Morally Refuse Fetal Surgery?*, 79 CALIF. L. REV. 499 (1991); Kristina Holmgren & Nils Uddenberg, *Abortion Ethics—Women's Post Abortion Assessments*, 73(6) ACTA OBSTETRICIA ET GYNECOLOGICA SCANDINAVICA 492 (1994).
[20] For this notion, *see* Donald H. Regan, *Justifications for Paternalism*, in NOMOS XV: THE LIMITS OF LAW 189 (J.R. Pennock & J.W. Chapman eds., 1974); J.W. Oakley, *Utilitarian Paternalist or Both? The State in England and the English*, 14(1) PROSE STUDIES 21 (1991); Jonathan Seglow, *Mill (1806–1873), in* INTERPRETING MODERN POLITICAL PHILOSOPHY 180 (A. Edwards & J. Townshend eds., 2002).

society. The utilitarian paternalist would not see the result specifically from the point of view of the woman or of the fetus and would not require an increase in happiness of any individual woman. It would be enough for such a utilitarian paternalist that the amount of social happiness would increase if the decision were to be made by the state rather than the woman to enable a healthy baby to be born. The aim of the restrictions placed on the pregnant woman would be to prevent her actions from inflicting harm on herself (prevention of the gain inherent in motherhood) or on the fetus (prevention of danger to the life of the fetus): restricting her freedom and her autonomy are in her best interest and of society as a whole.

Two problems arise from this theory. First, it may be argued that the woman cares about herself more than society cares about her because a person is closest to oneself; second, it may be assumed that the woman knows better than the state what is good for her. The paternalist will tend to support letting the state decide in her place, based on the assumption that in this way, general good on average will increase, "overcoming" the problem of the woman knowing best what is good for her. A quite contrary, paternalistic approach may argue that allowing the woman to fulfill her desire is a goal that should be advanced even if doing so will cause her harm (psychological, for not becoming a mother, or physical), harm to the viable fetus, or end its life. Although this approach seems anti-paternalistic, it is not. In my opinion, "the utilitarian of wishes" will calculate all the wishes existing at a given time and ascribe significance to the wishes of the woman and the wellbeing of the fetus. Such utilitarians will remove from the calculation certain wishes they judge to be "irrational," "strange," "not clear enough," or "inconsistent with the other wishes of the same person." Therefore, although it seems as if significance is being ascribed to the woman's wishes, in practice, this paternalistic theory does not take her into consideration; rather, it claims that the woman's wish to abort, which is likely to cause her and destroy the fetus, is not a wish at all because a person cannot harbor a desire to harm herself or her offspring.

Paternalism assumes that everyone is rational and therefore a woman's wish to have an abortion, destroying life, should be discounted. If we accept this viewpoint, we also ascribe irrationality to an adult who chooses not to receive medical treatment and withholds informed consent to it, signing his death warrant. Again, such a wish should be invalidated. This theory, then, is likely to destroy the basis of the doctrine of informed consent. Thus, accepting this extreme view is to return to pure paternalism, undermining decades of development of individual autonomy. For example, it would be a return to the view that anyone who refuses to receive painful chemotherapy must be treated forcibly because by refusing the individual is acting irrationally.[21]

Another school of thought that justifies the paternalistic attitude is deontology, which holds that human beings bear moral responsibility. A pregnant woman is in a certain physical condition that involves her being "used" to accommodate another human being, which is considered to automatically impair her decision-making skills. Therefore, the deontological paternalists would claim that her autonomy should be restricted and that a decision should be made in her stead. Kant's theory is an example of the deontologist perception: if a woman in this state is incapable of taking responsibility, it also implies that she has some sort of cognitive deficiency.

Cognitive deficiencies are defects in the ability of rational thinking[22] and reflect a failure in "practical inference,"[23] a process in which we make

---

[21] For the problematic collision between autonomy and this painful coercive medical treatment, *see* Michael H. Shapiro, *Legislating the Control of Behavior Control: Autonomy and the Coercive Use of Organic Therapies*, 47 S. CAL. L. REV. 237 (1974); Danny Scoccia, *Paternalism and Respect for Autonomy*, 100(2) ETHICS 318 (1990); Titiavan Kleffens et al., *The Medical Practice of Patient Autonomy and Cancer Treatment Refusals: A Patients' and Physicians' Perspective*, 58(11) SOCIAL SCIENCE & MEDICINE 2325 (2004).

[22] For a discussion of this issue, *see* Barbara Kellerman, *Allison Redux: Three More Decision-Making Models*, 15(3) POLITY 351 (1983); VIVIEN COELHO, CREATING AMBIENT INTELLIGENCE: APPLICATIONS AND DESIGN GUIDELINES FOR THE HOME (2012), http://130.216.33.163/courses/compsci705s1c/exams/SeminarReports/SeminarReport vcoe002.pdf; Robert C. Roberts & Ryan West, *Natural Epistemic Defects and Corrective Virtues*, 192(8) SYNTHESE 2557 (2015).

[23] For this philosophic notion, *see* Georg Henrik von Wright, *Practical Inference*, 72(2) PHILOSOPHICAL REVIEW 159 (1963); A.J. Kenny, *Practical Inference*, 26(3) ANALYSIS 65

certain assumptions about ourselves and the world, based on which we infer what we should do. Regarding a pregnant woman, the assumption is that a defect exists in her judgment regarding whether to continue or terminate the life of another being. The problem raised by this assumption also has ramifications regarding the cognitive skills of an invalid: is it justifiable to intervene in the decision of an ill person? The answer appears to be negative.

Kant's interpretation of autonomy is that every person can legislate his own ethical laws and act accordingly. A person's choice of actions according to these laws is autonomous and not enforced because it is the person himself making the ethical laws; these laws are chosen by the individual to express her essence as a rational and free agent. According to this view, the pregnant woman may not possess the ability for rational thought owing to her physical, hormonal, and mental state during the course of the pregnancy, therefore any choice she makes involving a decision to continue with the pregnancy, to terminate, or to refrain from undergoing a C-section, even at the expense of the fetus's life, does not express her essence as a rational and free agent, and therefore these are not autonomous actions. Autonomy means having personal control, and if the woman is considered unable to have personal control over an action, she is considered devoid of autonomy, and the Kantian prohibition of intervention in a person's autonomous life[24] does not apply. When a woman has no discretion and no autonomy, the deontologist will suggest the rational laws of the state should be applied for her sake.

The deontological theories introduced the ideal of independent human beings. How could it be then that the paternalists took those theories

---

(1966); G.H. von Wright, *On So-Called Practical Inference*, 15(1) ACTA SOCIOLOGICA 39 (1972).

[24] *See, e.g.*, David Garland, *The Birth of the Welfare Sanction*, 8 BRIT. J.L. & SOC'Y 29 (1981); Harry Van der Linden, *Kant, the Duty to Promote International Peace, and Political Intervention*, 2(1) PROCEEDINGS OF THE EIGHTH INTERNATIONAL KANT CONGRESS 71 (1995); Georg Cavallar & August Reinisch, *Kant, Intervention and the "Failed State,"* 2 KANTIAN REV. 91 (1998).

and changed Kant's strict individualism,[25] bringing it closer to the totalitarian doctrine that demands adherence to the commands of the state? The deontological paternalist must explain why it is justified to intervene in the absolutely non-autonomous actions of people: humans are intelligent beings, but their rationality is incomplete owing to lack of information, haste, illness, pregnancy, tension, etc., and there is no perfect overlap between the idea of autonomy and that of complete rationality, as claimed by the Kantian perception. The deontologist paternalist would maintain that adult individuals are mature enough to be autonomous even if their actions are likely to be carried out in a defective and flawed manner, and regardless, there should be no intervention in their actions.

The attitude toward a pregnant woman as an irrational person may be said to stem from a narrow perception of rationality. A broad perception of this term could also interpret a woman's behavior in this state as rational, as far as the woman is concerned, compared to other pregnant women in general. Another counterclaim is that autonomous individuals construct their lives by means of choices, and that a connection between past choices and present ones exists. This means that a person is autonomous if she remakes her choices daily, unrelated to the past, even relinquishing the option to shape her life based on her personal choices.

Consider Mill's example of the choice of a person who willingly sells himself into slavery. Paternalists would not justify intervention in an autonomous decision of this kind made by choice even if it involved relinquishing freedom forever—and accordingly, they cannot justify intervention in a woman's freedom.

It may also be argued that paternalists aim to promote the woman's best interest (directly or indirectly), promote the best interest of the fetus

---

[25] For a discussion of this perception, *see, for example,* David Garland, *The Birth of the Welfare Sanction*, 8 BRIT. J.L. & SOC'Y 29 (1981); Robert P. George, *Natural Law*, 52 AM. J. JURIS. 55 (2007); Robert P. George, *Natural Law*, 31 HARV. J.L. & PUB. POL'Y 171 (2008).

(directly), and protect whomever society considers to be weak. A human being is defined, among other methods, by means of the terms "eligibility" and "responsibility."[26] Society perceives the fetus not as a "human being" but rather as a "potential human being" who cannot shoulder responsibility and is incapable of using its rights for its best interest. Infringing on the woman's autonomy for the benefit of a non-person would mean that the human status (of the mother) is valued less than that of a potential human. An extreme paternalistic perception of the woman's status may achieve this result, implying that society perceives a pregnant woman as a "lesser human being." It is doubtful that those in favor of paternalism intended such an outcome.

1.3 The right of physicians and the extent of their judgment

The loss of autonomy may take on several forms and exist on different levels: a person may relinquish independence of judgment regarding a specific, single issue or various types of issues. When an ill person turns to a physician for care, he commits to agree to any treatment decided upon by the physician.[27] In this instance, the patient voluntarily agrees to relinquish his autonomy. Should the physician be called a paternalist? Can the physician force his judgment on the patient, claiming that the patient agreed to it by the mere fact of having agreed to medical care? And, if so, what is the extent of the physician's discretion? When someone follows the instructions of a professional with authority (the physician), he relinquishes his personal judgment or the right to take action based on this judgment, on the strength of the

---

[26] For the nexus of these notions in the context of abortion, *see* Randall A. Lake, *The Metaethical Framework of Anti-Abortion Rhetoric*, 11(3) SIGNS: JOURNAL OF WOMEN IN CULTURE AND SOCIETY 478 (1986); Rebecca J. Cook, *Human Rights and Reproductive Self-Determination*, 44 AM. U. L. REV. 975 (1995); Rebecca J. Cook & Bernard M. Dickens, *Human Rights Dynamics of Abortion Law Reform*, 25(1) HUM. RTS. Q. 1 (2003).

[27] For a discussion of this point, *see* O. O'Neill, *Paternalism and Partial Autonomy*, 10 JOURNAL OF MEDICAL ETHICS 173 (1984); Mark Siegler, *The Progression of Medicine: From Physician Paternalism to Patient Autonomy to Bureaucratic Parsimony*, 145(4) ARCH INTERN MED. 713 (1985); J. Nessa & K. Malterud, *Tell Me What's Wrong with Me: A Discourse Analysis Approach to the Concept of Patient Autonomy*, 24 JOURNAL OF MEDICAL ETHICS 394 (1998).

assumption that the physician has made a professional medical assessment that specific actions should be taken. Following the acceptance of the medical authority's discretion, the person undergoing the action considers himself exempt from using his discretion. The situation is different when autonomy is relinquished in decision making to comply with the authority of the state.

If one agrees with the argument supporting the paternalism of physicians toward their patients, I could also agree with the paternalism of the state toward a pregnant woman.[28] Concerning education, health, and other issues, the state is akin to a professional authority, and it legislates to regulate these and other areas in the lives of its citizens. It may be assumed that the state should have discretion regarding the choices of a pregnant woman. In the case of professional authorities, the reasons for voluntarily obeying orders reflect the content of these orders.[29] They are not the result of the ethical principle that professional authorities must shape their instructions using their best relevant judgment, but rather on an evidence-based presumption that they actually do so. In the case of state authority, the reasons for obeying rules may also be ethical, based on the content of the rules.

By obeying the law, we accept the fact that it obligates us to do something as prescribed (or refrain from doing so), even if we do not agree with it. This is the main dilemma in the duty to carry out the legislature's orders, at least where we are concerned: if there is a duty to obey the orders of the legislature and prevent a certain behavior of the pregnant woman, or to obligate her to behave in a specific way, this duty is based on the content of the law itself, and not on a personal

---

[28] For a discussion of this point, *see* Susan S. Mattingly, *The Maternal–Fetal Dyad: Exploring the Two-Patient Obstetric Model*, 22(1) OBSTETRIC MODEL 13 (1992); J. Wyatt, *Medical Paternalism and the Fetus*, 27 JOURNAL OF MEDICAL ETHICS ii15 (2001); E. ETTORRE, REPRODUCTIVE GENETICS, GENDER AND THE BODY (2002).

[29] *See, e.g.*, Stanley Milgram, *Some Conditions of Obedience and Disobedience to Authority*, 18(1) HUMAN RELATIONS 57 (1965); Neil Lutsky, *When Is "Obedience" Obedience? Conceptual and Historical Commentary*, 51(3) JOURNAL OF SOCIAL ISSUES 55 (1995); W. Bradley Wendel, *Civil Obedience*, 104 COLUM. L. REV. 363 (2004).

evaluation of it. Thus, professional and state authorities are comparable, therefore, denying the woman's autonomy can be justified in this case.[30]

2. A Family in a Dilemma

2.1 Constitutional law: The right to be or not to be a parent

According to the prevailing view, childbirth and fertility are private matters.[31] The decision whether or not to be a parent[32] derives from one's autonomous status;[33] the right to parenthood is a fundamental one that derives from the right to control over one's body and the right to ascribe value to one's life, freedom, and security. Every human being has a right to become a parent, and the state is not permitted to restrict this right or forbid anyone from becoming a parent by means of natural reproduction. The fundamental right to parenthood extends to every human being, including those whose parenthood may be considered invalid in advance, such as people with mental or intellectual disabilities.[34] The contrasting view of this right is society's duty not to intervene in a way that would impose restrictions upon it.[35] Is the

---

[30] PNINA LIFSHITZ-AVIRAM, INFORMED CONSENT OF A MINOR TO MEDICAL TREATMENT (2006) (Heb.).

[31] Yehezkel Margalit, *Scarce Medical Resources?—Procreation Rights in a Jewish and Democratic State* (2011), https://ssrn.com/abstract=1807908. For a discussion of this article, *see, for example,* AVISHALOM WESTREICH, ASSISTED REPRODUCTION IN ISRAEL: LAW, RELIGION AND CULTURE (2018); YEHEZKEL MARGALIT, DETERMINING LEGAL PARENTAGE—BETWEEN FAMILY LAW AND CONTRACT LAW 125 n.88 (2019).

[32] For this fundamental constitutional right, *see, e.g.,* Tracey S. Pachman, *Disputes Over Frozen Preembryos & the "Right Not to Be a Parent,"* 12 COLUM. J. GENDER & L. 128 (2003); Glenn Cohen, *The Constitution and the Rights Not to Procreate,* 60 STAN. L. REV. 1135 (2008); Glenn Cohen, *The Right Not to Be a Genetic Parent?,* 81 S. CAL. L. REV. 1115 (2008).

[33] For a discussion of this basic human right, *see* Daniel Statman, *The Right to Parenthood: An Argument for a Narrow Interpretation,* 10(3–4) ETHICAL PERSPECTIVES 224 (2003); Robin Levi et al., *Creating the "Bad Mother": How the U.S. Approach to Pregnancy in Prisons Violates the Right to Be a Mother,* 18 UCLA WOMEN'S L.J. 1 (2010); Yehezkel Margalit, *To Be or Not to Be (A Parent)?—Not Precisely the Question; The Frozen Embryo Dispute,* 18 CARDOZO J.L. & GENDER 355 (2012).

[34] Clause 18, Penal Law.

[35] The right to bring up children and educate them in accordance with the parents' conception derives from the right to be a parent. In the present situation, the right of

importance of parenthood merely a biological need based on the primal inclination to give birth for purposes of genetic continuity or is it a social and political need? Therefore, should it be stipulated as a right?

In the *Nahmani v. Nahmani* case, Israel Supreme Court Justice Dalia Dorner wrote:

> In human society, one of the strongest expressions of an aspiration without which many will not regard themselves free in the fullest sense of the word is the aspiration to parenthood. We are not speaking merely of a natural biological need. We are speaking of a freedom which, in human society, symbolizes the uniqueness of man. "Any person who does not have children is considered a dead person," said Rabbi Yehoshua ben Levi (Babylonian Talmud, Tractate Nedarim, 64b). Indeed, whether man or woman, most people regard having children as an existential necessity that gives meaning to their lives.[36]

When accepting the theory that the state is compelled to intervene in the right to parenthood, the question arises whether the individual's right to parenthood also includes the obligation of the state to help the person carry out this right, i.e., to cover the costs of the necessary procedures when parenthood cannot be achieved naturally. Some claim that the various new reproductive technologies, including sperm and egg donations, surrogates, fertility preservation, IVF, prevention of illness, and parenthood of different types—e.g., single parents, same-sex parents, parenting in late age—all disassociate society from the

---

society to intervene in this freedom is imposed only after the birth of the infant, because then it becomes an actual person with its own rights and duties. Thus, from the moment of birth, society is under an obligation to protect the child and prevent it from any harm, whether psychological, spiritual, or physical, according to the principles recognized by society. Based on this social obligation, many laws have been legislated, aiming to protect minors and sometimes even the fetus inside its mother's womb.

[36] CFH 2401/95 Nahmani v. Nahmani, Israel Law Reports [1995–96] 1, 62, http://ww3.lawschool.cornell.edu/AvonResources/RuthNahmaniv.DanielNahmani.Ddf
.

biological model of reproduction and therefore justify intervention by society and state.[37]

Some scholars[38] define the right to parenthood as the right of every person to make every possible effort, including those who can do so only by technological means (without violating the rights of others) to create offspring with a genetic or gestational connection[39] with at least one of the parents intending to raise it.

2.2 Relationships in the family and parenting abilities

Parenthood is unquestionably a right. Above, I explained that the state is prevented from intervening in the right to natural procreation because this is a fundamental right. Here I show that a complete lack of intervention may be to the detriment of the newborn child. The right to be a parent is not contingent on having parenting abilities or skills. The fact that one is capable of becoming a parent biologically in no way ensures that the individual is capable of performing the parental duties well or even properly. Society has yet to solve the legal and ethical dilemma arising from the right of every person to parenthood, which

---

[37] Yaniv Ron El, *The Limits of Reproductive Freedom from a Liberal Perspective: The Case of Sex Selection,* 32 TEL AVIV U. L. REV. 391 (2010) (Heb.).

[38] This statement is hotly debated in the scholarly literature. *See, e.g.,* Lori B. Andrews, *The Legal Status of the Embryo,* 32 LOY. L. REV. 357, 360 (1986); Ann M. Massie, *Symposium on John A. Robertson's Children of Choice: Regulating Choice: A Constitutional Law Response to Professor John A. Robertson's Children of Choice,* 52 WASH & LEE L. REV. 135 (1995); MARY WARNOCK, MAKING BABIES: IS THERE A RIGHT TO HAVE CHILDREN? 85 (2002); Richard F. Storrow, *The Bioethics of Prospective Parenthood: In Pursuit of the Proper Standard for Gatekeeping in Infertility Clinics,* 28 CARDOZO L. REV. 2283, 2295–99 (2007).

[39] For the unique relationship between the gestational mother and the fetus, *see, e.g.,* BARBARA KATZ ROTHMAN, RECREATING MOTHERHOOD 44, 97–105, 238–39 (1989); MARSHALL H. KLAUS & JOHN H. KENNELL, MATERNAL-INFANT BONDING 1–15 (1976); H. Marshall & Jeanne Schuler, *Baby M and the Politics of Gender,* 74 TELOS 126, 130 (1987–1988); Anne Goodwin, *Determination of Legal Parentage in Egg Donation, Embryo Transplantation, and Gestational Surrogacy Arrangements,* 1992 FAM. L.Q. 275 (1992).

can conflict with the fundamental right of a child to be protected from neglect or abuse by the parent.[40]

A debate on whether natural reproduction in cases of proven lack of parenting abilities should be prohibited is not within the ambit of this book. But arguably, the topic of parenting abilities is relevant in a discussion on preventing abortions and on enforced Parents do not always understand the essential aspects of childcare. Behavior patterns learned by a parent from others do not always suit the needs of a given child, and sometimes ignorance and lack of a suitable personal model might be harmful to the child.[41]

To discuss the nature of parenting abilities, a definition of a "good" parent is needed. In the past, a parent who provided for the child's physical needs was considered a good parent; today, the parent-child relationship is the important factor, and parents are expected to care about the child's emotional intelligence and wellbeing no less than the child's IQ.[42] Some maintain that because the term "parenting" has not

[40] *See, for example,* the more general inevitable contradiction between parental and children's rights: Ferdinand Schoeman, *Parental Discretion and Children's Rights: Background and Implications for Medical Decision-Making,* 10(1) JOURNAL OF MEDICINE AND PHILOSOPHY: A FORUM FOR BIOETHICS AND PHILOSOPHY OF MEDICINE 45 (1985); Annette R. Appell & Bruce A. Boyer, *Parental Rights vs. Best Interests of the Child: A False Dichotomy in the Context of Adoption,* 2 DUKE JOURNAL OF GENDER LAW & POLICY 63 (1995); Samantha Brennan & Robert Noggle, *The Moral Status of Children: Children's Rights, Parents' Rights, and Family Justice,* 23(1) SOCIAL THEORY AND PRACTICE 1 (1997).

[41] This issue reminds me of the unforgettable discussion of parenting licensing by Hugh Lafollette, *Licensing Parents,* 9(2) PHILOSOPHY AND PUBLIC AFFAIRS 182 (1980). For a discussion of his unique and problematic proposal, *see, among others,* Claudia Pap Mangel, *Licensing Parents: How Feasible?,* 22(1) FAM. L.Q. 17 (1988); David L. Chadwick, *Licensing Parents: Can We Prevent Child Abuse and Neglect?,* 273(22) JAMA 1798 (1995); SHOULD PARENTS BE LICENSED? DEBATING THE ISSUES (Peg Tittle ed., 2004).

[42] DANIEL GOLDMAN, EMOTIONAL INTELLIGENCE (1995). For an academic discussion of this central human intelligence, *see, e.g.,* John D. Mayer, *Emotional Intelligence,* 9(3) IMAGINATION, COGNITION AND PERSONALITY 185 (1990); John D. Mayer & Glenn Geher, *Emotional Intelligence and the Identification of Emotion,* 22(2) INTELLIGENCE 89 (1996); THE HANDBOOK OF EMOTIONAL INTELLIGENCE: THEORY, DEVELOPMENT, ASSESSMENT, AND APPLICATION AT HOME, SCHOOL, AND IN THE WORKPLACE (Reuven Bar-On & James D.A. Parker eds., 2000).

been defined yet, it is impossible to unequivocally establish what constitutes a good parent.[43]

When the law allows everyone, whatever their mental and cognitive abilities, to bring children into the world, there will inevitably be emotionally unbalanced parents who will harm their children; parents with childish or immature personalities who will place their own needs in the center and seek their own gratification before that of the child; parents who will concern themselves only with their image as giving parents instead of cultivating a reciprocal relationship with their child;[44] parents who assign a particular role for their child to fulfill, as when a child is brought into the world to replace someone who has died, or is intended for a parent's self-realization, where the parent does not see the child as a separate entity.

Sociologists specializing in the family field consider procreation to be of key importance. According to the "correct" order of things, the family is created for the sake of the child, but often this order becomes disrupted, and we see children brought into the world for the sake of the family. An example is when pregnancy is used as a means to force a marriage or prevent a divorce. In some cases, if the child does not "meet expectations," the parents transfer their disappointment or anger onto the child. Sometimes a child is used as a scapegoat to defuse

---

[43] 3 MARC. H. BORNSTEIN, HANDBOOK OF PARENTING, HANDBOOK OF PARENTING: BEING AND BECOMING A PARENT (2005). For a discussion of this book, *see* Nancy Eisenberg et al., *Parental Socialization of Emotion,* 9(4) PSYCHOLOGICAL INQUIRY 241 (1998); Greg J. Duncan & Jeanne Brooks-Gunn, *Family Poverty, Welfare Reform, and Child Development,* 71(1) CHILD DEVELOPMENT 188 (2003); Judith G. Smetana et al., *Adolescent Development in Interpersonal and Societal Contexts,* 57(1) ANNUAL REVIEW OF PSYCHOLOGY 255 (2006).

[44] Disabled children cast a shadow on the parental image because their birth raises doubts about the parents' ability to create a perfect baby. The number of disabled children who are rejected, neglected, or abused is especially high in cases when parents see their children as a reflection of themselves, and not as individuals in their own right.

tensions in a family. At other times the child chooses to become the scapegoat to save the family.[45]

Many researchers refute the popular perception that the parents' psychological disturbance is the only cause of child abuse.[46] The number of mentally defective parents who abuse their children is very high: research carried out in Israel showed that some 50% of parents suffering from mental retardation abuse their children. In discussions with parents like these and after following up on the reasons that led to abuse, it appears that the abuse resulted from a low frustration threshold, inability to control urges, and inability to assess the result of actions. Abusive parental behavior toward a child is also liable to occur as a result of at least two types of stressful conditions that lead to a lack of control: a difficult socioeconomic situation (caused by immigration, unemployment, or termination of employment) and a crisis or stress in the family, including pregnancy, birth, adolescence, divorce, or illness.

We have seen that new technological means and different family units exist today, and therefore a child can be brought into the world even without parents being married or even without sexual intercourse. People can plan to become parents when they are ready, considering only their own interests, more or less. The fundamental right to procreate has expanded over the years. At first. it applied only to married couples,[47] but today it can apply to single people, with the

---

[45] Ezra F. Vogel & Norman W. Bell, *The Emotionally Disturbed Child as a Family Scapegoat,* (10)3 CAN. J. PSYCHIATRIC NURSING 5 (1968). *See also* CARLFRED B. BRODERICK, UNDERSTANDING FAMILY PROCESS: BASICS OF FAMILY SYSTEMS THEORY 261 (1st ed. 1993); MAGGIE SCARF, INTIMATE PARTNERS: PATTERNS IN LOVE AND MARRIAGE 442 (2008); PHILIP BARKER & JEFF CHANG, BASIC FAMILY THERAPY (6th ed. 2013).

[46] M.L. BLUMBERG, PSYCHOPATHOLOGY OF THE ABUSIVE PARENT (1974). For a discussion of this book, *see, e.g.,* Hilda Parker & Seymour Parker, *Father–Daughter Sexual Abuse: An Emerging Perspective,* 56(4) AMERICAN JOURNAL OF ORTHOPSYCHIATRY 531 (1986); CHILDREN AT RISK 141 (Robert Ammerman & Michel Hersen eds., 1990); L.M. Youngblade & J. Belsky, *Social and Emotional Consequences of Child Maltreatment, id.* 109.

[47] *See* Griswold v. Connecticut, 381 U.S. 479 (1965), in which the court rejected a criminal injunction on married couples to use birth control. *See also* Catherine G. Roraback, Griswold v. Connecticut*: A Brief Case History,* 16 OHIO N.U. L. REV. 395 (1989); Mary L. Dudziak, *Just Say No: Birth Control in the Connecticut Supreme Court*

specific ruling of the court that the right to privacy is granted to every individual. This includes freedom from unjustified state intervention in an individual's decision whether or not to give birth.[48]

As noted, in extreme cases, preventing official intervention may harm the viable fetus and the newborn child, and therefore the time may be ripe to think in a somewhat paternalistic way. Alongside preventing abortion in the viable stage, forcing medical treatment on a woman during pregnancy, and obligating her to undergo a C-section against her will, it is time to consider the possibility of intervention even in the private lives of individuals to prohibit pregnancy in cases where it is liable to harm the fetus or the newborn.

2.3 A fetus or a child with disabilities

I proceed to examine the place of the disabled child in the family to confirm a theory according to which even a child with disabilities has a constitutional right to be born, a right equal in importance to that of the woman over her body. The converse is that an individual is allowed to reproduce even if there is an acute concern that the child will not be healthy and even if the progenitor is mentally challenged.[49] The question is: What is a disability? For legal purposes, a disability can be physical, mental, psychological, emotional, cognitive, developmental, or a combination of several of these. A person or child suffering from

---

before Griswold v. Connecticut, 75 IOWA L. REV. 915 (1990); Janet L. Dolgin, *The Family in Transition: From* Griswold *to* Eisenstadt *and Beyond*, 82 GEO. L.J. 1519 (1994).

[48] See, among others, John A. Robertson, Procreative Liberty and the Control of Conception, Pregnancy, and Childbirth, 69 VA. L. REV. 405 (1983); John A. Robertson, Embryos, Families, and Procreative Liberty: The Legal Structure of the New Reproduction, 59 S. CAL. L. REV. 942 (1986); Douglas NeJaime, Griswold's Progeny: Assisted Reproduction, Procreative Liberty, and Sexual Orientation Equality, 124 YALE L.J. F. 340 (2014–15).

[49] *See* MARGALIT, DETERMINING LEGAL PARENTAGE, *supra* note 32, at 119. Conversely, in the ethical-philosophical literature, one finds calls to restrict the birthrate of mentally challenged or abusive parents in the name of preserving the conceived child's interests and welfare. *See* Elike-Henner W. Kluge, *Sterilization of the Mentally Severely Handicapped: A Violation of the Right to Have Children?*, *in* SHOULD PARENTS BE LICENSED? *supra* note 42, 243, 246, and the other chapters in the book.

one or more disabilities is referred to as one "with disability." In our social culture, the term "disabled person" has a negative, even patronizing connotation.[50]

Impairment may be expressed in bodily functions or body structure, in carrying out activities, and in daily functioning. Disabilities include blindness, deafness, and dysfunction of olfaction or gustation; they may stem from a lack of ability to sense heat, cold, or pain, impairment of growth, intellectual or physical ability, mental illness, mental retardation, and the effects thereof. A disability or defect may cause a person to be limited in carrying out activities compared to his peers. A fetus suspected of having a disability or a defect such as those described above is more likely than any other to be aborted even in the viable stage.

Physicians face acute dilemmas when it comes to establishing what constitutes a disability for which an abortion is recommended. Some defects that appear to be serious during pregnancy, after birth, turn out to be lighter than expected, and it often happens that a pregnancy is terminated after identifying a minor defect.

Families have both external and internal limits: the external limits are intended to provide privacy and must be stable yet flexible so that the family can connect with third parties. The internal limits make a distinction between the role of the parents and that of the children, and help balance their relationships. A child with disabilities places specific and often difficult responsibilities on the family. Such children need extra protection at the expense of the other children in the family, strongly depend on the parents taking care of them, and impose burdens on parents, taking time and resources away from their siblings. Often, the family finds it difficult to continue functioning as a balanced

---

[50] The main concern in this regard is the problematic attempt to produce only "perfect" babies. *See, for example,* Ruth F. Chadwick, *The Perfect Baby: Introduction,* in ETHICS, REPRODUCTION AND GENETIC CONTROL (Ruth F. Chadwick ed., 1987); GLENN MCGEE, THE PERFECT BABY: A PRAGMATIC APPROACH TO GENETICS (1997); GLENN MCGEE, THE PERFECT BABY: PARENTHOOD IN THE NEW WORLD OF CLONING AND GENETICS (2000).

structure. This must be made clear when claiming that the viable fetus has a right to be born even if it is disabled or has a defect.

In his book, *My Left Foot*, the writer and artist Christy Brown[51] described a balanced structure, writing about how he blended into the daily life of his siblings despite being paralyzed and unable to talk. His brothers and their friends let him join in their activities, carried him on their backs, or wheeled him around in an improvised cart.

When a child is born with disabilities, it creates an increasing dependence on resources within and outside the family—mainly physicians, therapists, and teachers. Giving birth to such a child may even cause a marital crisis and require the family structure to readjust.[52] Different parents react differently to the birth of a child with defects. Dealing with the complexity of decision-making regarding children with special needs is important to our discussion because of their large numbers.[53] Having given birth to a child with special needs, parents are likely to feel that a heavy burden has been placed on their shoulders. A family that raises a disabled child needs assistance and a great deal of help from other parties, especially access to sources of information related to diagnosis and treatment, daily physical exercise, education,

---

[51] CHRISTY BROWN, MY LEFT FOOT (1969). For the relation of this book with the abortion dilemma, *see, for example,* COLIN BARNES, DISABLING IMAGERY AND THE MEDIA: AN EXPLORATION OF THE PRINCIPLES FOR MEDIA REPRESENTATIONS OF DISABLED PEOPLE (1992), https://disability-studies.leeds.ac.uk/wp-content/uploads/sites/40/library/Barnes-disabling-imagery.pdf; Jack A. Nelson, *The Media Role in Building the Disability Community,* 15(3) JOURNAL OF MASS MEDIA ETHICS 180 (2000); Wendy Chrisman, *A Reflection on Inspiration: A Recuperative Call for Emotion in Disability Studies,* 5(2) JOURNAL OF LITERARY & CULTURAL DISABILITY STUDIES 173 (2011).

[52] HELEN A. FEATHERSTONE, DIFFERENCE IN THE FAMILY—LIFE WITH A DISABLED CHILD (1980). For a discussion of this book, *see* Michael Ferrari et al., *The Family and the Child with Epilepsy,* 22(1) FAMILY PROCESS 53 (1983); Monica Cuskelly, *Adjustment of Siblings of Children with a Disability: Methodological Issues,* 21(2) INTERNATIONAL JOURNAL FOR THE ADVANCEMENT OF COUNSELLING 111 (1999); Isack Kandel & Joav Merrick, *The Birth of a Child with Disability: Coping by Parents and Siblings,* 3 SCIENTIFIC WORLD JOURNAL 741 (2003).

[53] ANN S. KIMAN, CRISIS: PSYCHOLOGICAL FIRST AID FOR RECOVERING AND GROWTH (1978). Some 18 million people with special needs lived in the US as of 2016.

therapy, and rehabilitation. Such a family also needs social support to reorganize itself to cope with the new situation. Professionals may have different opinions, from blaming the parents for the medical and psychological misfortunes of the child[54] to sidelining the parents entirely while focusing on therapies for him.[55]

Featherstone[56] described three factors that are liable to widen the rift between the parents whose child has been born with disabilities, rapidly leading to a family crisis: fear, fatigue, and anger. Fear inhibits communication; fatigue lowers the level of patience and makes it difficult to find solutions; and although the source of anger is the child because the parents do not allow themselves to be angry with their child, they take it out on one another. When the child is severely disabled, and the question arises whether to institutionalize him or to take medical action, parents must choose between their responsibilities toward the child and their obligations to the rest of the family. When the parents do not agree, conflict may ensue. For the family to find a balance, there must be cooperation between the parents. When a child with special needs is born, parents may have serious doubts about the quality and value of their parenthood.

Parents of children with special needs look to their healthy children to reinforce their faith in themselves as good parents, capable of giving birth and raising children without defects. To meet this need, parents try to prove to themselves that they are "okay" by clinging to their healthy children or by bringing additional healthy children, without

[54] MARGARET S. MAHLER, ON CHILD PSYCHOSIS AND SCHIZOPHRENIA: PSYCHOANALYTIC STUDY OF THE CHILD 286–380 (1952). *See also* Guy Da Silva, *The Role of the Father with Chronic Schizophrenic Patients: A Study in Group Therapy*, 8(3) CANADIAN PSYCHIATRIC ASSOCIATION JOURNAL 190, 201 (1963); Allan F. Mirsky, *Israeli High-risk Study: Editor's Introduction*, 21(2) SCHIZOPHRENIA BULLETIN 179, 179 (1995); Edward F. Foulks, *Advocating for Persons Who Are Mentally Ill: A History of Mutual Empowerment of Patients and Profession*, 27(5) ADMINISTRATION AND POLICY IN MENTAL HEALTH AND MENTAL HEALTH SERVICES 353, 359–60 (2000).

[55] BRUNO BETTELHEIM, LOVE IS NOT ENOUGH: THE TREATMENT OF EMOTIONALLY DISTURBED CHILDREN (1950).

[56] FEATHERSTONE, *supra* note 55.

special needs, into the world. As a result, healthy children often suffer. Their relationship with the parents and the child with special needs is influenced by the attitude of the parents but is not similar to it. The majority attempt to hide the existence of this sibling from other people, envy the attention this child receives, are afraid of becoming "infected," and feel under pressure because of the additional burden on the parents' shoulders.

The parents themselves must renounce their self-determination and free time to care for the child, which leads to frustration and feelings of guilt. The parents are in a constant state of indecision and must find a balance between the contradictory tasks of adaptations. A conflict exists between the immediate needs of the child and future plans, between showering affection on the child and feelings of disappointment and resentment, between continuing to function day-to-day and giving in to pain and anger, between wanting to take full responsibility for the child and the need to start depending on others. Changes take place in all areas of family life, including work habits, social life, sexual activity, relationships with the extended family, and expressions of emotion.

I have yet to find comprehensive anthropological research on how parents relate to a child with disabilities, but it is clear that the relationship is based on their cultural perception of the world.[57] The social definition of a newborn as a "non-person" also forms the basis of the phenomenon of infanticide—intentionally killing a newborn with the agreement of the parents, family, or community,[58] making it less difficult to deal with infanticide on a psychological level.

---

[57] See Chapter 3, *supra*, n. 98.

[58] For the correlation between infanticide and abortion, *see, e.g.*, Michael Tooley, *Abortion and Infanticide*, 1 PHILOSOPHY AND PUBLIC AFFAIRS 44 (1972); R. Sauer, *Infanticide and Abortion in Nineteenth-Century Britain*, 32(1) POPULATION STUDIES 81 (1978); JONATHAN GLOVER, CAUSING DEATH AND SAVING LIVES: THE MORAL PROBLEMS OF ABORTION, INFANTICIDE, SUICIDE, EUTHANASIA, CAPITAL PUNISHMENT, WAR AND OTHER LIFE-OR-DEATH CHOICES (1990).

In some societies, taking the life of a child with certain characteristics that conflict with their religious ideals (for example, twins or a child with a defect) is not considered a crime. This perception is widespread in the Tonga and the Bantu of Southeast Africa and Malaya. For the Masi, a baby born without a nose is considered a demon who will wreak havoc in the future, therefore it is killed. Among the Hausa in northern Nigeria, a baby with a defect is immediately thrown into the river, and in Borneo, the baby's neck is broken. There is also a tendency to kill a newborn that is not considered "a person." For example, Foucault defined "a real person" by criteria based on financial capability, the ability to make love, circumcision, and fertility. Therefore, a sterile woman is not "a real person," just as someone who has not yet been circumcised and therefore not considered an adult cannot distinguish between good and evil. Because an androgyne is sterile and unable to be circumcised, he is not "a real person," and it is customary to kill such a baby immediately after birth.[59]

These perceptions exist not only in African tribes. In ancient Greece, Rome, and Egypt, it was customary to kill an infant born with a defect: an infant found to be weak or disabled by the council of elders was thrown into a deep valley. Plato also recommended that a chronically ill person should be put to death. The infanticide of female babies was widespread in many societies for hundreds of years. Boys are much more valuable than girls for the Rajputs of Kalafur in India because they are needed for religious duties. At the beginning of the 19th century, this preference was still expressed by the killing of female babies. The British sought to do away with this custom, and it became less prevalent but still exists. Even today, male children receive preferential medical treatment, which explains why the rate of female infantile mortality is double that of boys.

Many incidences of violence have been known toward those who are physically "ugly," and children with certain physical characteristics,

---

[59] MEIRA WEISS, CONDITIONAL LOVE: PARENTS' ATTITUDES TOWARDS THE HANDICAPPED (1994).

such as dark skin, who are considered of a lower cultural status, are known to have been victims of infanticide. The literature describes two groups from Madagascar with similar physical characteristics apart from the color of their skin: one light, the other dark. A dark-skinned child born in a light-skinned group was put to death even if his parents were not in doubt, in the belief that if left alive, the child would turn into a sorcerer, a leper, a thief, or be guilty of incest.[60]

Regarding cases of abuse, Sheleff argued that parents feel a basic hostility toward their children.[61] Regarding the "Oedipus complex,"[62] Sheleff maintained that Freud ignored the first part of the Greek story and did not emphasize that the initial aggressive impulse was that of the father (Laius) toward his son (Oedipus). As in primitive society, in our times as well, a child with a defect, whose appearance is associated with the image of an animal or a monster, is exposed to maltreatment by his parents. Like our ancestors, we are affected by what we see. Acceptance or rejection of a child with disabilities depends on the interpretation of the body image.

Symbolic interpretation of the body is a mental mechanism that triggers the dynamic process of acceptance or rejection. A review of the literature on infanticide revealed that children whose deformed looks are reminiscent of an image of an animal are usually subjected to severe harm. In Mexico, for example, infants with "animal-like" faces are

---

[60] *Ibid.*

[61] Leon Sheleff, *Generations Apart: Adult Hostility to Youth*, 89 AM. J. SOC. 509 (1981). For a discussion of this landmark article, *see, for example*, MARTIN DALY & MARGO WILSON, HOMICIDE: FOUNDATIONS OF HUMAN BEHAVIOR (1988); MIRIAM M. JOHNSON, STRONG MOTHERS, WEAK WIVES: THE SEARCH FOR GENDER EQUALITY 288 n.6 (1988); FRIENDS IN SCHOOL: PATTERNS OF SELECTION AND INFLUENCE IN SECONDARY SCHOOLS 270 (Joyce Levy Epstein & Nancy Karweit eds., 2014).

[62] For a discussion of the possible correlation between this term and the hostility of parents toward their children, *see* Leon Shaskolsky Sheleff, *Beyond the Oedipus Complex: A Perspective on the Myth and Reality of Generational Conflict*, 3(1) THEORY AND SOCIETY 1 (1976), https://link.springer.com/content/pdf/10.1007/BF00158478.Pdf; Benjamin Shmueli, *What Has Feminism Got to Do with Children's Rights—A Case Study of a Ban on Corporal Punishment*, 22 WIS. WOMEN'S L.J. 177 (2007) *passim*; Robert M. Galatzer-Levy, *Women and Children Last*, 69(1) PSYCHOANALYTIC STUDY OF THE CHILD 108 (2015).

killed, and according to Evans-Pritchard,[63] such defect is often reminiscent of an animal or a limb of an animal, which relates to a violation of the totem of the sacred animal:

> I once met a man who had a foot with only three withered toes. I was told that his grandmother had an ostrich totem. Her son-in-law injured the ostrich, and her daughter gave birth to this child who has a defect in his feet... Ostriches, or rather the spirit of ostriches, stamped the ostrich shape on the child.

Research undertaken by Meira Weiss over the course of six years on the topic of how parents see their disabled or sick children sheds light on this issue.[64] The study revealed that about half the babies who were discovered to have defects after birth (50.8%) were abandoned by their parents immediately or soon after the birth: parents of these babies refused to take them home and most of them did not even visit them in the hospital. Some of the babies were sent home under the protection of the law against child abandonment, in a police van or hospital ambulance. Weiss concluded that parents tend to reject a child who is physically deformed, as it is considered a "non-person." Sometimes parents who abandon their children at the hospital take upon themselves a different type of responsibility for the life of the child or decide to care for him outside the home. Weiss made a distinction between two important aspects of parental behavior: one is the degree of intimacy or territorial distance with which parents treat their children

---

[63] Quoted in MEIRA WEISS, THE CHOSEN BODY: THE POLITICS OF THE BODY IN ISRAELI SOCIETY (2002). *See also* MEIRA WEISS, CONDITIONAL LOVE: PARENTS' ATTITUDES TOWARDS THE HANDICAPPED (1994); AVIAD E. RAZ, COMMUNITY GENETICS AND GENETIC ALLIANCES: EUGENICS, CARRIER TESTING AND NETWORKS OF RISK (2009). Dor Yesharim is a non-profit organization founded by the Ashkenazi ultra-Orthodox community to test young men and women of marriageable age for genetic diseases. The organization provides data relating to genetic compatibility. Aviad Raz researched ultra-Orthodox women regarding the lack of transparency of data provided by Dor Yesharim, which revealed that even ultra-Orthodox women request access to information about themselves when tests for carrying certain diseases are involved.

[64] Ibid.

and the other is the perception of parental responsibility toward the children.

Weiss's research discusses the limits we take for granted in our lives. Cultural norms direct us to relate to parental love as a given and an unconditional obligation. In my book on informed consent of minors to medical treatment, I showed that this is not the case. Parents do not necessarily and in all situations love their children unconditionally.[65] Having studied several cases, Weiss also showed that parental love is not an absolute norm. The encounter with the child with a disability puts to the test the perception of the essence of a human being and questions whether the child is identified as a person. A child with a defect poses a threat to the parents and makes them anxious that the defect will reflect on them. It may be that we need the "non-person" to define what a "person" is.

In many societies, relationships between parents and children are considered extremely intense.[66] Cultural norms define the relationship of the woman with the fetus or the child and predict the situations in which the woman would perceive the child as a "non-person," leading to abuse. Following the birth of a child with a defect, the parents may not have yet formed a parent-child relationship, so the bond between them is a bond between strangers. Weiss observed closely the relationships between parents and their children who deviated from the norm as a result of illness after a connection had already been established between them. Parent-child relationships offer an

---

[65] For a discussion of whether we, as a responsible society, may trust parents to fulfill their moral duties when it is reasonable but not certain that they will, *see* Herbert L.A. Hart, *Legal and Moral Obligation*, in ESSAYS IN MORAL PHILOSOPHY 82, 103–04 (Abraham I. Melden ed., 1958); HERBERT L.A. HART, THE CONCEPT OF LAW 165–67 (1961); DAVID ARCHARD, CHILDREN: RIGHTS AND CHILDHOOD 103 (1993); *see also* the other references enumerated by MARGALIT, DETERMINING LEGAL PARENTAGE, *supra* note 32, at 79–82.

[66] For the argument that there is an almost mystical bond between the mother and her fetus, *see* KLAUS & KENNELL, *supra* note 40; Janet L. Dolgin, *Solomon's Dilemma: Exploring Parental Rights: The "Intent" of Reproduction: Reproductive Technologies and the Parent–Child Bond*, 26 CONN. L. REV. 1261 (1994); Margaret F. Brinig, *A Maternalistic Approach to Surrogacy: Comment on Richard Epstein's Surrogacy: The Case for Full Contractual Enforcement*, 81 VA. L. REV. 2377, 2383 n. 22 (1995).

appropriate field to test violent reactions to disabilities and reveal the cultural guidelines determining whether or not a child should be isolated or nurtured, live at home, be quarantined, or be sentenced to death. Findings from the anthropological literature often show that choosing violent behavior is perceived as a legitimate solution to the problem of a child with special needs.

The behavior of many parents reflects the perception that the child is defined as belonging to them only if he is not defective in any way and will not endanger their social status. If their child was born with a defect or has become disfigured, he is different from a normal human child and therefore not considered their child.[67] Even if abandoning such babies at the hospital or transferring them to an institution shortens their life, the parents have no sense of committing violence or cruelty because they relate to these babies as they would to a foreign or strange creature.[68]

Weiss's research examined how parents influence the body image of their children. Both mothers and fathers tended to reject a child with defects that threatened their self-definitions. The research shows that the mothers were more active than the fathers in adopting behavior patterns that had been chosen by the couple. When the parents cared for the child, the mother shouldered most of the care, and when that child was abandoned or rejected, the woman was more adamant and decisive about it. This may be explained by the preconceived idea and

---

[67] For the inevitable correlation between the quest for the perfect baby and the attempt to abort the fetus, *see* RUTH F. CHADWICK, *The Perfect Baby: Introduction*, *in* ETHICS, REPRODUCTION AND GENETIC CONTROL 93 (RUTH CHADWICK ed., 1993); GLENN MCGEE, THE PERFECT BABY: PARENTHOOD IN THE NEW WORLD OF CLONING AND GENETICS (2000); Larissa Remennick, *The Quest for the Perfect Baby: Why Do Israeli Women Seek Prenatal Genetic Testing?*, 28(1) SOCIOLOGY OF HEALTH & ILLNESS 21 (2006).

[68] For a discussion of the reprehensible practice of abandoning babies, among others, because of medical problems, *see* Lorraine Sherr & Natalie Hackman, *Abandoned Babies—Abandoned Issue*, 15(2) COUNSELLING PSYCHOLOGY QUARTERLY 153 (2002); Annette R. Appell, *Safe Havens to Abandon Babies, Part I: The Law*, 5(4) ADOPTION QUARTERLY 59 (2002); Annette R. Appell, *Safe Havens to Abandon Babies, Part III: The Effects*, 6(2) ADOPTION QUARTERLY 67 (2002).

social structure where the woman is less likely to work outside the home and is perceived as responsible for raising the child.

The psychoanalytical explanation could also help provide insight into the phenomenon. The pregnant woman makes an emotional and material investment in building the nest. She becomes attached to the fetus by imagery that portrays the child as perfect. Such dreams of a child that has not yet been born are normal: during pregnancy, she sees the child as having characteristics similar to her own or other beloved relatives. The woman idealizes the child based on her idealization. Thus, in her expectations of the child, she makes a greater narcissistic investment than the father, and for her, the crisis is likely to be greater when such expectations are dashed. It is important for the mother to prove that her child is perfect; she is prepared to invest in the infant as long as the defect is invisible and does not harm her self-image; but when the defect is apparent, the child threatens her and her body integrity more than the father.

Today, the perception of disability has shifted away from being a personal tragedy. The medical model relates to the disabled person as an invalid or one whose life is destined to be full of suffering, leading to an overabundance of tests. Eugenics raises the prospect of giving birth to babies who are free of disabilities. Disability studies challenge this perception. They consider disabilities to be a social phenomenon: more than a physical defect of a person, disability is the social phenomenon reflecting the physical aspect, and society exacerbates the defect by excluding the disabled.[69] When no access is provided to a certain place, the disabled are made more aware of their disabilities.

---

[69] For a discussion of the abortion dilemma through the prism of disability studies, *see* Keith Sharp & Sarah Earle, *Feminism, Abortion and Disability: Irreconcilable Differences?*, 17(2) DISABILITY & SOCIETY 137 (2002); Janice McLaughlin, *Screening Networks: Shared Agendas in Feminist and Disability Movement Challenges to Antenatal Screening and Abortion*, 18(3) DISABILITY & SOCIETY 297 (2003); Marsha Saxton, *Disability Rights and Selective Abortion*, *in* THE DISABILITY STUDIES READER 105 (Lennard J. Davis ed., 2006).

Society broadcasts to them that they are not wanted and "worth less."[70] This social attitude conveys a message to the woman to abort a being that will be less valuable.

The borderline between "normal" and "disabled" is not clear. Some people argue that a fetus with Down's syndrome or Tay-Sachs will have a poor quality of life because of the defect, and it would therefore be advisable to terminate the pregnancy. But what about people who are destined to be obese, short, deaf, or dumb? Multiple tests are available now to establish whether a fetus has a defect. Fetal selection based on the rights of the woman, considering the pregnancy as "conditional," makes it possible to reject fetuses with defects. This is harmful to a society that cultivates tolerance, empathy, and compassion for special needs.

Disability, like beauty, is in the eye of the beholder.[71] The fertility revolution and the nearly limitless abilities of medical detection should not be used to allow a woman to expel a defective viable fetus from her body. Preventing the woman from doing so does not detract from her autonomy but rather impresses upon her that she must accept this human being growing within her. Only if this potential human being will suffer as a result of illness or defect should a viable fetus be aborted. The significance of a lack of tolerance toward the "different other" is that it influences us as humans and affects us as a society in all walks of life - work, economy, politics. Whatever we see as different, limited, or other, is rejected and cast aside. Society loses patience and tolerance and

---

[70] For a discussion of the possible correlation between "being worth" less, disability, and abortion, *see* Ralph Sue, *"Existence Without Life": Disability and Genetics*, 1 AUSTRALIAN DISABILITY REVIEW 3 (1995); Janet Radcliffe Richards, *How Not to End Disability*, 39 SAN DIEGO L. REV. 693 (2002); Rosamund Scott, *Prenatal Testing, Reproductive Autonomy, and Disability Interests*, 14(1) CAMBRIDGE QUARTERLY OF HEALTHCARE ETHICS 65 (2005).

[71] For the various definitions of disability, *see* Lisa Eichhorn, *Major Litigation Activities Regarding Major Life Activities: The Failure of the Disability Definition in the Americans with Disabilities Act of 1990*, 77 N.C. L. REV. 1405 (1999); Matilde Leonardi et al., *The Definition of Disability: What Is in a Name?*, 368(9543) THE LANCET 1219 (2006); Kenneth A. Kavale, *A Time to Define: Making the Specific Learning Disability Definition Prescribe Specific Learning Disability*, 32(1) LEARNING DISABILITY QUARTERLY 39 (2009).

becomes indifferent, even alienated from suffering, chaos, and loss. Society relates to the other according to its exterior form and does not always check the inner self, intelligence, thoughts, and desires of the other. A society that alienates itself becomes an alienated society.[72]

2.4 "Forbidden" conduct during pregnancy

> How is that? You don't even know me. I've worked and I'm a good mother. That doesn't matter, says the system. You use drugs, brother. And that's the real deal. So out of the clear blue sky. The obnoxious, unidentifiable, anonymous creature elopes with my son. But that's alright, says Uncle Sam. You defaulted your rights the moment you picked up.[73]

I mentioned that the pregnant woman and the fetus inside her are sometimes considered one entity. In my opinion, they are separate entities. If the pregnant woman decides not to abort in the first trimester, I believe that she is morally obligated to ensure the health and proper development of the fetus.[74] A woman who takes unnecessary risks that are likely to endanger the fetus defaults on her moral obligation toward it. The pregnant woman's moral obligation is to care

---

[72] For a discussion of this notion, *see* PAULO FREIRE, CULTURAL ACTION FOR FREEDOM 2 (1970), www.thinkingtogether.org/rcream/archive/110/CulturalAction.pdf; Jaap Kuiper, *The Scientists Will Save the World: Environment Education in an Alienated Society*, 15 SOUTHERN AFRICAN JOURNAL OF ENVIRONMENTAL EDUCATION 39 (1995); URSULA A. FALK & GERHARD FALK, AGEISM, THE AGED, AND AGING IN AMERICA: ON BEING OLD IN AN ALIENATED SOCIETY (1997).

[73] DAISY OATMAN, HOMELESS POET (1990). The poem appears in CLARICE FEINMAN, THE CRIMINALIZATION OF A WOMAN'S BODY §§157 (1992). For a discussion of the latter source, *see* Wendy Chavkin, *Women and Fetus: The Social Construction of Conflict*, 3(2) WOMEN & CRIMINAL JUSTICE 71 (1992); Lisa Maher, *Punishment and Welfare: Crack Cocaine and the Regulation of Mothering*, 3(2) WOMEN & CRIMINAL JUSTICE 35 (1992); Delila Amir & Orly Biniamin, *Abortion Approval as a Ritual of Symbolic Control*, 3(2) WOMEN & CRIMINAL JUSTICE 5 (1992).

[74] During pregnancy, the fetus should be considered as "a child who will be born" and not "a potential child." These definitions are quoted from MARGARET ATWOOD, THE HANDMAID'S TALE (2012).

for the good health of the viable fetus and to undergo the appropriate tests during pregnancy to avoid causing damage.

The woman's womb provides the viable fetus with "accommodation," therefore she has a duty to avoid conduct that might be harmful to the guest in the environment in which it develops. She should avoid drinking alcohol, smoking cigarettes,[75] taking drugs, and ingesting unnecessary medications that are harmful to the fetus. She should avoid working in dangerous conditions, such as those that involve pollution, uncleanliness, or are subject to chemical emissions. She should do everything necessary to ensure the normal development and good health of the fetus. I suggested that there is—or should be—liability for third-party damages toward the newborn for prenatal harm. Most legal systems do have provisions for the newborn to receive compensation for prenatal damage on condition that it was a viable fetus when the damage happened, and it was born alive.[76]

A child should be able to make a claim for prenatal damage against the woman because of her "forbidden" conduct during pregnancy if the child can prove a causal connection between the behavior and the damage. A woman, by the act of becoming pregnant, undertakes to care

---

[75] For the correlation between smoking and causing possible defects in the fetus, *see* Bernstein et al., *supra* note 40, at 986; CENTERS FOR DISEASE CONTROL AND PREVENTION, *supra* note 40; Lisa Wood et al., *Indigenous Women and Smoking During Pregnancy: Knowledge, Cultural Contexts and Barriers to Cessation*, 66(1) SOCIAL SCIENCE & MEDICINE 2378 (2008).

[76] *See* Jorgensen v. Meade Johnson Lab., 483 F 2d 237 (1973); Renslow v. Mennonite Hospital, 367 N.E. 2d 1250 (1977). In the *Jorgensen* case, the damage was caused to the fetus resulting from birth-control pills taken by the woman before becoming pregnant, and the US court decided that if a causal connection could be established between the act or the negligence this would be considered harm that deserves compensation, without conclusive importance accorded to the time when the tort took place. In the *Renslow* case, the child prosecuted the hospital for damage caused to him by a blood transfusion his mother had been given eight years before the birth. The law in Australia, Canada, the US, and the UK establishes that a live newborn can claim damages caused to him when still in a fetal stage. *See also* BONNIE STEINBOCK, LIFE BEFORE BIRTH: THE MORAL AND LEGAL STATUS OF EMBRYOS AND FETUSES §§ 165–89 (2011).

for the fetus. If she reneges on this undertaking, the child should be able to sue her after birth for breach of her legal obligation.

Under current laws, if the pregnant woman causes deliberate harm to the fetus, she can be sued for damages by the child; but if she causes harm unwittingly, or because of lack of care or negligence, the child may not be able to claim damages. If a pregnant woman is in the habit of smoking, taking drugs, working with dangerous materials, drinking alcohol in large quantities, taking medications, etc., causing harm to the fetus, I argue that the fetus who has been harmed should be allowed to claim damages from her after being born, even if we do not define fetal rights as we define human rights.[77]

It is in the interests of society that pregnant women know that from the minute they are aware of carrying "the beginnings of a human being," there are limitations on their conduct and even some loss of autonomy. In this case, loss of autonomy is proportional. In *Gordin v. Gordin*,[78] a Michigan court for the first time recognized this rationale in a claim of a child who prosecuted his parents for prenatal injury. During pregnancy, the woman took medication that caused the child's teeth to darken. The court determined that the woman defaulted on her obligation to care by not checking that she was pregnant before taking the medication, and by not notifying the physician that she was taking it when she discovered that she was pregnant. In *Stallman v. Youngquist*,[79] the court rejected the claim of a child who prosecuted a

---

[77] For a discussion of the interaction between parental immunity and abortion, *see* Marjorie M. Shultz, *Abortion and Maternal-Fetal Conflict: Broadening Our Concerns*, 1 S. CAL. REV. L. & WOMEN'S STUD. 79, 82 n.7, 83 (1992); Kerry Lorraine McBride, *Minor's Right to Divorce His or Her Parents: Fundamental Liberty Interest and Standing of a Minor Who Is Dependent on the Courts to Bring Termination of Parental Rights Proceedings*, 17 J. JUV. L. 68, 70–1 (1996); Janet Malek & Judith Daar, *The Case for a Parental Duty to Use Preimplantation Genetic Diagnosis for Medical Benefit*, 12(4) AMERICAN JOURNAL OF BIOETHICS 3 (2012).

[78] Gordin v. Gordin, 102 Mich 301 N.Y. 2d 869 (1980).

[79] *See* Stallman v. Youngquist, 531 N.E. 2d 355 (1988) for a historical review of the development of the rationale of wrongful birth. For an academic discussion of this substantial verdict, *see* Gregg R. Brown, *Prenatal Rights—The Intersection of Parental Immunity and Prenatal Rights: The Nonfamily Activity Exception or Traditional Concepts of*

woman for damage caused to him as a fetus as a result of her negligent driving. The court claimed that placing responsibility for damages on a pregnant woman violates her autonomy. In two cases, *Chenault v. Huie,*[80] in which a child suffered from developmental defects because the woman was taking drugs during pregnancy, and *Dobson v. Dobson,*[81] in which a road accident caused a child to be born with physical and mental defects, the court ruled that the obligations of a pregnant woman to a fetus were moral, not legal.

In most Western countries, a woman cannot be tried if her prohibited conduct causes her fetus to be damaged. There is a well-known example of a claim filed by authorities seeking to forcibly commit a woman to drug rehabilitation following the birth of two addicted children, where it was feared that the fetus she was carrying would be born in the same condition. The appeals court filed the claim and ordered enforced commitment for the woman, citing mental disturbance, but the decision was overturned by the high court.[82] Legal systems worldwide are unclear whether a pregnant woman should be under a legal obligation to care for the fetus during pregnancy, or has only a moral duty toward the fetus.[83]

Some believe that there is a "unique symbiotic relationship"[84] and even total dependence between the woman and the fetus, so an event that

---

Negligence—Stallman v. Youngquist, 129 Ill. App. 3d 859, 473 N.E.2d 400 (1st Dist. 1984), 10 S. ILL. U. L.J. 749 (1985); Anthony Jackson, *Action for Wrongful Life, Wrongful Pregnancy, and Wrongful Birth in the United States and England,* 17 LOY. L.A. INT'L & COMP. L.J. 535, 559–60 (1995); Kathryn S. Banashek, *Maternal Prenatal Negligence Does Not Give Rise to a Cause of Action,* Stallman v. Youngquist, 125 Ill. 2d 267, 531 N.E.2d 335 (1988), 68 WASH. U. L. Q. 189 (1990).

[80] Chenault v. Huie, 989 S.W. 2d 474 (1999).

[81] Dobson v. Dobson, 2 S.C.R. 753 (1999). *See also* Teresa Foley, Dobson v. Dobson*: Tort Liability for Expectant Mothers,* 61 SASK. L. REV. 177 (1998); Nelson, Erin, *Case Comment:* Dobson v. Dobson (Litigation Guardian), 8(3) HEALTH L. REV. 30 (2000); Ernest J. Weinrib, *The Passing of* Palsgraf, 54 VAND. L. REV. 803, 810 n.17 (2001).

[82] Rosamund Scott, *Maternal Duties Toward the Unborn? Sounding from the Law of Tort,* 8 MED. L. REV. 1 (2000).

[83] Chenault v. Huie.

[84] *See* Remy v. Macdonald, 801 N.E. 2d 260 (2003). For a discussion of this landmark case in the legal literature, *see* Kristi Kleiboeker, *Encouraging Responsibility During*

takes place during pregnancy should be considered predestined: "That this is so, is not a pregnant woman's fault: it is a fact of life."[85] The same is true when the woman causes deliberate harm or has been negligent. In the case of *Winnipeg Child and Family Services v. D.F.G.,*[86] the state requested an order that would force the woman to undergo rehabilitation from glue sniffing, but the Canadian High Court did not recognize the obligations of a pregnant woman. Some think[87] that the woman's right to autonomy over her body is a principle that should not be upheld over the right of the fetus to be born, even if they agree that the fetus has a right to begin life without defects arising from a violation of the obligation to care for it, including violations on the part of the mother. But in some places, the legal world already recognizes that a child has the right to be born healthy.[88]

The woman's autonomy concerning her obligation to care for the fetus is valid. Yet, she has a legal obligation of care toward the fetus that should eliminate or limit the use of drugs, cigarettes, alcohol, or medicine, exposure to dangerous materials, and so on. I am aware of the claim that the standard of care imposed on the woman would be too strict, but I do not see this as problematic or undermining the woman's

---

Pregnancy Through Amending the Unborn Victims of Violence Act, 83 WASH. U. L. Q. 1621, 1629 n.56, 1630 n.62, 1647 n.181 (2005); Kirsten Rabe Smolensky, *Creating Children with Disabilities: Parental Tort Liability for Preimplantation Genetic Interventions,* 60 HASTINGS L.J. 299, 322 n.130, 325 n.155 (2008); Christopher J. Wiener, *Transgenerational Tort Liability for Epigenetic Disease,* 13 DEPAUL J. HEALTH CARE L. 319, 326 n.41 (2011).

[85] Stallman v. Youngquist.

[86] Winnipeg Child and Family Services v. D.F.G., 3 S.C.R. 925 (1997).

[87] *See* Harrison v. Stephens, H.C.A. 16 [2006]; Waller v. James H.C.A. 15 [2006]. This Australian court ruled that doctors should not be made to pay damages for wrongful life and that life with a defect should not be weighed against lack of life. After the French court ruled that compensation should be granted for wrongful life, the French law was revised to prevent these rulings from recurring. For a discussion of this matter, *see* M.A. Duguet, *Wrongful Life: The Recent French Cour de Cassation Decisions,* 9 EUR. J. HEALTH 139 (2002).

[88] For the ethical-philosophical difficulties of this argument, whether indeed a fetus has the right to be born healthy, what is known as the non-identity problem, *see* Glenn Cohen, *The Constitution and the Rights Not to Procreate,* 60 STAN. L. REV. 1135, 11131 n.48 (2008); Glenn Cohen, *Beyond Best Interests,* 96 MINN. L. REV. 1187 (2011–12).

status. In *Gordin*,[89] the court ruled that the woman's conduct must be reasonable during pregnancy, but she is not duty-bound to do everything to protect the fetus. If a woman had to avoid employment that might endanger the health of the fetus, it may place her financial situation at risk and possibly lead to her going hungry, causing harm to herself and the fetus. This is not what I propose.

A woman is not merely a "container" or a "hotel" for the fetus for nine months. Obligating the woman to avoid deliberately harmful or negligent conduct—driving in an unreasonable way, smoking, taking drugs[90] — does not undermine the woman's autonomy, but rather strengthens her status as someone who is concerned for the health of a being for whom she is responsible. Some scholars claim that recognizing the woman's obligation to care for the fetus creates symbolic significance, and women who engage in potentially reckless conduct are selfish and irresponsible. Others claim that irresponsible and negligent behavior, such as drinking alcohol, taking drugs, or smoking stems from addiction and needs treatment. In such cases, "a claim for damages" is not appropriate because the harmful conduct was unintentional.

It has also been argued that a pregnant woman is obligated to undergo regular tests during pregnancy.[91] Certain authors maintain that tests

---

[89] *Supra* note 79.

[90] For the correlation between taking drugs during the pregnancy and defects of the fetus, *see* John O. Forfar & Matilda M. Nelson, *Epidemiology of Drugs Taken by Pregnant Women: Drugs That May Affect the Fetus Adversely*, 14(4) CLINICAL PHARMACOLOGY & THERAPEUTICS 632 (1973); Michael J. Tueth, *Psychotropic Medications During Pregnancy: Risk to the Fetus*, 270(18) JAMA 2177 (1993); Margaret S. Chisolm & Jennifer L Payne, *Management of Psychotropic Drugs During Pregnancy*, 352 BMJ h5918 (2016).

[91] Margery W. Shaw, *Conditional Prospective Rights of the Fetus*, 5 JOURNAL OF LEGAL MEDICINE 63 (1984). For a discussion of this landmark article, see, e.g., Michael A. Shekey, *Comment: Criminal Liability of a Prospective Mother for Prenatal Neglect of a Viable Fetus*, 9 WHITTIER L. REV. 363 (1987) *passim*; Patricia King, *Should Mom Be Constrained in the Best Interests of the Fetus*, 13 NOVA L. REV. 393, 395 n.5 (1989); Bonnie Steinbock, *Maternal–Fetal Conflict and in Utero Fetal Therapy*, 57 ALB. L. REV. 781, 789 n.38 (1994).

can be initiated to establish the scope of the woman's duty of care,[92] and that the relationship between the woman and the fetus is a special one because the fetus is dependent on the woman. Others claim that separate rights of autonomy might harm women's interests.[93] In my opinion, the opposite is true: the dependence of the fetus does not mean that its rights are assimilated into her rights. A newborn infant is also dependent on the woman who gave birth to it and is likely to remain dependent on her for a long time until reaching the stage of independence. This does not mean that as a result, this newborn's rights are not separate from its mother's. A newborn is defined as a person and therefore has complete legal human rights, including the right to its own autonomy.

Although the rights of a viable fetus and the rights of a newborn are not the same, I still maintain that the viable fetus has rights that are not diminished or compromised because of its dependence on the woman for life and development. In other words, the dependence of the fetus on the woman does not eliminate her duty to care for him; it does not eliminate the right of the fetus to claim damages if the duty was breached resulting in the child being born disabled; it does not eliminate, in my opinion, the duty of the state to bring criminal charges against the woman, if she behaved in a harmful way. It is wrong to conflate negligent driving by a pregnant woman with conduct involving substance abuse, imbibing alcohol, etc. These behaviors are not "predestined." The duty of a pregnant woman to the fetus in the viable stage must be legal, not merely moral.

---

[92] *See, for example,* Carl Ann Simon, *Parental Liability for Prenatal Injury,* 14 COLUM J.L. & SOC. PROBS. 47, 85 (1979) ("The conduct of the reasonably prudent expecting parent under like circumstances"). For a discussion of this article, *see* Elizabeth F. Collins, *An Overview and Analysis: Prenatal Torts, Preconception Torts, Wrongful Life, Wrongful Death, and Wrongful Birth: Time for a New Framework,* 22 J. FAM. L. 677, 679 n.12 (1983); Dorothy E. Roberts, *Crime, Race, and Reproduction,* 67 TUL. L. REV. 1945, 1958 n.59 (1992–93); Tony Hartsoe, *Person or Thing—In Search of the Legal Status of a Fetus: A Survey of North Carolina Law,* 17 CAMPBELL L. REV. 169, 256 (1995).

[93] Dawn Johnsen, *The Creation of Fetal Rights: Conflict with Woman's Constitutional Rights to Liberty, Privacy, and Equal Protection,* 95 YALE L.J. 599 (1986).

There are many reasons for and against the law of torts when it comes to the relationship between parents and their children.[94] Providing immunity to parents from their children's lawsuits is tantamount to violating the rights of the children. The court must make a distinction between different behaviors of a pregnant woman and decide which of these should allow the child who was harmed as a fetus to sue the mother for damages. Admittedly, any conduct of hers is liable to affect the fetus, and her autonomy will be restricted.

When a woman becomes pregnant not as the result of violence, she has effectively imposed on herself a restriction on her autonomy.[95] A standard of care must be set for every pregnant woman in the stage of pregnancy when she is aware of a fetus inside her. She should be expected to refrain from smoking, imbibing alcohol, and taking drugs. She should be expected to stop taking medication that may harm the fetus, and generally, act as a reasonable person with respect to the rights

---

[94] *See* Joseph J. Basgier, *Children's Rights: A Renewed Call for the End of Parental Immunity and Arguments for the Further Expansion of a Child's Right to Sue,* 26 L. & PSYCHOL. REV. 123 (2002); T. Allen-Mills, Honey, *I've Been Sued by the Kids,* SUNDAY TIMES, Mar. 17, 1996. For an additional academic discussion of this point, *see* Gail D. Hollister, *Parent–Child Immunity: A Doctrine in Search of Justification,* 50 FORDHAM L. REV. 489 (1982); David Fisher, *Parental Rights and the Right to Intimate Association,* 48 HASTINGS L.J. 399 (1997); Irene Hansen Saba, *Parental Immunity from Liability in Tort: Evolution of a Doctrine in Tennessee,* 36 U. MEM. L. REV. 829 (2006).

[95] For a discussion of the pregnant woman's autonomy vs. the obvious required restrictions for keeping the fetus healthy, *see* Judith Kahn, *Of Woman's First Disobedience: Forsaking a Duty of Care to Her Fetus—Is This a Mother's Crime,* 53 BROOK. L. REV. 807 (1987); Pamala Harris, *Compelled Medical Treatment of Pregnant Women: The Balancing of Maternal and Fetal Rights,* 49 CLEV. ST. L. REV. 133 (2001); Michael Ulrich, *With Child, Without Rights: Restoring a Pregnant Woman's Right to Refuse Medical Treatment Through the HIV Lens,* 24 YALE J.L. & FEMINISM 303 (2012)

of another. The mother and child are not the same person,[96] and the status and rights of each should be assessed separately.[97]

It is legitimate to expect a family to provide a child with a good life and protection, but every family undergoes crises, and pregnancy is a stressful time for the family. Events may transpire that are not in the best interest of the fetus. Although the expectation is that every family will give the best to their children, there are stressful situations when this becomes impossible, such as divorce, death, domestic violence, etc. In stressful circumstances, the family may not behave ideally toward its children, and in the case of pregnancy, the decision to have an abortion may sometimes be understandable. There are many cases reported in the literature when the parents' judgment affecting their children was faulty, resulting in a love-hate relationship in the family and legal cases brought by children against parents.[98] Because the woman has a moral obligation toward the viable fetus she is carrying, it should be possible to take legal action against her both in the civil courts (torts) and in the criminal courts if she inflicted harm on the fetus.

---

[96] Lifshitz-Aviram, *supra* note 31. For a discussion of the problematic method for receiving informed consent for a minor for medical treatment, *see* also Lois A. Weithorn & Susan B. Campbell, *The Competency of Children and Adolescents to Make Informed Treatment Decisions*, 53(6) CHILD DEVELOPMENT 1589 (1982); Committee on Bioethics, *Informed Consent, Parental Permission, and Assent in Pediatric Practice*, 95(2) PEDIATRICS 314 (1995), http://pediatrics.aappublications.Org/content/pediatrics/95/2/314.full.pdf; Lawrence Schlam & Joseph P. Wood, *Informed Consent to the Medical Treatment of Minors: Law and Practice*, 10 HEALTH MATRIX 141 (2000)

[97] Lifshitz-Aviram, *supra* note 31, at 233.

[98] FYODOR DOSTOYEVSKY, THE BROTHERS KARAMAZOV (1958); LEV TOLSTOY, KREUTZER SONATA (1975).

Chapter 5
Eugenics: In sorrow thou shalt *not* bring forth boys and girls

This chapter addresses the dangers of eugenics, some of which remain relevant today. The topic of eugenics has been extensively relevant to current selection practices. Historically, the notion of eugenics was associated with practices of the Nazi regime in Germany but as I show in this chapter, it was also relevant in the UK, the US, and elsewhere in the earlier part of the last century.[1]

The word "eugenics" derives from two Greek words: *genes* (to be born) and *eu* (good or fitting), referring to improved offspring. A discussion of the rights of a viable fetus would be incomplete if it did not deal with the danger posed by eugenics, which can eventually lead to the elimination of fetuses considered "unfit," "retarded," "defective," and the like.[2]

Terminating a pregnancy in general and at the viable stage in particular, out of fear of giving birth to a defective child raises social-ethical issues about the exercise of control over the next generation—the choice of what "type" of people we want in society, and not necessarily choosing to prevent suffering. In general, eugenic practices were government-led coercive pursuits aimed at improving the human race.

---

[1] D Kevles "Eugenics and Human Rights" (1999) 319 BMJ 435, 436-7.

[2] For a discussion of the close interaction between eugenics and abortion, *see, for example,* John R. Jr. Harding, *Beyond Abortion: Human Genetics and the New Eugenics,* 18 PEPP. L. REV. 471 (1991); ANN FARMER, BY THEIR FRUITS: EUGENICS, POPULATION CONTROL, AND THE ABORTION CAMPAIGN (2008); Darrin P. Dixon, *Informed Consent or Institutionalized Eugenics—How the Medical Profession Encourages Abortion of Fetuses with Down Syndrome,* 24 ISSUES L. & MED. 3 (2008).

Meira Weiss[3] maintains that the "genetic panic" in Israeli society is an expression of a collective ideal that worships bodies that are healthy, strong, in good shape, and perfect. Yael Hashiloni-Dolev[4] is of a different opinion and explains the differences in attitude between Israel (where opposition to fetal selection and genetic intervention in the next generation is minimal) and other Western countries (where opposition is strong) by the difference between the status accorded to the fetus in Israel and in Western countries. In Israel, the fetus is considered part of the woman's body whereas in Western societies—mainly following Christian-Catholic precepts—it is considered a living being, autonomous, with equal human rights to those of adults.

For some decades, there has been almost worldwide consensus that it is necessary to limit the birth rate, especially in populous countries. To achieve this goal, enforced sterilization, government-approved abortion, and the dilution of weaker populations have been practiced in several countries. The intention behind the growing number of medical tests is to ensure not only the birth of a healthy child but also of a perfect one, limiting the birth rate of individuals who are imperfect according to existing standards set by society.

Over 25 years ago, Heyd used the term "genethics" to describe "the problems inherent in the ethics of creating human beings, determining their number and identity"[5] because these issues concern yet unborn human beings rather than those who have already been born. According to Heyd, modern medical technologies that enable the early

---

[3] MEIRA WEISS, THE CHOSEN BODY: THE POLITICS OF THE BODY IN ISRAELI SOCIETY (2002). *See also* MEIRA WEISS, CONDITIONAL LOVE: PARENTS' ATTITUDES TOWARDS THE HANDICAPPED (1994); AVIAD E. RAZ, COMMUNITY GENETICS AND GENETIC ALLIANCES: EUGENICS, CARRIER TESTING AND NETWORKS OF RISK (2009).

[4] YAEL HASHILONI-DOLEV, THE FERTILITY REVOLUTION 75 (2013) (Heb.).

[5] *See* DAVID HEYD, GENETHICS: MORAL ISSUES IN THE CREATION OF PEOPLE (1992). For a discussion of this often-quoted book, *see* Tim Mulgan, *The Demands of Consequentialism* (1995) (PhD thesis, University of Oxford); Nicholas Agar, *Liberal Eugenics*, 12(2) PUBLIC AFFAIRS QUARTERLY 137, 138 n.5 (1998); Partha Dasgupta, *Population and Resources: An Exploration of Reproductive and Environmental Externalities*, 26(4) POPULATION AND DEVELOPMENT REVIEW 643 (2000).

discovery of genetic diseases and prevent the birth of babies carrying them have given rise to ethical dilemmas regarding the type of life we desire for the child. The growing number of prenatal tests attests to women's desire to create life only if it has a certain "threshold" value. Heyd maintains that it will not be long before society can positively design the characteristics of the newborn with genetic engineering, not merely to prevent the birth of babies with defects. Society appears to be moving in the direction of cloning, as described by Aldous Huxley in *Brave New World*?[6] A book titled *Who Should Play God?*[7] opens with the following dedication: "To Aldous Huxley, for his foresight." Some of the events predicted by Huxley's book in 1932 have come to pass, and what we consider today to be science fiction will quite likely materialize in the future.

Eugenics is rooted in a social-biological philosophy concerned with how the development of genetics, aiming to find a way to "enhance" humankind, may affect the mental and behavioral characteristics of human beings.[8] We must ask ourselves to what degree we think it appropriate to make selection decisions of this type and what limitations we should impose on our choices, especially from week 24 of gestation onward.

Sir Francis Galton, a British scientist, coined the term "eugenics" in 1883[9] when he adopted genetic methods to improve humankind. He

---

[6] ALDOUS HUXLEY, BRAVE NEW WORLD (1932). For a discussion of the concept of this iconic book in relation to abortion and eugenics, *see* William T. Vukowich, *The Dawning of the Brave New World—Legal, Ethical, and Social Issues of Eugenics*, 1971 U. ILL. L.F. 189 (1971); Diane Wiener et al., *Mentalism, Disability Rights and Modern Eugenics in a "Brave New World,"* 24(5) DISABILITY & SOCIETY, 599 (2009); Leo Lucassen, *A Brave New World: The Left, Social Engineering, and Eugenics in Twentieth-Century Europe*, 55(2) INTERNATIONAL REVIEW OF SOCIAL HISTORY 265 (2010).

[7] TED HOWARD & JEREMY RIFFKIN, WHO SHOULD PLAY GOD? THE ARTIFICIAL CREATION OF LIFE AND WHAT IT MEANS FOR THE FUTURE OF THE HUMAN RACE 1 (1977).

[8] Primitive belief in eugenics led to the Spartan practice of throwing weak or defective babies off a cliff.

[9] *See, e.g.*, D.J. Galton & C.J. Galton, *Francis Galton: And Eugenics Today*, 24 JOURNAL OF MEDICAL ETHICS 99 (1998); Nicholas W. Gillham, *Sir Francis Galton and the Birth of*

claimed that characteristics such as mental weakness are genetic and typical of people of low social status. He intended to enhance the human race by preventing certain genetic states. According to him, positive eugenics meant encouraging the birth of newborns with what were considered to be positive character traits to "promote" successful populations.[10] By contrast, negative eugenics intended to prevent the increase of problematic populations, among others, by sterilizing people considered to have negative characteristics, and in other cases by killing the sick and disabled, not only embryos and fetuses.

At the beginning of the 1920s, centers for eugenics research were established and functioned successfully in Europe and the US. The first centers started to operate in 1904, in Germany, and later in England. During the 1920s and 1930s, tens of thousands of mentally defective people in Sweden were sterilized. The most extensive program was organized in the US. The large waves of immigration from Europe to the US before and after World War I led to a concern that there would be a change in the demographic makeup of the country. As a result, a Eugenics Record Office was established that employed people in the fields of medicine, law, and others to keep track of immigrants. The office collected data about immigrants and conducted campaigns to increase awareness about "racial responsibility," which included avoiding intermarriage. Immigrants from Eastern Europe were prevented from entering the US. It was at this time that the psychologist

---

Eugenics, 35(1) ANNUAL REVIEW OF GENETICS 83 (2001); Nicholas W. Gillham, A LIFE OF SIR FRANCIS GALTON: FROM AFRICAN EXPLORATION TO THE BIRTH OF EUGENICS (2001).

[10] *Ibid*, p.72: "Attempts to fertilize upper-class women with sperm from Nobel prize winners did not result in the births of geniuses or especially talented people. A similar experiment was carried out in the US in the 1950s;" *see also* DAVID PLOTZ, THE GENIUS FACTORY: THE CURIOUS HISTORY OF THE NOBEL PRIZE SPERM BANK (2005), in which he described his disappointing results. "Ultimately, these experiments merely led to ordinary people." For a discussion of this book, *see* J. Thomas Oldham, *How an Eccentric Eyeglass Manufacturer Revolutionized Assisted Reproduction in the U.S.: A Review of* The Genius Factory *by David Plotz*, 39 FAM. L.Q. 781 (2005); Kimberly D. Krawiec, *Sunny Samaritans and Egomaniacs: Price-Fixing in the Gamete Market*, 72 LAW & CONTEMP. PROBS. 59 (2009); Dov Fox, *Choosing Your Child's Race*, 22 HASTINGS WOMEN'S L.J. 3, 4 n.4 (2011).

Henry Goddard coined the word "moron," meaning a person "infected" with "defective genes."

In 1966, when Indira Gandhi asked President Johnson for humanitarian aid, he made it conditional on establishing a birth rate quota for India. To control the birth rate, the government offered money to anyone willing to refrain from having children, which resulted in the sterilization of three million Indians in 1973. Under the regime of Gandhi's son, Sanjay, acquiring land, water, electricity, food coupons, etc. was conditional upon sterilization. According to estimates, one-quarter of Indian women of reproductive age underwent sterilization between 1966 and 1977, the majority without their consent and some even without their knowledge, in hospitals managed by the Indian health services.[11]

About one-third of all women in Puerto Rico underwent sterilization until 1975 in their country. At various times, in other countries there have been drives to reduce the birth rate among weaker populations, similar to population control attempted in the US. Hindus in India tried to prevent the birth of Muslims and the unclean; the Singhalese in Sri Lanka tried to prevent the birth of Tamils; the Spanish in Peru wanted to prevent the birth of the Incas; the Serbs in Kosovo attempted to prevent the birth of Albanians, and so on.

Eugenics was also popular with the Nazis.[12] In 1933, legislation was passed that prohibited termination of pregnancy in general, but made it compulsory to undergo sterilization and termination of pregnancy

---

[11] *See, e.g.*, Brint Dillingham, *Indian Women and IHS Sterilization Practices*, 3 AM. INDIAN J. 27 (1977); Jane Lawrence, *The Indian Health Service and the Sterilization of Native American Women*, 24(3) AMERICAN INDIAN Q. 400 (2000); Myla Vicenti Carpio, *The Lost Generation: American Indian Women and Sterilization Abuse*, 31(4) SOC. JUS. 40 (2004), https://www.jstor.org/stable/pdf/29768273.pdf.

[12] For the close connection between the Nazi's perspective and eugenics practice, *see, e.g.*, Henry P. David et al., *Abortion and Eugenics in Nazi Germany*, 14(1) POPULATION & DEV. REV. 81 (1988); Robert N. Proctor, *Eugenics in Hitler's Germany*, *in* DEAF PEOPLE IN HITLER'S EUROPE 32 (Donna F. Ryan ed., 2002); RICHARD WEIKART, FROM DARWIN TO HITLER: EVOLUTIONARY ETHICS, EUGENICS, AND RACISM IN GERMANY (2004).

based on eugenic considerations. Sterilization was forced upon people with genetic diseases such as mental illness, learning disabilities, physical deformities, epilepsy, blindness, deafness, and alcoholism. The Nazis began to implement their plan of euthanasia, called T-4, during 1939-1941. At first, some 500 babies were put to death by injection of luminal or morphine, and tests were carried out on their brains. By 1941, more than 79,000 people with mental illnesses had been put to death in gas chambers in six extermination camps; by November 1942, some 90,000 had been starved to death, and more than 300,000 people had undergone sterilization.[13] Yael Hashiloni-Dolev[14] showed that the Nazi state forced motherhood on Aryan women under the eugenics plan known as Lebensborn, initiated by Heinrich Himmler. According to this plan, women of the upper class were imprisoned in a mating farm and forced to copulate with SS officers to produce a superior generation. The children who were born were also held at the Lebensborn mating farm. Others who met the racial criteria were simply snatched from their parents by a special military unit under the auspices of the eugenics project. Between 1939 and 1941 more than 100,000 people were put to death under this plan, the majority of them inmates in institutions.[15]

Although the original aims of the eugenics concept were positive, intended to prevent suffering and improve the human race, its interpretation by the Nazis turned it into a concept to be avoided at all

---

[13] YAEL HASHILONI-DOLEV, THE FERTILITY REVOLUTION 75 (2013) (Heb.). For a discussion of this book, *see, e.g.*, TAMAR NOVICK, MILK & HONEY: TECHNOLOGIES OF PLENTY IN THE MAKING OF A HOLY LAND, 1880–1960 (University of Pennsylvania, ProQuest Dissertations Publishing (2014), https://search.proquest.com/openview/d8a5e12799a52d183c28923d1147afi51/12pq; origsite=gscholar&cbl=18750&diss=y; Daphna Birenbaum-Carmeli, *Thirty-five Years of Assisted Reproductive Technologies in Israel*, 2 RBMS ONLINE 16 (2016); Naomi Gershoni & Corinne Low, *The Impact of Extended Reproductive Time Horizons: Evidence from Israel's Expansion of Access to IVF* 11, UNIVERSITY OF PENNSYLVANIA POPULATION CENTER WORKING PAPER (PSC/PARC), 2017–15. https://repository.upenn.edu/psc_publications/15.

[14] *Ibid.*

[15] HASHILONI-DOLEV, *supra* note 12, at 73.

costs. At the same time, other approaches exist today that have sought to revert to the original positive aspects of eugenics.

The Jewish psychiatrists who came from Germany to the Land of Israel in the 1930s brought with them the eugenics theory as well as difficult treatments, like electric shock, insulin injections, and lobotomies.[16] For example, in 1944, Kurt Levenstein delivered a lecture at a conference held by the Association of Neurologists in Tel Aviv in which he recommended preventing people suffering from various psychological and neurological disorders—from alcoholism to manic depression and epilepsy—from having children. He suggested accomplishing this, among others, by preventing pregnancy, terminating pregnancy, and sterilization. Levenstein, then, joined the proponents of eugenics.

The views of the sociologist Aviad Raz countervail those of Kurt Levenstein.[17] Raz describes a change in the perception of eugenics to a utopian and liberal concept, which emphasizes its current advantages. Liberal eugenics expands the birthing freedom of every woman because it allows her to decide the fate of the fetus.[18] Even if termination is permitted in the case of defects and severe illnesses that cause great suffering, minor defects—shortsightedness, deafness, or obesity—are insufficient to warrant termination of the pregnancy.

I hold a different opinion. With the development of human abilities and the advancement of the human genome, genetic science will continue to expand.[19] With our ability to map the human genome, we

---

[16] Lobotomy is a surgical procedure in which the synapses to and from the frontal lobes of the brain are disconnected, under the assumption that these lobes are the emotional centers and that numbing them will blunt the emotions affecting mental patients. This procedure is no longer in use.

[17] RAZ, *supra* note 2.

[18] For a discussion of this modern notion of liberal eugenics, *see,* for example, Nicholas Agar, *Liberal Eugenics*, 12(2) PUB. AFF. Q. 137 (1998); Elizabeth Fenton, *Liberal Eugenics and Human Nature: Against Habermas*, 36(6) HASTINGS CENTER REPORT 35 (2006); NICHOLAS AGAR, LIBERAL EUGENICS: IN DEFENCE OF HUMAN ENHANCEMENT (2008).

[19] For a discussion of the recent most advanced and challenging practices of genetic science, *see, e.g.,* F. Ann Ran et al., *Genome Engineering Using the CRISPR-Cas9 System*, 8 NATURE PROTOCOLS 2281 (2013); Le Cong et al., *Multiplex Genome Engineering Using*

will be able to see more and more personality traits and behavioral indications, in addition to foreseeing severe illnesses. According to liberal eugenics, women will be able to choose to terminate their pregnancy based on genetic potential even if it is uncertain but probable, and the trend toward eugenics will become increasingly popular.

I find it unacceptable that the present legal situation allows women to terminate their pregnancy whether the fetus has a defect or for any other reason, even at the viable stage. I find it unacceptable that women can choose whether to give birth to a child based on specific characteristics. The woman's choice and the fertility revolution, which enable her to decide when, how many, and with whom she wants to reproduce must be limited by the right of the viable fetus to be born, even if the fetus has a disability that is not likely to become a severe disease. Women's autonomy must be limited not only after the child is born but also before birth. Women have a right to choice and autonomy, but this does not include the choice of the type of child she wants to bring into the world, based on their taste, preference, religion, sexual preference, what they may consider a life worth living, and the like.

More than anything, choosing fetal characteristics is an expression of an extremist society in which humans are "manufactured." Soon humans will be created by IVF rather than by means of sexual relations. Soon characteristics detected by a preimplantation genetic diagnosis test (PGD) that parents consider to be negative will be a reason for rejecting any fetus. A cold and mechanized futuristic society of this kind I find frightening.[20] "Genetic diagnostics" and "fetal selection" are terms

---

CRISPR/Cas Systems, SCIENCE (2013); Patrick D. Hsu et al., *Development and Applications of CRISPR-Cas9 for Genome Engineering*, 157(6) CELL 1262 (2014). *See also* Tara R. Melillo, *Gene Editing and the Rise of Designer Babies*, 50 VAND. J. TRANSNAT'L L. 757 (2017); Chen Wang et al., *Gene-Edited Babies: Chinese Academy of Medical Sciences' Response and Action*, 393 (10166) THE LANCET 25 (2019).

[20] *See* the PRESIDENT'S COMMISSION FOR THE STUDY OF ETHICAL PROBLEMS IN MEDICINE AND BIOMEDICAL AND BEHAVIORAL RESEARCH, SPLICING LIFE: THE SOCIAL AND ETHICAL ISSUES OF GENETIC ENGINEERING WITH HUMAN BEINGS (1982). For a discussion of the conclusions of this commission, *see* S.J. Youngner & E.T. Bartlett, *Human Death*

generally associated with sinister regimes, which turn children into a commodity.[21]

and High Technology: The Failure of the Whole–Brain Formulations, 99(2) ANN INTERN. MED. 252 (1983); Ronald Bayer, *Ethics, Politics, and Access to Health Care: A Critical Analysis of the President's Commission for the Study of Ethical Problems in Medicine and Biomedical and Behavioral Research*, 6 CARDOZO L. REV. 303 (1984); P. J. Greco & K.A. Schulman, *The Patient Self-Determination Act and the Future of Advance Directives*, 115(8) ANN. INTERN. MED. 639 (1991).

[21] For an outline of articles that touch on the problems of such commercialization and commodification, in addition to the references enumerated in this section, *see* Glenda Labadie-Jackson, *The Reproductive Rights of Latinas and Commercial Surrogacy Contracts English Translation*, 14 TEX. HISP. J.L. & POL'Y 49, 60 n.109 (2008). *See also* Pamela Laufer-Ukeles, *Mothering for Money: Regulating Commercial Intimacy*, 88 IND. L.J. 1223 (2014) *and more broadly* Ram Rivlin, *The Puzzle of Intra-Familial Commodification*, 67(1) UNIV. TORONTO L.J 68 (2017) (discussing custody agreements and divorce negotiation).

Chapter 6
Can a Delicate Balance be Found?

I have argued in this book that the rights of a viable fetus should be considered almost equal to those of "one that is born," at least from a moral point of view. This position may be controversial, although other authors subscribe to it. For example, Alessandra Piontelli[1] quotes Freud in her book:[2] "There is much more continuity between intra-uterine life and earliest infancy than the impressive caesura[3] of the act of birth would have us believe."[4] The editor of the book noted that Piontelli observed 11 fetuses in the wombs of their mothers using three-dimensional ultrasound scans and followed up on their development from birth to the age of 4 years. Her main finding is that there is a remarkable continuity of behavior before and after birth, and that every fetus, just like every human being, is unique.[5]

A *National Geographic* program aired in 2005 showed amazing footage of the journey of the human fetus from the moment of conception until birth. The film was made from the perspective of the fetus and focused

---

[1] Dr. Alessandra Piontelli, trained in medicine and neuropsychiatry in Italy, works as a pediatric psychiatrist in the UK.

[2] ALESSANDRA PIONTELLI, FROM FETUS TO CHILD: AN OBSERVATIONAL AND PSYCHOANALYTICAL STUDY (2003). For a discussion of this book, *see* JOAN RAPHAEL-LEFF, PREGNANCY: THE INSIDE STORY (2001); KAY MILTON, LOVING NATURE: TOWARDS AN ECOLOGY OF EMOTION (2002); DEBORAH MARKS, DISABILITY: CONTROVERSIAL DEBATES AND PSYCHOSOCIAL PERSPECTIVES (2014).

[3] ALESSANDRA PIONTELLI, FROM FETUS TO CHILD. It is known that the fetus can hear and react to noises in the intrauterine environment.

[4] SIGMUND FREUD, INHIBITION, SYMPTOMS AND ANXIETY §§ 138 (James Strachey ed., 1990). For a discussion of this important book, *see, e.g.*, Austin Sarat, *Living in a Copernican Universe: Law and Fatherhood in a Perfect World*, 43 N. Y. L. SCH. L. REV. 843, 849 n.34 (1999); Austin Sarat, *Imagining the Law of the Father: Loss, Dread, and Mourning in the Sweet Hereafter*, 34 LAW & SOC'Y REV. 3, 17 (2000); ON FREUD'S INHIBITIONS, SYMPTOMS AND ANXIETY (Samuel Arbiser & Jorge Schneider eds., 2013).

[5] For example, she describes twins that hit one another in the womb and continued doing so during their childhood; other twins stroked each other and continued this behavior as children.

on the development of its primary senses in the course of the pregnancy. It used advanced photography and four-dimensional ultrasound to show the behavior of the fetus inside the womb. In the 32nd week, the fetus is already fully developed. From this stage, during deep sleep, its eye movements are similar to those of an adult; it is woken by a touch or a loud noise; it makes characteristic and unique movements; it reacts to sounds; it feels pain (during amniocentesis or a blood test taken from the skull, the fetus reacts with a jolt from the prick of the needle). Fetal behavior changes according to the stimuli.

In the previous chapters, I discussed the importance that society places on regular prenatal checkups and diagnoses. I showed that by doing so, society strives for perfect human beings, not necessarily healthy humans. This distorted perception of a "perfect child" is the reason for the increasing number of prenatal diagnoses, with tests and close follow-ups before birth. I showed that this perception turns the medical system into "defensive medical care" and harms the principle of the sanctity of life. I spoke of eugenics, which encourages the "selection" of fetuses and rejects those with disabilities, whatever the stage of pregnancy. As I pointed out, eugenics has been practiced not only by repressive regimes but in the US and other countries as well. It would be dangerous to reawaken such views in contemporary society.

We must initiate a dialogue about fetal rights at the legal, moral,[6] ethical,[7] and philosophical levels that recognize that from 24 weeks onward the fetus is almost a person and should be entitled to almost the

---

[6] For the moral dimensions of abortion, *see,* among others, THE MORALITY OF ABORTION: LEGAL AND HISTORICAL PERSPECTIVES (John Thomas Noonan ed., 1970); ABORTION: MORAL AND LEGAL PERSPECTIVES (Jay L. Garfield & Patricia Hennessey eds., 1984); BONNIE STEINBOCK, LIFE BEFORE BIRTH: THE MORAL AND LEGAL STATUS OF EMBRYOS AND FETUSES (2011).

[7] The ethical and philosophical literature concerning this issue is enormous. See the following landmark books: BARUCH A. BRODY, ABORTION AND THE SANCTITY OF HUMAN LIFE: A PHILOSOPHICAL VIEW (1975); CHRISTOPHER KACZOR, THE ETHICS OF ABORTION: WOMEN'S RIGHTS, HUMAN LIFE, AND THE QUESTION OF JUSTICE (2011).

same rights as those of a newborn.[8] Determining that the viable fetus is a beginning of a person would balance its rights with the rights of the woman to autonomy.[9] Fetal rights would enable the state to prevent the fetus from being destroyed at the viable stage if there is no high probability of a serious defect. Such rights would enable the state to compel women to undergo surgery on the fetus during the pregnancy to prevent the defect or to heal it and enable it to be born, as long as the surgery and the continuation of the pregnancy do not place the woman in danger. These rights would allow the state to enforce a C-section if the fetus's life is at risk, again, if such surgery would not endanger the mother's life.

1. Voluntary Termination of Pregnancy at the Viable Stage: Destroying the Fetus

The consequences of terminating a pregnancy at the viable stage are far-reaching. It amounts to giving birth to a viable fetus that has been killed.[10] The fetus is destroyed by inserting a long needle through the wall of the abdomen and the uterine wall until it reaches the amniotic fluid sac. The needle penetrates the chest wall of the fetus, and potassium chloride (KCI) is injected into its heart causing it to stop beating. At the end of this procedure, an induced birth is performed,

[8] For seminal books dealing with fetal rights, *see* CYNTHIA R. DANIELS, AT WOMEN'S EXPENSE: STATE POWER AND THE POLITICS OF FETAL RIGHTS (1996); FETAL RIGHTS: A NEW ASSAULT ON FEMINISM (Claudia Malacrida & Jacqueline Low eds., 2008); RITA JOSEPH, HUMAN RIGHTS AND THE UNBORN CHILD (2009).

[9] For the modern discussion of the woman's right to abort her fetus, *see,* for example, JOHN KENYON MASON, THE TROUBLED PREGNANCY: LEGAL WRONGS AND RIGHTS IN REPRODUCTION (2007); N.E. H. HULL & PETER CHARLES HOFFER, ROE V. WADE: THE ABORTION RIGHTS CONTROVERSY IN AMERICAN (2010); SITAL KALANTRY, WOMEN'S HUMAN RIGHTS AND MIGRATION: SEX-SELECTIVE ABORTION LAWS IN THE UNITED STATES AND INDIA (2017).

[10] For a discussion of fetal rights at this stage, *see* Mary Anne Wood & Lisa Bolin Hawkins, *State Regulation of Late Abortion and the Physician's Duty of Care to the Viable Fetus*, 45 MO. L. REV. 394 (1980); Alan Zaitchik, *Viability and the Morality of Abortion*, 10(1) PHIL. & PUB. AFF. 18 (1981); Laurence H. Tribe, *The Abortion Funding Conundrum: Inalienable Rights, Affirmative Duties, and the Dilemma of Dependence*, 99(1) HARV. L. REV. 330 (1985).

and the "contents" are expelled by means of medication. Perhaps this explains why Western countries absolutely prohibit such terminations or subject them to severe restrictions. Israeli law bans the procedure unless it is carried out in extraordinary circumstances stipulated by penal law: the committee for termination of pregnancy can authorize or reject a request for a termination at its discretion, The guidelines for using discretion of this nature were set out in the Director General's circulars.[11]

Guidelines in force in Israel conveniently summarize criteria close to those accepted worldwide, with some modifications, for assessing fetal defects, classified into *mild, moderate,* and *severe*.[12] A mild handicap is described as a physical or developmental handicap the severity of which does not impair the ability to blend in with society and does not create dependence on others. A moderate handicap is described as a physical or developmental handicap that impairs the ability to function in society, but the level of severity does not necessarily require lifelong dependence on others. A mild handicap can be a defect in a fetus whose mental and emotional development is expected to be completely normal; a minimal physical handicap that is usually a skeletal defect or

[11] The Termination of Pregnancy Committee at the Viable Stage works in conjunction with the Ministry of Health, *Director General: Termination of Pregnancy Committee at the Viable Stage No. 23/07* (19.12.2007), www.health.gov.il/hozer/pdf mk-23 2007 (Heb.).

[12] In fields such as genetics, cardiology, nephrology. For an extensive discussion of the unique Israeli regulation, *see,* e.g., Dan Shnit, *Induced Abortion in Israeli Law,* 15 ISRAELI Y.B. HUM. RTS. 155 (1985); Yael Yishai, *Abortion in Israel: Social Demands and Political Responses,* in 6 WOMEN IN ISRAEL 287 (Yael Azmon & Dafna N. Israeli eds., 1993); Yael Yishai, *The Hidden Agenda: Abortion Politics in Israel,* 22 J. SOC. POL'Y. 193 (1993); Noga Morag Levine, *Abortion in Israel: Community, Rights, and the Context of Compromise,* 19 L. SOC. INQUIRY 313 (1994); Larissa I. Remennick & Rosie Segal, *Sociocultural Context and Women's Experiences of Abortion: Israeli Women and Russian Immigrants Compared,* 3 CULTURE, HEALTH & SEXUALITY 49 (2001); Larrisa I. Remennick & Amir Hetsroni, *Public Attitudes About Abortion in Israel: A Research Note,* 82 SOC. SCI. Q. 420 (2001); Nitzan Rimon-Zarfaty & Aviad Raz, *Abortion Committees as Agents of Eugenics: Medical and Public Views on Selective Abortion Following Mild or Likely Fetal Pathology,* in KIN, GENE, COMMUNITY: REPRODUCTIVE TECHNOLOGIES AMONG JEWISH ISRAELIS 202 (Daphna Birenbaum-Carmeli & Yoram S. Carmeli eds., 2010); L. Ariella Zeller & Elana Maryles Sztokman, *Abortion in Israel: When the Nation Enters the Womb,* 10 LILITH (2011–12).

deformation such as missing a hand, a shorter thigh bone, clubfoot, a cosmetic defect in the makeup of the face such as cleft lip,[13] asymmetry or distortion of the shape of the ear, etc. These are defects that involve discomfort and limit functioning, but they do not significantly affect the quality of life and ability of the person born with these defects to live an independent life and blend in with society. According to the Director General's circular permission should not be granted for a termination because of a mild functional handicap.

A moderate handicap is a handicap the severity of which does not require lifelong dependence on others, like a severe handicap. In other words, a moderate handicap means that the person has mobility and is able to have a meaningful life at both mental and emotional levels, for example, a heart or lung defect that allows a reasonable quality of life and life expectancy, but restricts certain physical efforts or a defect in the digestive tract that prevents ingestion of certain foods.[14]

A severe handicap is described as a physical or developmental handicap the severity of which necessitates lifelong help of others. According to the Director General's circular, the expression "requires lifelong help of others" means total lifelong physical dependence (e.g., help in getting dressed, eating), or a mental or emotional handicap (e.g., lack of ability to function and exist independently). Examples of severe handicaps include structural abnormalities in the brain, blindness,

---

[13] For a discussion of the morality of aborting a fetus with a cleft lip, *see* Bertram S. Kraus et al., *Malformations Associated with Cleft Lip and Palate in Human Embryos and Fetuses*, 86(3) AM. J. OBSTETRICS & GYNECOLOGY (1963); J.C. Bear, *Spontaneous Abortion, Sex Ratio and Facial Cleft Malformations*, 13 (1) CLINICAL GENETICS 1 (1978); J.C. Bear, *Additional Data on Spontaneous Abortion and Facial Cleft Malformations*, 24(6) CLINICAL GENETICS 407 (1983).

[14] For an academic discussion of the various types of disability and the abortion dilemma, *see*, for example, Ralph Althouse & Nicholas Wald, *Survival and Handicap of Infants with Spina Bifida*, 55 ARCHIVES OF DISEASE IN CHILDHOOD 845 (1980); Gail Geller et al., *Attitudes toward Abortion for Fetal Anomaly in the Second vs. the Third Trimester: A Survey of Parisian Obstetricians*, 13(8) PRENATAL DIAGNOSIS 707 (1993); Souhail Alouini et al., *Termination of Pregnancy for Mild Foetal Abnormalities: Opinions of Physicians*, WebmedCentral 2(3) OBSTETRICS & GYNAECOLOGY (2011), https://www.webmedcentral.com/article_view/1770

missing both hands, or genetic syndromes related to a significant developmental disorder.

Israel is the worldwide leader in pregnancy tests for the detection of fetal defects. Some tests are invasive, others are not. Some may harm the woman and others may even harm the fetus (such as radiation to the fetus from a CT scan to diagnose minor flaws in the vertebrae or bones). Some provide the woman with conclusive information and others provide her with statistical data. Although it is not yet possible to make a definite prognosis of every possible defect, whether minor or major, according to the expectations of the pregnant woman, current tests are sufficient to abort a fetus with a high probability of a healthy birth and a meaningful life.

Heyd writes in Ethics and Medicine:[15]

> Prometheus stole fire from the gods and gave it to man. His great sin in this act was the sin of pride, hubris. The audacious pretension of knowledge that crosses the lines of what is permitted, the attempt to compete with the powers of the gods, constituted the crime for which Prometheus was sentenced to endless suffering by Nemesis, the goddess of vengeance. According to one of the accepted interpretations of the story of Prometheus, man's hubris embeds with it the seed of punishment: the actual digging for knowledge and the power attached thereto takes its revenge on the prideful person. The social philosopher Ivan Illich perceives that this myth of Prometheus is a powerfully symbolic expression of the history of modern medicine. Medicine expresses man's boastful pretensions to achieve divine control by overcoming man's morbidity, and at the same time containing the punishment for these pretensions. According to Illich, Nemesis is clothed in a

[15] DAVID HEYD, ETHICS AND MEDICINE 22 (2011) (Heb.).

> doctor's white coat and hence the name of his book, *Medical Nemesis*.[16]

Nemesis wears the doctor's white coat and the coat, or cloak, of modern society in this book as well. An overabundance of tests establishing defects, morbidity, and genetic mapping allows modern society and medicine to decide which fetuses will live and which will not, with a slight nod from the state. The sin of hubris is given free rein.[17]

As Heyd[18] related over a decade ago, in the course of an argument about terminating pregnancies, a question was put to liberals (who allow termination at any stage) whether they would allow these abortions if the pregnancy were in a transparent womb. The assumption was that if those in favor of termination at any stage were to see the viable fetus, they would not reject its status and rights as a person and would not authorize its destruction. Today the fetus can be monitored by ultrasound in its mother's womb during pregnancy and can be

---

[16] IVAN ILLICH, MEDICAL NEMESIS (1975). For the most recent discussion of this remarkable book, *see, among others,* Tom Sanders & Diane Roberts, *Social Representations of Diagnosis in the Consultation*, 52(6) SOCIOLOGY 1185 (2018); Fran Toye et al., *A Meta-Ethnography of Health-Care Professionals' Experience of Treating Adults with Chronic Non-Malignant Pain to Improve the Experience and Quality of Health Care*, NAT'L INST. FOR HEALTH RES. (HEALTH SER. & DELIVERY RES.) (2018), https://core.ac.uk/download/pdf/157620169.Ddf; Richard Berlin et al., *Systems Medicine Disease: Disease Classification and Scalability Beyond Networks and Boundary Conditions*, 6 FRONTIERS IN BIOENGINEERING BIOTECHNOLOGY 112 (2018), https://www.frontiersin.org/articles/10.3389/fbioe.2018.001 12/full.

[17] For a discussion of the fears of "playing God" and hybris regarding this sensitive issue, *see* U.S. CATHOLIC Conference, Congregation for the Doctrine of the Faith, Instruction on Respect for Human Life in Its Origin and on the Dignity of Procreation, Donum Vitae (1987), *and more briefly*, Marjorie Maguire Shultz, *Reproductive Technology and Intent-Based Parenthood: An Opportunity for Gender Neutrality*, 1990 WIS. L. REV. 297, 329–30 (1990); Yehezkel Margalit, DETERMINING LEGAL PARENTAGE—BETWEEN FAMILY LAW AND CONTRACT LAW 184 (2019).

[18] HEYD, *supra* note 19, at 61.

observed in various states: asleep, moving, sucking its fingers.[19] Termination at the viable stage is an extreme expression of hybris.

The opposite is argued by the feminist viewpoint, according to which "the legal system methodically and systematically harms the intrinsic right of women to life, personal protection and body integrity."[20] This argument derives from an attitude whereby the right of a woman to control her fertility is an important and basic aspect of the right of a woman over her body.[21] Orit Kamir[22] discusses control over fertility:

> The woman has a right to behave during her pregnancy in a way that endangers the fetus. Is she justified to behave in this way in the context of her freedom of action and her rights over her body or does she have an obligation to the fetus or to society to be careful and minimize as much as possible any danger to the fetus? For example, should a woman who drinks alcohol, smokes cigarettes, or takes drugs during her pregnancy be exposed to a claim—by the newborn or by society—for danger to the fetus in her womb?

Kamir considers the right to terminate a pregnancy as a fundamental aspect of the right to control fertility. By contrast, regarding control over fertility, I see the main right of the woman only as the right not to

---

[19] PIONTELLI, *supra* note 2. As noted, Alessandra Piontelli observed fetuses in the wombs of their mothers using ultrasound scans and followed their development from birth to age 4.

[20] ORIT KAMIR, FEMINISM, RIGHTS AND LAW 91 (2002) (Heb.) (that silence in and of itself does not create a false representation). For a discussion of this research, *see* e.g., Irit Koren, *The Bride's Voice: Religious Women Challenge the Wedding Ritual*, 10(2) NASHIM 29 (2005); Efrat Shoham, *Gender, Traditionalism, and Attitudes Toward Domestic Violence Within a Closed Community*, 49(4) INT'L J. OFFENDER THERAPY & COMP. CRIMINOLOGY 427 (2005); Ilan Tamir & Yair Galily, *Women's Sports Coverage in Israel: Perception Versus Reality*, 3(1) INT'L J. SPORT COMM. 92 (2010).

[21] For a discussion of this basic human right, *see, e.g.*, ROSALIND POLLACK PETCHESKY, ABORTION AND WOMAN'S CHOICE: THE STATE SEXUALITY AND REPRODUCTIVE FREEDOM (1990); Jennifer Denbow, *Abortion: When Choice and Autonomy Conflict*, 20 BERKELEY J. GENDER L. & JUST. 216 (2005); Robin West, *From Choice to Reproductive Justice: De-constitutionalizing Abortion Rights*, 118 YALE L. J. 1394 (2008–09).

[22] KAMIR, *supra* note 25, at 129.

conceive. Kamir thinks that "the feminist struggle focuses on the woman's freedom of choice and her right over her own body."[23] I do not question this perception so long as it does not affect the rights of another human being. I believe that a viable fetus is a person, and I maintain that it has rights based on the sanctity of life and the prohibition of murder.[24]

We have seen that there is an ongoing intolerance of people with disabilities or those who are "imperfect." A society that considers that a fetus with a handicap should be destroyed is a society that considers a handicapped person as one whose life is less valuable because of the handicap. To decide that it is preferable for a handicapped fetus to die rather than live with its handicap leads to a dangerous slippery slope. I maintain that society should respect the rights of people with disabilities from the moment the disability is discovered, already in the fetal stage, and not from the moment of birth. Advances in technology should not lead to distorted ethical philosophies that approve of the destruction of less-than-perfect fetuses based on prenatal tests,[25] some of which are described below.

Genetic diseases can be diagnosed by non-invasive and invasive techniques to assess the state of the fetus *in utero* during the different stages of pregnancy. They include chorionic villus sampling,

---

[23] *Id.* at 131.

[24] When conception is the result of incest, rape, or a relationship based on force, preference should be given to the right of the woman over that of the fetus, but in these cases, the pregnancy can be terminated in the initial stages and there is no need to wait until the fetus is viable. For a unique discussion whether a rapist should be deprived of his parenthood right following the delivery of a child resulting from rape, *see* NORVIN RICHARDS, THE ETHICS OF PARENTHOOD 4 (2010) ("Imagine a rapist who impregnates his victim. He is the biological father of the child, but surely that fact gives him no rights at all where the child is concerned").

[25] See, e.g., Mordechai Shohat et al., *Prenatal Diagnosis of Down Syndrome: Ten Year Experience in the Israeli Population*, 122A(3) AM. J. PUB. HEALTH 215 (2003); Carron Sher et al., *Factors Affecting Performance of Prenatal Genetic Testing by Israeli Jewish Women*, 120A(3) AM. J. PUB. HEALTH 418 (2003); Larissa Remennick, *The Quest for the Perfect Baby: Why Do Israeli Women Seek Prenatal Genetic Testing?*, 28(1) SOC. HEALTH & ILLNESS 21 (2006).

cordocentesis, fetal biopsy, fetal liver tissue biopsy, and fetal muscle tissue biopsy. Earlier I described the use of ultrasound imaging to detect fetal defects, discover congenital heart defects, confirm the length of the pregnancy, identify multifetal pregnancies, and discover intrauterine growth retardation.[26]

The aim of these tests, and especially ultrasound scans, is to discover defects in all body systems, including the skull and various parts of the brain, the face and neck area, the spine, the chest, the digestive tract, the sexual and renal organs, the heart and blood vessels, the abdominal wall, the skeleton, and the limbs. Early discovery of defects in IVF, while the fetus is still *in vitro,* has been a blessing as it can prevent what could be prolonged and severe suffering by the newborn and his family. At the same time, early detection of defects can lead to difficult legal and ethical issues that have no solution yet about whether the parents or others have a moral right to decide to have an abortion based on the seriousness of the defect.

Instead of performing a "selection" of fetuses, a social and legal system should be in place to support people with handicaps, including financially. A society that knows how to respect people who are different is also one that is tolerant, ethical, moral, and deserving. Medical technology develops at such a pace that society must catch up to formulate moral and ethical approaches that are adequate for processing the data that technology presents it with. Prenatal genetic diagnosis (PGD),[27] often used in statistical prediction, is becoming

---

[26] For an academic discussion of the required follow-up and prenatal diagnosis during the pregnancy, *see,* among others, Aliza Kolker & B. Meredith Burke, *Grieving the Wanted Child: Ramifications of Abortion after Prenatal Diagnosis of Abnormality,* 14(6) HEALTH CARE FOR WOMEN INT'L 513 (1993); A. Asch, *Prenatal Diagnosis and Selective Abortion: A Challenge to Practice and Policy,* 89(11) AM. J. PUB. HEALTH 1649 (1999); Emily Jackson, *Abortion, Autonomy and Prenatal Diagnosis,* 9(4) SOC. & LEGAL STUD. 467 (2000).

[27] For a discussion of the interaction between PGD and abortion, *see,* for example, David A. Luthy et al., *Prenatal Genetic Diagnosis and Elective Abortion in Women over 35: Utilization and Relative Impact on the Birth Prevalence of Down Syndrome in Washington State,* 7(3) AM. J. MED. GENETICS 375 (1980); Asch, supra note 31; C. Cameron & R. Williamson, *Is There an Ethical Difference Between Preimplantation Genetic Diagnosis and Abortion?,* 29 J. MED. ETHICS 90 (2003).

increasingly prevalent. Genetic prediction involves uncertainty regarding findings and even information about illnesses for which a cure may be found in the future. At the same time, defensive medicine calls for the destruction of fetuses that have a statistical chance of a defect or a specific illness even in the distant future.

In the Israeli *Hammer v. Amit* case,[28] Justice Rivlin wrote:

> Quantification of the damage of a person with a disability—by comparing it with the possibility that he would not have been born at all or by comparing it to a person with no disability—is itself a violation of the value of his life and of the presumption, which is not to be negated, that the value of the lives of people with disabilities is absolute, not relative… The very decision that there are situations in which it would have been better for a person not to have been born because he has a defect contains a problematic social-moral statement that contradicts fundamental values of society regarding human dignity and the sanctity of life.[29]

He went on to say:

> Naturally, the point of view of the parents usually changes after the birth of their child. Naturally, once their child has been born, his parents love him. The disability only intensifies the love. Nevertheless, they are often capable—and the court is also capable—of separating their present love for their child from their sincere statement that if they had been given a choice in advance, before their child was born and became a person, they

[28] CA 1326/07 Hammer v. Amit (28.05.2012), versa.cardozo.yu.edu/sites/default/files/upload/opinions/Hammer%20v.%20Amit.pdf. For a discussion of this landmark verdict, *see* Paola Frati et al., *Preimplantation and Prenatal Diagnosis, Wrongful Birth and Wrongful Life: A Global View of Bioethical and Legal Controversies*, 23(3) HUM. REPROD. UPDATE 338 (2017); Barbara Pfeffer Billauer, *Abortion, Moral Law, and the First Amendment: The Conflict between Fetal Rights & Freedom of Religion*, 23 WM. & MARY J. WOMEN & L. 271, 285 n.70 (2017).

[29] *Hammer v. Amit*, at para. 27, 28 of Justice Rivlin's ruling.

> would have chosen not to bring into the world a child with a disability like his.[30]

David Heyd believes that there should be no discussion about the rights of a nonexistent being.[31] In my opinion, this approach can lead to the destruction of a fetus in the viable stage for any reason, not only being a result of incest, endangering the life of the mother or the fetus, or a defect that will prevent the newborn from living a life with dignity. This danger must be prevented. A fetus is a being that does exist, even if its existence is minimal. It has its identity and interests, and at the viable stage, these interests might conflict with those of the woman carrying it.

I have shown that in certain cases, Israeli legislation considers the fetus as a being with rights. In 2000, several Knesset members proposed a bill for the definition of a person or human being.[32] In Section 1 of the bill it is stated:

Amendment of Interpretation Law.

> In the Interpretation Law of 1981, in section 4 after "when relating to a human being" add "including a human creature, a fetus from the day it is created."

In Section 2 of the bill it is stated:

---

[30] *Id.* at para. 38 of Justice Rivlin's ruling.

[31] For this issue of the nonidentity problem, *see* David Heyd, *The Right Not to be Born with a Defect* DILEMMAS IN MEDICAL ETHICS 255 (2005). MARGALIT, *supra* note 22, at 121 n.82, 249 n.257.

[32] Private Bill No. 985 was presented to the chairman of the Knesset and vice-chairmen on March 1, 2000. For an academic discussion of the Israeli legislation regarding abortion, *see,* among others, Yael Yishai, *Abortion in Israel: Social Demands and Political Responses,* in 6 WOMEN IN ISRAEL 287, 292 (Yael Azmon & Dafna N. Israeli eds., 1993); Naomi Chazan, *Israel at 70: A Gender Perspective,* 23(3) ISR. STUD. 141 (2018), Project MUSE, muse.jhu.edu/article/699549; Shulamit Almog & Sharon Bassan, *The Politics of Pro and Non Reproduction Policies in Israel,* 14 J. HEALTH & BIOMEDICAL L. 27 (2018).

> In the Penal Law, 1977, instead of section 308, add: "... from the day the fetus is created it is considered a person."

A note attached to the bill states that drafting the competence law, according to which a person is competent to hold rights and liabilities from birth till death, does not imply that the fetus—a "potential" person—lacks rights. The note also indicates that the legal wording does not detract from the possibility that the fetus is a person, yet the law tied the validity of its rights and liabilities to a certain period of time, from the end of the birth to its dying day. Because the law does not define "the end of the birth," it is open to interpretation. In the clarifications, different dictionary definitions are brought for the term "fetus" in its various states of development, including the definition of a fetus as an organism. Based on these definitions, the drafters of this bill reached the conclusion that "when relating today to the law of human rights, the fetus should also be taken into consideration. One can venture to claim that a fetus is a person." The bill did not pass and I think that today, more than 20 years after this bill, it should be redrafted. Today, with progress in different fields such as genetics, genomics, and maternal-fetal medicine, the status of the fetus, at least during the viable stage, should be redefined by legislation.

Hashiloni Dolev,[33] in her research on the history of the policy of pregnancy terminations in Israel, notes that in contrast to Germany, Israel has adopted a liberal position reflected in its very high number of authorized pregnancy terminations. Yonatan Davis presented data from the Israeli Ministry of Health[34] showing that the rate of abortions

---

[33] YAEL HASHILONI DOLEV, A LIFE (UN) WORTHY OF LIVING: REPRODUCTIVE GENETICS IN ISRAEL AND GERMANY (2007). For a discussion of this book, *see,* among others, Roy Gilbar, *Between Unconditional Acceptance and Responsibility: Should Family Ethics Limit the Scope of Reproductive Autonomy*, 21 CHILD & FAM. L.Q. 309, 321 n.64, 324 n.80 (2009); Silke Schicktanz et al., *The Cultural Context of End-of-Life Ethics: A Comparison of Germany and Israel*, 19 CAMBRIDGE Q. HEALTHCARE ETHICS 381, 381 n.3 (2010); Daphne Barak-Erez, *IVF Battles: Legal Categories and Comparative Tales*, 28 DUKE J. COMP. & INT'L L. 247, 250 n.5 (2018).

[34] Yonatan Davis, *The Question of the Causal Connection in "Wrongful Birth" as a Consequence of the* Hammer v. Amit *Case*, MED. & L. 54 (Special Issue, Jan. 2015) (Heb.).

is lower in Israel than in most European countries. As noted, data from the Central Bureau of Statistics in Israel show that in 2010, 99.1% of the requests to terminate a pregnancy were authorized,[35] and data from 2011 and 2012 were similar.[36]

Some may contend that a woman has an uninterrupted right over her body, at any stage of pregnancy. But for reasons of social balance, some rights should take precedence over others. In our case, a fetus that can survive in an environment other than its mother's womb should be given rights that occasionally override those of the woman who carries it. One may object that the woman will be the one bringing up the handicapped child, therefore we should distinguish between theory and practice. The state must put in place a system to help parents bring up a handicapped child, with appropriate financial support.

In balancing the rights of the woman over her body against those of the viable fetus, in some cases, the termination of pregnancy will be justified even at the viable stage of the fetus. When this happens, it should be in the best interests of the fetus,[37] based on objective criteria: for example, if the life expectancy of the fetus as a newborn is certain to be very short, if it is expected to live with severe disabilities and endure endless suffering, or if it will be severely mentally challenged or have a terminal illness abortion should be justified.

I see no difference between human rights and the rights of a viable fetus. This is the appropriate balance between the rights. Legal acknowledgment of human value, sanctity of life, freedom,[38] and the

---

[35] Central Bureau of Statistics "Terminations of Pregnancies" is available on the Bureau website: www.cbs.gov.il/reader/cw_usr_view_SHTML?ID=752.

[36] In 2011, 20,945 women requested to terminate their pregnancy and 20,576 requests were granted. In 2012, 21,689 women applied to the committee for termination of pregnancy and 20,063 of these requests were granted.

[37] Israel Basic Law: Human Dignity and Freedom, recognizing the value of man, the sanctity of life and freedom.

[38] Basic Law: Human Dignity and Freedom. For a discussion of this substantial law, *see*, e.g., Aharon Barak, *A Constitutional Revolution: Israel's Basic Laws*, 4 CONST. F. 83, 83–84 (1993); Eyal Benvenisti, *The Influence of International Human Rights Law on the Israeli Legal System: Present and Future*, 28(1) ISR. L. REV. 136 (1994); David Kretzmer, *The New*

right of people with disabilities to equality[39] must lead to a new medical, social, and ethical discourse on the subject of the rights of the viable fetus. This expresses the dilemma and thesis at the heart of this book. The question is the weight to be attached to the interests of the fetus to be born healthy against the interests of the woman whose task it will be to bring up a child with a handicap.[40]

In practice, the level of the future handicap often cannot be properly estimated.[41] We have seen that prenatal follow-up can detect defects, but it is doubtful that statistical accuracy of the prediction regarding the functional ability of a fetus with a defect is high. Often the physicians do not know whether the defect is caused by a known syndrome, or it is random.[42] An ultrasound scan may raise suspicions of a genetic syndrome and lead to additional tests.[43] One frequently recommended genetic test is for detecting the deafness gene. Prenatal genetic tests today allow for the discovery of anomalies in sex

---

Basic Laws on Human Rights: A Mini Revolution in Israeli Constitutional Law?, 26(2) ISR. L. REV. 238 (1992).

39 Law of Equal Rights for People with Disabilities. *See also* ANN FRYE, DISABLED AND OLDER PERSONS AND SUSTAINABLE URBAN MOBILITY: THEMATIC STUDY PREPARED FOR GLOBAL REPORT ON HUMAN SETTLEMENTS 38 (2013), https://unhabitat.org/wp-content/uploads/2013/06/GRHS.2013.Thematic.Disabled.and.Older.Persons.pdf; EDNA ZAFRIR & STAN NICOLAE CRISTIAN, MORE THAN A RAMP: IS THE ACADEMY ACCESSIBLE? 340 (2018), https://www.futureacademy.org.uk/files/images/upload/ERD2017F41.pdf.

40 Because the father has no legal status and because of single-parent families, we are not dealing with the burden on the family unit but on the birth mother alone. According to the penal law and directives from the Israeli Ministry of Health, the father of the fetus has no legal status in the eyes of the committee for termination of pregnancies and his informed consent is not required to terminate the pregnancy. *See* C.A. 413/80 Roe v. Doe, P.D. 35(3), 57, 95-96. For a discussion of this landmark ruling, *see* Daphna Hacker, *Single and Married Women in the Law of Israel—A Feminist Perspective*, 9 FEMINIST LEGAL STUD. 29, 44 n.23 (2001).

41 YIGAL WOLMAN, ULTRASOUND IN BIRTH MOTHERS (2006) (Heb.) noted that when discovering a defect, such as club foot, there is a 10%-14% chance of finding other innate abnormalities, and even if this is the only defect, the chances of finding chromosomal defects are 6%-22%. This is a defect in the foot, and many doctors are sure that it does not warrant an abortion. Some 25% of cases are discovered by means of ultrasound and approximately 10% are mistakenly diagnosed.

42 Of heart defects, 20% are known to be connected to Down's syndrome.

43 An ultrasound scan may raise suspicion of a genetically based syndrome that requires additional tests such as amniotic fluid or a specific cardiac US.

chromosomes that might cause sterility in the future. Fetuses that test positive for these syndromes should not be sentenced to death.

2. The Right of the Fetus "Over Its Own Body"

Another topic that restricts women's autonomy and requires a balancing of rights is the administration of medical treatment to women against their will during pregnancy to improve or ensure the good health of the viable fetus. I discussed the question of whether it is acceptable to force a woman to undergo a C-section without her informed consent. This issue involves an open conflict between human rights and the rights of the "beginnings of a person."

In the previous sections, I described the positive law; here I establish new guidelines for how the law should be interpreted or drafted in the future to reflect a justified paternalistic viewpoint and fulfill a social-ethical function. In the last few decades, considerable progress has been made in technology and science, enabling a better understanding of fetal anatomy[44] and physiology, and more accurate detection of fetal deformities and pathologies during pregnancy. This brought a significant change in modern obstetrics, reflected, among others, in the change of its name from "high-risk pregnancy" to "maternal-fetal" medicine.[45] Until recently, modern medicine provided only the diagnostics for detecting fetal defects and pathologies but has been unable to offer solutions for treatment apart from terminating the pregnancy. Today, the option of intrauterine treatment makes it possible to correct or improve different fetal conditions inside the

---

[44] For a discussion of this emerging field, *see*, for example, J.C. Weinreb et al., *Human Fetal Anatomy: MR Imaging*, 157(3) RADIOLOGY 715 (1985); S.M. McCarthy et al., *Obstetrical Magnetic Resonance Imaging: Fetal Anatomy*, 154(2) RADIOLOGY 427 (1985); D. Levinee et al., *Fetal Anatomy Revealed with Fast MR Sequences*, 167 AM. J. ROENTGENOLOGY 905 (1996).

[45] For an academic discussion, *see*, e.g., Ian A. Greer, *The Challenge of Thrombophilia in Maternal Fetal Medicine*, 342(6) N. ENGL. J. MED. 424 (2000); Vassilios Fanos et al., *Metabolomics Application in Maternal–Fetal Medicine*, BIOMED. RES. INT. (2013); Mary E. D'Alton et al., *Putting the "M" Back in Maternal–Fetal Medicine*, 208(6) AM. J. OBSTETRICS & GYNECOLOGY 442 (2013).

womb by means of medication or surgery. Below is a survey of several modern treatments for a variety of disorders.

2.1 Intrauterine treatments

The types of treatment provided during fetal life can be placed into three categories: interventions related to the type of birth or when it should take place to provide the best treatment for the newborn, medical treatment, and surgery.

3. Types of Birth Interventions

Interventions related to the type of birth or when it should take place include an elective C-section in cases where defects are likely to interfere with the procedure of normal birth and in cases where an immediate surgical solution is required for a fetal defect under sterile conditions. Such cases include, among others, a serious defect in the abdominal wall, hydrocephalus (accumulation of fluid in the brain cavity causing a significant increase in the size of the fetal head), spinal defects, and spinal tumors. Cases that require premature birth include renal and urethral disorders, hydrops fetalis, and a significant disorder in intrauterine growth.

3.1 Medical treatment

The group of neural tube defects (NTDs) affects the development of the spinal canal, often leading to severe neurological disability. Today, treatment with folic acid before the pregnancy and during the first trimester is known to reduce the risk of developing these defects by 80%.[46]

---

[46] See Susana Manrique et al., *Maternal Anaesthesia in Open and Fetoscopic Surgery of Foetal Open Spinal Neural Tube Defects*, 36(3) EUR. J. ANAESTHESIOLOGY 175 (2019); Ma'atem B. Fofou-Caillierez et al., *Vitamin B-12 and Liver Activity and Expression of Methionine Synthase Are Decreased in Fetuses with Neural Tube Defects*, 109(3) AM. J. CLINICAL NUTRITION 674 (2019); Philippe Lemay et al., *Whole Exome Sequencing Identifies Novel Predisposing Genes in Neural Tube Defects*, 7(1) MOLECULAR GENETICS & GENOMIC MED. E00467 (2019).

Women suffering from congenital adrenal hyperplasia (CAH) require treatment with steroids in the first weeks of pregnancy to ensure the proper sexual development of the fetuses. If a male fetus develops, the treatment can be discontinued; if it is female, treatment should continue.[47]

Fetal thyrotoxicosis is a defect that may develop in fetuses whose mothers suffer from hyperthyroidism. The mother should be treated with medication that suppresses the activity of the thyroid in order to treat the fetus.[48]

In extreme cases, hypothyroidism in the fetus can be treated with an intrauterine drip of hormone replacement.

The fetal respiratory system reaches maturity at a relatively late stage in the pregnancy. Therefore, when born prematurely, fetuses are more prone to respiratory disorders after birth. Many studies have proven that treatment with steroids for women who are liable to give birth prematurely significantly reduces the risk of respiratory problems in the newborn.

Hydrops fetalis is a fetal syndrome that may occur for several reasons, one of which has to do with the development of antibodies of the fetal red blood cells, resulting in the destruction of the red blood cells and fetal anemia. Treating pregnant women with blood type Rh with an

---

[47] For an up-to-date discussion of this defect, *see* Alessandro Prete et al., *Diagnosis and Management of Congenital Adrenal Hyperplasia in Children and Adults*, ADVANCED PRACTICE IN ENDOCRINOLOGY NURSING 657 (Sofia Llahana et al., 2019); Maria I. New et al., *Fertility in Patients with Nonclassical Congenital Adrenal Hyperplasia,* 111(1) FERTILITY & STERILITY 13 (2019); Maria I. New & Zev Rosenwaks, *Introduction: Contemporary Perspectives on Congenital Adrenal Hyperplasia: Impacts on Reproduction,* 111(1) FERTILITY & STERILITY 4 (2019).

[48] For the most recent discussion, *see,* e.g., Myrthe M. van Dijk et al., *Maternal Thyrotropin Receptor Antibody Concentration and the Risk of Fetal and Neonatal Thyrotoxicosis: A Systematic Review,* 28(2) THYROID 789 (2018); Stephanie L. Samuels et al., *Neonatal Thyrotoxicosis,* 45(1) CLINICS IN PERINATOLOGY 31 (2018); Wilburn D. Bolton & Jennifer M. Perkins, *Thyrotoxicosis in Pregnancy, in* THYROID DISEASE & REPRODUCTION 117 (Jennifer Lipkowitz Eaton ed., 2019).

antibody known as anti-D reduces the risk of the destruction of red blood cells in the next pregnancy.

Neonatal alloimmune thrombocytopenia (NAIT) is a disproportion between the antibodies of the paternal and maternal platelets, causing destruction of the fetal platelets and a greater tendency for bleeding, especially cerebral hemorrhage. In such cases, the woman can be treated with intravenous immunoglobulin and steroids to reduce the risk to the fetus.

Fetal arrhythmias are mainly benign disorders that disappear by themselves, although in certain cases they can be treated with drugs, such as Digoxin.

3.2 Surgical treatment

Surgical treatment is divided into three groups of intervention: minimally invasive procedures by means of guided ultrasound, laparoscopic procedures, and open surgery.

The ultrasound-guided procedures include inserting a drain to remove fluids accumulating in the fetus into the amniotic fluid cavity, and to perform cordocentesis and intrauterine blood transfusion for the fetus. Laparoscopic procedures include mainly cauterizing fetal blood vessels in the placenta to reduce the risk of death and neurological disabilities in twins, although recently this type of procedure was used to correct a spinal defect. Open surgery is carried out in a few medical centers in the world, where the aim is to correct severe problems, such as spinal defects. Naturally, the more significant the surgical intervention, the greater the risk of complications such as intrauterine infection, premature rupture of membranes, premature birth, and fetal death.

Obstructive uropathy is performed when there is an obstruction in the urinary tract and urine collects in the bladder and kidneys, which can lead to kidney failure. In these cases, the fetal bladder can be drained by means of guided ultrasound by inserting a drain from the fetal bladder into the amniotic sac. This reduces the pressure until birth, when the urinary system can be corrected surgically.[49]

Hydrocephalus is the result of an obstruction in the spinal cord, with spinal fluid collecting in the fetal brain and exerting pressure on the brain tissue. It can result in defective development of the fetal brain and a noticeable growth in the size of the head. In these cases, a drain can be inserted into the brain chambers to draw off the excess fluid.

Hydrothorax is an accumulation of fluids in the lungs of the fetus, and it may damage the development of the lungs. In these cases, a drain can be inserted to draw out excess fluid into the amniotic sac.[50]

Neural tube defects in the spinal canal can be treated with open surgery with a high success rate of up to 50% reduction in neurological disability, although there is a high risk of premature birth. There have been reports of therapeutic trials on defects of this type using laparoscopy.

Fetal anemia may cause fetal edema. It can be treated by inserting a needle into the umbilical cord using ultrasound guidance and an intrauterine blood transfusion into the fetus. Two or three transfusions

---

[49] For the most recent discussion of this fetal anomaly, *see,* among others, Colin J. Down et al., *Practical Management of Fetal Obstructive Uropathy*, 5(1) J. FETAL MED. 37 (2018); Mustafa Z. Mahmoud, *Real Time Brightness Mode Ultrasound in Determining the Causes and Complications of Obstructive Uropathy* 19 J. BIOL. SCI. 181 (2019), https://www.researchgate.net/profile/Mustafa Z Mahmoud/publication/329717620 Real Time Brightness Mode Ultrasound in Determining the Causes and Complications of Obstructive Uropathy/links/5 c65193945851582c3e6f9dd/Real-Time-Brightness-Mode-Ultrasound-in-Determining-the-Causes-and-Complications-of-Obstructive-Uropathy.pdf; Mukesh Chandra Arya et al., *Transcaval Ureter: A Rare Embryological Anomaly of Inferior Vena Cava Causing Obstructive Uropathy*, 30(2) UROLOGICAL SCI. 86–88 (2019), http://www.e- urol-sci.com/preprintarticle.asp?

[50] See, e.g., Rodrigo A. Mon et al., *Outcomes of Fetuses with Primary Hydrothorax That Undergo Prenatal Intervention (Prenatal Intervention for Hydrothorax)*, 221 J. SURGICAL RES. 121 (2018); Ruben S.G.M. Witlox et al., *Neonatal Management and Outcome After Thoracoamniotic Shunt Placement for Fetal Hydrothorax*, 103 ARCHIVES OF DISEASE IN CHILDHOOD F245 (2018); Fumio Suyama et al., *Fetal Lung Size After Thoracoamniotic Shunting Reflects Survival in Primary Fetal Hydrothorax with Hydrops*, 44(7) J. OBSTETRICS & GYNAECOLOGY RES. 1216 (2018).

are usually enough to transfer red blood cells to the fetus that will suffice until birth.

Twin-to-twin transfusion syndrome. When fetuses share one placenta, there may be an asymmetrical transfer of blood from one fetus to the other, so that most of the blood flows to one of the fetuses (the "recipient"), which suffers from an excess blood supply, and drains from the other fetus (the "donor"), which suffers from fetal anemia. This phenomenon can be treated in different ways, and the currently accepted treatment is by laparoscopy, using a laser to cauterize the placental blood vessels connecting the blood supplies of the fetuses.

Congenital diaphragmatic hernia is a defect in the partition between the chest thorax and the heart, allowing the abdominal organs to migrate into the chest wall and preventing normal development of the lungs. The fetal windpipe can be obstructed by means of a balloon, enabling the lungs to grow and pressing the abdominal organs back in place.[51]

In some cases, the risks to the mother or the fetus are likely to be higher than the chances of a good prognosis. Furthermore, complications may occur in any medical intervention, including loss of the fetus. Some treatments are more effective than others, and the treatments listed above do not provide magic solutions to all possible fetal problems. There are instances when the termination of pregnancy is the best option available.[52]

---

[51] *See* also Pramod S. Puligandla et al., *Diagnosis and Management of Congenital Diaphragmatic Hernia: A Clinical Practice Guideline*, 190(4): CMAJ E103–E112 (2018); Matthew Harting, *Aggressive Surgical Management of Congenital Diaphragmatic Hernia: Worth the Effort? A Multicenter, Prospective, Cohort Study*, 267(5) ANNALS OF SURGERY 977 (2018); Christopher J. McLaughlin et al., *Congenital Diaphragmatic Hernia, Clinical Algorithms, in* GENERAL SURGERY 487 (Salvatore Docimo & Eric M. Pauli eds., 2019).

[52] The chapter dealing with the intrauterine treatment of a fetus was written by Dr. Amir Aviram and is based mainly on Shelley C. Springer, *Prenatal Diagnosis and Fetal Therapy*, MEDSCAPE WEBSITE (updated 28.04.2014) (http://emedicine.medscape.come/article/936318-overview). For the most recent overview of this field, *see* Maria Laseca Modrego et al., *Prenatal Diagnosis of Foetal Labial Fusion*, 37(2) J. OBSTETRICS & GYNAECOLOGY 243 (2017); Amirhossein Moaddab et al.,

4. The Viable Fetus: A Human Being inside a Human Being

Applying medical treatment to a fetus in the womb of its mother raises additional ethical and moral questions, first and foremost regarding the identity of the patient—whether it is the woman or the fetus. Additional questions are: Can a woman refuse medical treatment for the fetus inside her body even if doing so endangers the fetus? Can a woman refuse medical treatment for the fetus inside her body even if there is no risk to herself, but it would save, help heal, or alleviate the illness of the fetus after the birth? Can a woman be forced to undergo medical treatment of any kind for the benefit of the fetus? Can a woman be forced to undergo a C-section to give birth to a healthy fetus?

I maintain that the viable fetus, which is expected to live an independent life on its own or with medical assistance, has rights that sometimes override those of the woman. Going even further, when treating pregnant women, physicians must take into consideration that they have two patients with a biological connection and must consider the health of both the woman and the viable fetus. Most pregnant women would probably agree to a certain amount of personal risk to give birth to a healthy child, but the controversy concerns women who refuse treatment for the benefit of the fetus during the pregnancy or refuse to undergo a C-section despite the medical need for it to save the fetus.

Advanced medical technology allows physicians to treat the viable fetus to save its life or improve its quality of life. Contrary to claims that a viable fetus has no legal status, is not a person, and therefore legally unfit and not entitled to rights, I maintain that a viable fetus is a person at least from the moral point of view, and must therefore be protected. In most countries, the legal status of the fetus develops as the stages of

---

Ethical Issues in Fetal Therapy, 43 BEST PRAC. & RES. CLINICAL OBSTETRICS & GYNAECOLOGY 58 (2017); International Society for Prenatal Diagnosis et al., *Joint Position Statement from the International Society for Prenatal Diagnosis (ISPD), the Society for Maternal Fetal Medicine (SMFM), and the Perinatal Quality Foundation (PQF) on the Use of Genome-Wide Sequencing for Fetal Diagnosis*, 38(1) PRENATAL DIAGNOSIS 6 (2018).

pregnancy progress. The stage of viability must signify a change in its legal status. Several physicians agree, including Noga Blickstein:

> Sometimes, the interests of the fetus, the "patient," conflict with those of the woman. However, the physician's duty to the fetus is absolute, in the same way as the physician's duty to the woman. This duty is meant in a positive sense, i.e., the physician has a duty to treat the fetus (including follow-up) in the best possible way, even when it is still inside the womb. The physician, however, is restricted by the mother, owing to her autonomy over her body, from providing it with invasive means. In any event, the physician is never duty-bound to harm a viable fetus or to destroy it, even if this is what the mother wants. The only exception (and some disagree) is when there is absolutely no doubt that a serious defect exists, and when proved without a shadow of a doubt that the defect would prevent it from having a decent life.[53]

The viable fetus and the woman are not a single entity.[54] The fetus is a patient, and its right to be born, and to be born healthy, should be

---

[53] Prof. Blickstein's opinion, as quoted by Justice Menahem Raniel in (Tel Aviv (831/08) *Dahan (minor) v. State of Israel Ministry of Health* (Nevo 5.2.12) (Heb.), in which the plaintiff was born by C-section in the 28th week of pregnancy with partial moderate CP known as spastic diplegia. The plaintiff claimed, among others, that the mother did not give informed consent for a C-section and that the operation could have been avoided, increasing the chances that the plaintiff would have died. She therefore sued for battery, which was rejected. For a recent discussion of this medical problem, *see* Yanxin Zhang & Ye Ma, *Application of Supervised Machine Learning Algorithms in the Classification of Sagittal Gait Patterns of Cerebral Palsy Children with Spastic Diplegia, in* 106 COMPUTERS IN BIOLOGY AND MEDICINE 33 (2019); Samuel M.T. Jeffery et al., *Surgical Outcomes of Single-Level Bilateral Selective Dorsal Rhizotomy for Spastic Diplegia in 150 Consecutive Patients,* WORLD NEUROSURGERY (2019); Naglaa A. Zaky et al., *Role of Two Therapeutic Interventions on Balance in Children with Spastic Diplegia and Hemiparasis: A Comparative Study,* 6 PHYSICAL THERAPEUTIC REHABILITATION 2 (2019).

[54] See, e.g., Mary Anne Wood & Lisa Bolin Hawkins, State Regulation of Late Abortion and the *Physician's Duty of Care to the Viable Fetus,* 45 MO. L. REV. 394 (1980); Lawrence J. Nelson & Nancy Milliken, *Compelled Medical Treatment of Pregnant Women Life, Liberty, and Law in Conflict,* 259(7) JAMA 1060 (1988); Tu'uhevaha J. Kaitu'u-Lino et al., *Serum Concentrations of Soluble Flt-1 Are Decreased Among Women with a Viable Fetus and No*

protected. We have seen that a fetus, after being born, can take legal action against a third party if this caused prenatal damage. Under certain circumstances, a fetus has the right to inherit. Under others, it has the right to receive child support. If a woman refuses to provide informed consent for a C-section, at a stage when the fetus is viable and her refusal is liable to cause damage to the fetus, the woman should be forced to undergo the C-section. Penal law that does not protect the fetus by exacting a penalty for its destruction must be amended.

There is a gap between the protection extended to fetuses and human beings: legal policy states that the newborn should be protected from the instant it emerges from the womb. But the distinction between a newborn baby and a fetus at the viable stage, a few weeks before it emerges into the world, is spurious I have shown above that the conduct of a pregnant woman that endangers the fetus should be punished.[55] Likewise, this principle should be upheld also in cases where the woman refuses to provide the fetus with medical treatment or to undergo a C-section.

Other behaviors can harm the viable fetus, like taking drugs and medication ignoring their effect on the viable fetus. The fetus should be considered an entity in every respect for purposes of third-party claims—including against the woman—if it was treated with negligence and lack of care. Although these claims are recognized only following the birth of the fetus, in some cases in which the fetus was refused medical treatment or surgery there is no newborn, therefore I argue that a trustee should be able to sue in the name of the fetus.

The fetus has the right to prenatal treatment if the treatment does not pose a danger to the woman. A woman who denies this right must be held responsible both criminally and in civil court, for damages. When

---

Symptoms of Miscarriage Destined for Pregnancy Loss, PLOS ONE 7(2) e32509 (2012), https://journals.plos.org/plosone/article?id=10.1371/journal.pone.0032509.

[55] Linda C. Fentiman, *Pursuing the Perfect Mother: Why American's Criminalization of Maternal Substance Abuse Is Not the Answer—A Comparative Legal Analysis*, 15 MICH. J. GENDER & L. 389 (2009).

dealing with the potential rights of the fetus, the scope of the pregnant woman's autonomy over her body should be restricted. One person's autonomy does not justify harming the rights of another person or a potential person. Even those who are convinced that the woman's autonomy over her body is of utmost importance must agree that this autonomy should not be enjoyed at the expense of others. Both in England and the US, C-sections have been carried out against the woman's wishes by court order.[56]

The argument to the contrary is that even if the fetus can be considered an entity in itself, it is still difficult to recognize its claim against the woman who gave birth to it.[57] I am aware that enforcing a C-section by court order on a woman who refuses to undergo one raises complex ethical questions. One is the lack of consistency in legal policy that on one hand makes it necessary for any mature person to provide informed consent to a surgical procedure and on the other forces a mature pregnant woman to undergo surgery against her will. Another problem is that enforcing a C-section on the woman might be detrimental to the physician-patient relationship. The American College of Obstetrics and Gynecology published the following opinion on the matter:

> Obstetricians should refrain from performing procedures that are unwanted by pregnant women… The use of the courts to resolve these conflicts is almost never warranted.[58]

---

[56] For a discussion of this problematic coercive practice, *see,* for example, Monica K. Miller, *Refusal to Undergo a Cesarean Section: A Woman's Right or a Criminal Act*, 15 HEALTH MATRIX 383 (2005); V. Chandis & T. Williams, *The Patient, the Doctor, the Fetus, and the Court-Compelled Cesarean: Why Courts Should Address the Question Through a Bioethical Lens*, 25 MED. & L. 729 (2006); Theresa Morris et al., *Forced and Coerced Cesarean Sections in the United States*, 16(2) CONTEXTS 24 (2017).

[57] In countries where the legislature has already enacted legislation dealing with harm to the fetus, *see* Joanne Pedone, *Filling the Void: Model Legislation for Fetal Homicide Crimes*, 43 COLUM. J.L. & SOC. PROBS. 77 (2009); Andrew S. Murphy, *A Survey of State Homicide Laws and Their Potential Applicability to Pregnant Women Who Harm Their Own Fetuses*, 89 IND. L.J. 847 (2014).

[58] Mary Jo Ludwig, *Maternal–Fetal Conflict* (11.04.2008), https://deDts.washmgton.edu/bioethx/toDics/matem.html. *See also* Susan Markens et

In the case of ordinary surgical procedures, however, no potential person (fetus) is involved, and in any case, the physician-patient relation should not be adversely affected by external intervention, especially if it is appropriate. Regarding cases of claims for wrongful birth, Heyd noted:

> A human being that has yet to be created does not exist, it has no identity and no interests whatsoever, let alone rights against anyone—parent or advisor. It would however be misleading to consider the parents as guardians of the child when the parents themselves have not yet decided whether or not to bring the child into the world!... If the law were to aim to protect the rights of the fetus not to be born (under certain circumstances when a severe handicap is suspected), the law would obligate the mother and the doctors to carry out an abortion, thus protecting the right of the fetus not to be born. But naturally, no legal system works this way: abortions are an issue permitted by law, at best, but never enforced.[59]

The discussion about the fetus at the pre-viable stage diverges from the topic of this book, but even so, I beg to differ. We assume that if the woman has not sought an abortion, she wants the pregnancy and the child. The law does not protect the right of the fetus not to be born, on the contrary: by determining that the woman who wants to terminate a pregnancy should apply for permission to do so, the legislature expresses the opinion that there is supervision over the autonomy and choice of the woman, and to a certain extent, protection of the fetus.

---

al., *Feeding the Fetus: On Interrogating the Notion of Maternal-Fetal Conflict*, 23(2) FEMINIST STUD. 351 (1997); F. S. Oduncu et al., *Cancer in Pregnancy: Maternal-Fetal Conflict*, 129(3) J. CANCER RES. & CLINICAL ONCOLOGY 133 (2003); Robert M. Samstein et al., *Extrathymic Generation of Regulatory T Cells in Placental Mammals Mitigates Maternal-Fetal Conflict*, 150(1) CELL 29 (2012).

[59] Heyd, *supra* note 121 at 255.

I propose legislation that regulates the status of a fetus at the viable stage and provides it with rights.[60] Protection of a viable fetus as a future citizen is a proper objective as far as society and ethics are concerned. Providing medical treatment for a viable fetus to improve its quality of life or to save it during the pregnancy, without endangering the woman's life, is a good and correct outcome, and so is performing a C-section to save the life of the fetus with minimal risk to the woman.

In the chapter on paternalism, I showed that sometimes paternalistic attitudes are justified, for example, when enforcing the wearing of a helmet while riding a motorcycle and wearing a seatbelt when driving a car. In philosophical discourse about utilitarianism, the outcome becomes a guiding principle. In our case, the expected result of forcing a woman to undergo treatment with the aim to improve the health or save the life of a viable fetus is a good one. This principle should be affirmed in advance by the legislature, not retroactively by the court. As I showed above, the utilitarian attitude is that a good result is a result that causes more joy than suffering, when relating to joy in its entirety.

Sociological jurisprudence talks of the need for balance.[61] One method to establish balance is by the legislature deciding on the preferred interests; another method is for the court to balance interests based on a prior case. In the case of balancing the right of a woman over her body, which is the interest of the woman as an individual, and the right of a viable fetus over its body, the decision should take into account the

---

[60] See, e.g., William T. Muse & Nicholas A. Spinella, *Right of Infant to Recover for Prenatal Injury*, 36 VA. L. REV. 611 (1950); Bernice Bird, *Fetal Personhood Laws as Limits to Maternal Personhood at Any Stage of Pregnancy: Balancing Fetal and Maternal Interests at Post-Viability Among Fetal Pain and Fetal Homicide Laws*, 25 HASTINGS WOMEN'S L.J. 39 (2014); Ghodrati Fatemeh & Akbarzadeh Marzieh, *The Rights of the Fetus: Ensoulment as the Cut-off Point Legislation on Abortion Running Title: The Rights of the Fetus in Legislation Abortion*, 10(1) HEALTH SCI. J. 1 (2016).

[61] For a discussion of this field in relation to abortion, *see*, among others, Thomas H. Jr. Barnard, *An Analysis and Criticism of the Model Penal Code Provisions on the Law of Abortion*, 18 W. RES. L. REV. 540, 547 n.48, 559 n.114 (1967); David Fuqua, *Justice Harry A. Blackmun: The Abortion Decisions*, 34 ARK. L. REV. 276, 281 (1980); Allan Ides, *The Jurisprudence of Justice Byron White*, 103 YALE L.J. 419, 420 n.3, 429 n.47 (1993).

woman's point of view, of the viable fetus, of society (maintaining the right of a living or a potential individual to keep the body complete), and of the public (penalizing anyone who harms the completeness of another person's body). A formula for balance should establish the relative weight of the conflicting interests of the woman and the viable fetus.

Piontelli[62] observed 11 fetuses in the womb using ultrasound, after which she followed their development from birth until age 4. She presented detailed reports of her observations and descriptions of psychoanalytical treatment in small children, whose behavior in analysis clearly showed the effect of the experience they had had in the womb.[63] Being able to see the viable fetus using ultrasound technology reinforces its status and emphasizes its human aspect.[64]

The choice whether or not to perform the abortion is the woman's, but it is not necessarily a question of freedom of choice. With an abundance of tests to identify fetuses with defects at every stage of the pregnancy and the culture that encourages the choice of abortion at any stage the woman's choice seems to be strongly influenced by external pressures that exclude the interests of the viable fetus. Legislatures must make sure to provide a fair representation of these interests.

I recommend legislative intervention, based on an ethical consensus and social policy that justifies providing the viable fetus with rights on one hand, and imposes tort liability on women who violate these rights on the other. Society must apply standards of conduct to pregnant women. It must impose on them a legal, not only moral obligation to

---

[62] PIONTELLI, *supra* note 2, at 333.

[63] *Id.* on the back cover.

[64] For an academic discussion of this issue, *see*, for example, B. Jacquetin et al., *Intrauterine Exchange Transfusion of the Fetus Under Ultrasound Guidance: First Successful Report*, 1(4) FETAL DIAGNOSIS & THERAPY 180 (1986); Peter A. van Dam et al., *Application of Ultrasound in the Diagnosis of Heterotopic Pregnancy—A Review of the Literature*, 16(3) J. CLINICAL ULTRASOUND 159 (1988); Society for Maternal–Fetal Medicine Publications Committee et al., *Doppler Assessment of the Fetus with Intrauterine Growth Restriction*, 206(4) AM. J. OBSTETRICS & GYNECOLOGY 300 (2012).

provide the viable fetus with a proper environment for growth, enable it to be born, and to have a healthy life despite its disability, based on clear and defined[65] medical data regarding its condition.

I am aware of the claim that there is a unique symbiotic connection between the woman and the fetus, and courts should be mindful of it when interpreting the law. The courts should determine the obligation of pregnant women regarding the required caution and level of knowledge expected of them to prevent harm to the fetus over the course of the pregnancy or even in the pre-pregnancy stage. The autonomous right of the woman over her body should be restricted when there is another entity inside of her. The court should take into consideration the woman's background, culture, intellect, mental state, financial state, and health. The court should also take great care when imposing a duty: its extent, the appropriate standard, and the legal policy. The court can set standards for the reasonable pregnant woman and her conduct.[66]

The court must carefully balance the new rights of the fetus with those of the woman. Thus, the court may recognize negligence on the part of a woman that took place years before the pregnancy—for example, using drugs that endanger the fetus or choosing a place of work where

---

[65] As opposed to the perception raised in *Chenault v. Huie*, 989 S.W. 2d 474 (1999). For an academic discussion of this verdict, *see* e.g., Dana Hirschenbaum, *When Crack Is the Only Choice: The Effect of a Negative Right of Privacy on Drug-Addicted Women*, 15 BERKELEY WOMEN'S L.J. 327, 334 n.55 (2000); Edward Sylvester, Chenault v. Huie*: Denying the Existence of a Legal Duty Between a Mother and Her Unborn Children*, 31 AKRON L. REV. 107 (2000); Tsachi Keren-Paz, *On Mothers, Babies and Bathwater: Distributive Justice, Tort Law and Prenatal Duties*, 14(2) SOC. & L. STUD. 179 (2005).

[66] I am aware of the opposite claim, according to which the assessment of a reasonable person is unattainable when it comes to a pregnant woman: "The reasonable person standard, however, is not designed to apply to matters involving intimate, private, and personal decisions. The proposed solution of 'reasonable pregnant woman' does not resolve many issues presented by applying universal standards to parental conduct." *See* Joseph S. Badger, Stallman v. Youngquist*—No, You Can't Sue Mommy in Illinois: The Illinois Supreme Court Rejects Maternal Parental Civil Liability*, 11, N. ILL. U. L. REV. 409 (1990–91). For a discussion of this verdict, *see* Sandra L. Haley, *The Parental Tort Immunity Doctrine: Is It a Defensible Defense*, 30 U. RICH. L. REV. 575, 587 n.55 (1996).

there was a danger of developing a malignancy.[67] The court can make a distinction between pregnant women who drank reasonable or unreasonable amounts of alcohol if the child later experienced severe learning difficulties. The court can decide when using heavy narcotics that harm the newborn is a breach of legal duty that justifies a ruling of lack of maternal capability or when the refusal to allow medical treatment of the fetus during pregnancy, leading to death or irreversible damage to the newborn, is a breach of this duty.

The Western world does not generally recognize the woman's responsibility toward the fetus. At the same time, Tedeschi[68] describes a court case won by a child who was born suffering from syphilis with which the father had infected the mother, although elsewhere such claims were rejected. In the US, the court recognized the claim of the child who sued his mother because of his dental problems and the dark color of his teeth, damage caused by the medication she took during pregnancy. On the same issue the court ruled that there was no difference between a third party and the woman's responsibility toward the fetus, and she was ruled liable.[69] A child who sued his mother won in a case where the pregnant woman crossed a road negligently, without using a pedestrian crossing, and in the ensuing accident, the fetus was badly injured.[70] A court in Australia ruled that a

---

[67] If a woman's legal duty toward the viable fetus is recognized, there is concern that claims against the woman would be recognized regarding conduct prior to the pregnancy and during its course, and her legal duty would be much greater, to the extent of restricting her freedom and autonomy. For a discussion of this argument in relation to the abortion dilemmas, *see*, e.g., DOUGLAS WALTON, SLIPPERY SLOPE ARGUMENTS (1992); Eric Lode, *Slippery Slope Arguments and Legal Reasoning*, 87 CAL L. REV. 1469 (1999); G.A. den Hartogh, *The Slippery Slope Argument*, *in* COMPANION TO BIOETHICS 280 (2009) *passim*.

[68] Gad Tedeschi, *On the Problem of Damages for Wrongful Birth*, STUD. L. 269, 462 (1978) (Heb.).

[69] Gordin v. Gordin, 102 Mich. 301 N.Y. 2d 869 (1980) (The court in Michigan for the first time recognized the rationale in a claim of a child who prosecuted his parents for prenatal injury).

[70] Bonte v. Bonte, 136 N.H. 286 (1992). For a discussion of this ruling, *see* Stacie L. Lude, *After* Farley v. Sartin*: The Consequences of Declaring a Nonviable Fetus a Person for the Purpose of Wrongful Death*, 99 W. VA. L. REV. 339, 354 n.91 (1996); Teresa Foley, Dobson v. Dobson*: Tort Liability for Expectant Mothers*, 61 SASK. L. REV. 177 (1998); Christopher J.

fetus born with injuries caused by its mother's negligence that resulted in a traffic accident can sue her if she was negligent in general, not only toward the fetus.[71]

Feminists claim that the right to terminate a pregnancy is one of the fundamental rights of the woman. Assisted reproduction technologies enable every woman to have sexual relations without becoming pregnant and to choose whether she wants to avoid bringing children into the world.[72] But the moment she does decide to bring another person into the world, the woman has both a moral and legal responsibility toward the fetus.

Wiener, *Transgenerational Tort Liability for Epigenetic Disease*, 13 DEPAUL J. HEALTH CARE L. 319, 325 n.38 (2011).

[71] Bowditch. V. McEwan & Ors, [2002] QSA 172. *See also* Russell Smyth, *Trends in the Citation Practice of the Supreme Court of Queensland over the Course of the Twentieth Century*, 28 U. QUEENSLAND L.J. 39, n.123 (2009); Kate Wellington, *Maternal Liability for Prenatal Injury: The Preferable Approach for Australian Law?*, 18 TORT L. REV. 89, 90–95 (2010), http://sites.thomsonreuters.com.au/journals/files/2010/10/j19_v018_TORTLREV_pt02_wellington.pdf; ERIN NELSON, LAW, POLICY AND REPRODUCTIVE AUTONOMY 171 (2013).

[72] *See also* Margalit, *supra* note 22, at 115 ("In the modern era, however, following the revolution in contraceptive methods, an individual easily can prevent an undesirable pregnancy to a large extent by segregating procreation from the conjugal relationship while preserving his basic right to avoid a coerced parenthood").

Epilogue
Equipoise

Who is wise? He who sees the future.[1]

On June 24, 2022, a moral tectonic earthquake shook the US with the announcement of the Supreme Court decision in Dobbs v. Jackson Women's Health Organization overturning the landmark abortion case, Roe v. Wade. The overturning of the last five decades of legal practice regarding abortion came as a shock inside the US and throughout the world.[2] In 1973, in the US, there two decisive rulings were handed down by the Supreme Court regarding abortions: Roe v. Wade and Doe v. Bollton.[3] In these two rulings, for the first time in the history of the US, the legislature recognized a woman's constitutional right to induce the termination of pregnancy, making abortion legal in all 50 states. Every pregnant woman had the basic human autonomy to decide whether or not she wanted to continue the pregnancy. Sixteen years later, in Planned Parenthood v. Danforth, the Supreme Court reinforced this right when it decided that a woman who wanted to terminate a pregnancy did not have to get the consent of her parents, if she was a minor, or of her husband, if she is married.[4] Thus, it is possible to say that in the last 50 years, there has been widespread recognition of a

---

[1] Babylonian Talmud *Tamid* 32a, http://ancientworldonline.blogspot.co.il/2012/01/online-soncino-babylonian-talmud.html. *See also* Stephen D. Solender, *Pursuing Excellence in Jewish Communal Policy, Program, and Professional Practice in Times of Change,* J. JEWISH COMMUNAL SERVICE 35, 41 (1992).

2. Richard Storrow, The Leaked Draft Decision in Dobbs: Context and Content, L. PROFESSOR BLOG NETWORK (May 4, 2022), https://lawprofessors, typepad.com/reproductive-rights/2022/05/index.html [http://perma.cc/4479-TRLW];1.Glenn Cohen et al., What Overturning Roe v. Wade May Mean for Assisted Reproductive Technologies in the U.S. J. Am. Med. ASS'N 15 (July 5, 2022); Reva B. Siegel et al,. Equal Protection in Dobbs and Beyond: How States Protect Life Inside and Outside of the Abortion Context, 43 COLUM, J. GENDER & L. 1 2023.

[3] Roe v. Wade 410 U.S. 113 (1973); Doe v. Bolton 410 U.S. 179 (1973).

[4] Planned Parenthood v. Danforth, 428 U.S. 52 (1976).

woman's basic right to have an abortion. This right was stopped with the enactment of the Dobbs ruling, which stated that "the Constitution does not confer a right to abortion."

Some experts have called the year 2019 a critical year regarding the right to abortion. In the first half of this year alone, almost 60 pieces of legislation prohibiting abortion were enacted in 19 states in the US, decreeing 26 prohibitions on abortion. Since then there have been many prohibitions against abortion in other states. A law enacted in Texas in 2021 (SB8) bans abortions from the sixth week of pregnancy even in the case of rape. In the same year, 12 other states enacted similar laws banning abortions. With the wave of legislation that followed in the wake of Dobbs, the results take us back 50 years.

The present book does not favor this legislation. The legal situation after Roe is all or nothing. Pro-life or pro-choice. This book seeks to strike a balance between the rights of the woman over her body and the rights of the fetus—from the 24th week of pregnancy onward. Until week 24, a woman has full autonomous right over her body to terminate her pregnancy. Pro-choice. From week 24, the fetus has the full right to be born—full moral rights, similar to human rights. There must be a sweeping ban on abortions with the exception of the woman's life being at risk if the pregnancy is continued or the possibility of a lifelong disability and complete dependence and suffering for the fetus. Pro-life. To confirm this thesis, the book examined the different stages of development of the fetus while in the womb, the position of antiquity and of various religions in the matter, and whether the family is able to make objective decisions that take into account potential lives and moral rights. Many tests during pregnancy are intended not only for the benefit of the woman but also and especially for that of the fetus to be born. The book questions the ability of one person, the pregnant woman, to decide for another potential life, that of the fetus, at a developmental stage where it is able to survive outside the womb. The fetus lives inside the woman and is nourished by her, but it is viable and should be given legal rights. This is the essence of the book, which seeks to balance the two rights.

Legislation should be of the kind that the public can comply with. This book advocates this type of balancing legislation.

From the viable stage onward, the fetus has the moral status of a human being.[5] It should be considered an entity with interests that are its own and may be different from those of the woman carrying it. The woman has a legal obligation toward the viable fetus. Therefore, I adopt the individual-biological model of theoreticians who consider the fetus and the woman as two separate individuals.

Ronald Dworkin,[6] like others, maintained that it is not necessary to assign a moral status to the fetus to prohibit abortions. I argue that the discussion cannot be complete without determining the legal and moral status of a viable fetus, and that a dialogue on the matter should discuss the feminist view that women have ultimate rights over their bodies.

---

[5] On this topic, *see* YAEL HASHILONI-DOLEV, THE REPRODUCTIVE REVOLUTION 67 (2013) (Heb.), where she discusses models to help understand the connecting experience between the woman and the fetus: the individual-biological model and the social-contextual model. According to her, the fetus can be considered a human entity in the former model but not in the latter. For a discussion of her research, *see* Hagai Boas et al., *Between Individualism and Social Solidarity in Vaccination Policy,* https://ijhpr.biomedcentral.com/track/pdf/10. 1 186/s 13584-016-0119-y. For the almost mystical bond that exists between the surrogate mother and the fetus, *see* Margaret F. Brinig, *A Maternalistic Approach to Surrogacy: Comment on Richard Epstein's Surrogacy: The Case for Full Contractual Enforcement*, 81 VA. L. REV. 2377, 2383 n.22 (1995), discussed in Yehezkel Margalit, *In Defense of Surrogacy Agreements: A Modern Contract Law Perspective*, 20 WM. & MARY J. WOMAN & L. 423, 435 n.45 (2014).

[6] RONALD DWORKIN, LIFE'S DOMINION: AN ARGUMENT ABOUT ABORTION, EUTHANASIA, AND INDIVIDUAL FREEDOM X (2011), discussed in Elizabeth Harman, *The Moral Status of Early Fetuses and the Ethics of Abortion*, 28(4) PHIL. & PUB. AFF. 310, 313, 322–23 (1999), https://ethicslab.georgetown.edu/phil553/wordpress/wp-content/uploads/2015/01/Harman-Moral-Status-of-Early-Fetus es.pdf; John R. Meyer, *Human Embryonic Stem Cells and Respect for Life*, 26 J. MED. ETHICS 166, 167 n.11 (2000), http://jme.bmj.com/content/26/3/166.short.

Glaucon[7] claimed that the law is an agreement between people not to harm one another, the basis of the agreement being the desire of every person not to be harmed. Plato, in the name of Socrates, argued otherwise. According to him, the agreement is not a social contract between people but rather a political arrangement deriving from the nature of the world. Locke, as we have seen, maintained that in a natural state as well, a person has basic rights: the right to life, freedom, and ownership. The purpose of legislation, according to this perception, is to preserve these rights. Throughout the book, I have advocated that this model be used, and that the legal duty should be placed on the pregnant woman vis-à-vis the viable fetus.

The approach that favors restricting state intervention in the life of the individual as much as possible is conducive to legislation that establishes the status of the viable fetus and its right to life based on the principle of harm.[8] Extending the ability of the state to restrict the right of the woman over her body is justified for paternalistic reasons, too: a person's autonomy is not unlimited, certainly when another potential human life is involved. Justice Blackmun, who wrote the majority opinion, stated in *Roe v. Wade*:[9]

> We need not resolve the difficult question of when life begins. When those trained in the respective disciplines of medicine, philosophy and theology are unable to arrive at any consensus,

---

[7] PLATO, THE POLITEIA vol. II, 358-61 (1979). For a discussion of this dialogue, *see* CHARLES H. KAHN, PLATO AND THE SOCRATIC DIALOGUE: THE PHILOSOPHICAL USE OF A LITERARY FORM (1996).

[8] Note that these are cases where the woman is not in any danger; I agree that the woman's life comes before that of the viable fetus.

[9] *Roe v. Wade*, 410 U.S. 113 (1973) when the US Supreme Court allowed abortions to be performed during the first trimester, limited them during the second trimester, and prohibited them entirely during the third trimester. For a discussion of this landmark verdict, *see e.g.*, Nancy K. Rhoden, *Trimesters and Technology: Revamping* Roe v. Wade, 95 YALE L.J. 639 (1985–86); WHAT ROE V. WADE SHOULD HAVE SAID: THE NATION'S TOP LEGAL EXPERTS REWRITE AMERICA'S MOST CONTROVERSIAL DECISION (Jack M. Balkin ed., 2005); N.E.H. HULL & PETER CHARLES HOFFER, ROE V. WADE: THE ABORTION RIGHTS CONTROVERSY IN AMERICAN HISTORY (2010).

the judiciary, at this point in the development of man's knowledge, is not in a position to speculate as to the answer.[10]

The Court was aware of the difficulty in defining the status of the fetus vis-à-vis that of the woman who was detrimentally affected by legislation that prohibits abortion, therefore it stipulated that formal restrictions were justified during the third trimester of pregnancy only, when the fetus is at the advanced stage of intrauterine life. Lockhart[11] called this system the "principle of the rights of doubtful persons" (PRDF): when a conflict exists between an individual with a moral status, like a pregnant woman, and an individual with an uncertain moral status, the woman prevails.

The approach presented in this book does not dispute the PRDF approach and does not insist on reaching a conclusion or taking a stand in the debate in principle between those who oppose abortions (known as pro-life) and claim that the fetus has a moral status and those in favor of it (known as pro-choice),[12] who claim that the woman has a right to autonomy. I do not take issue with the right of the woman over her body; rather, I maintain that, as with every right, it is not absolute when

---

[10] For a discussion of this often-quoted statement, *see,* for example, John H. Ely, *The Wages of Crying Wolf: A Comment on* Roe v. Wade, 82 YALE L.J. 920, 920 n.9, 925 n.41 (1972–73); Gary B. Gertler, *Brain Birth: A Proposal for Defining When a Fetus Is Entitled to Human Life Status,* 59 S. CAL. L. REV. 1061, 1065 (1986); Jason M. Horst, *The Meaning of Life: The Morning-After Pill, the Question of When Life Begins, and Judicial Review,* 16 TEX. J. WOMEN & L. 205, 206 (2007)

[11] TED LOCKHART, MORAL UNCERTAINTY AND ITS CONSEQUENCES 127–29 (2000). For recent discussions of this book, *see* Maria Lasonen-Aarnio, *Enkrasia or Evidentialism? Learning to Love Mismatch,* PHIL. STUD. 1 (2018), https://link.springer.com/content/pdf/10.1007%2Fs11098-018-1196-2.pdf; Itai Sher, *Comparative Value and the Weight of Reasons,* 35(1) ECON. & PHIL. 103 (2019); RALPH WEDGWOOD, MORAL DISAGREEMENT AND INEXCUSABLE IRRATIONALITY (2019), https://www-bcf.usc.edu/~wedgwood/inexcusable_irrationality.pdf.

[12] For a discussion of this hotly debated issue, *see,* among others, RUTH COLKER, ABORTION AND DIALOGUE: PRO-CHOICE, PRO-LIFE, AND AMERICAN LAW (1992); KATHY RUDY, BEYOND PRO-LIFE AND PRO-CHOICE: MORAL DIVERSITY IN THE ABORTION DEBATE (1997); RANDY ALCORN, PRO-LIFE ANSWERS TO PRO-CHOICE ARGUMENTS (2009).

dealing with a viable fetus, therefore a balance must be achieved between their rights.

* * *

In the legal history of many jurisdictions, there have been attempts to make a distinction in law between the different stages of pregnancy. The difficulties raised in the past in passing legislation regarding the status of the fetus and distinguishing between the different stages of pregnancy should not hinder our efforts.

I like to believe, as did Freud, that a mother will always love her children, but I know that sometimes a mother can also hate them.[13] We have seen that some people believe that voluntary abortions should be prohibited out of hand, and others are of the opinion that they should be allowed at any stage of pregnancy. The present book did not deal with this discourse. Rather, it considered both the woman and the fetus in its intrauterine environment, and sought to achieve a balance of rights and enhanced regulation in the field of voluntary terminations of pregnancy at the viable stage.

I attempted to formulate a model that places a legal and moral obligation on the pregnant woman toward the viable fetus. The act of refusing to receive intrauterine medical treatment for the fetus at the viable stage (not providing informed consent even when minimal risk exists to the woman and a good chance of curing the fetus) can greatly reduce the rights of the fetus. Likewise, not carrying out a C-section

---

[13] Donald W. Winnicott, *Hate in the Counter-Transference*, 30 INT'L J. PSYCHO-ANALYSIS 69 (1949). Winnicott specified 18 reasons for a mother's possible hatred of her infant, including risk to the woman's body during pregnancy and birth and interference in the woman's private life. For a recent discussion of this book, *see* Johan Berg et al, *Countertransference in Swedish Psychotherapists: Testing the Factor Structure of the Therapist Response Questionnaire, Research, in* PSYCHOTHERAPY: PSYCHOPATHOLOGY, PROCESS AND OUTCOME (2019), https://www.researchinpsychotherapy.org/index.php/rpsy/article/view/331/297; MARK O'CONNE, THE PERFORMING ART OF THERAPY: ACTING INSIGHTS AND TECHNIQUES FOR CLINICIANS (2019); PATRICIA HARTE BRATT, MUTUAL GROWTH IN THE PSYCHOTHERAPEUTIC RELATIONSHIP: RECIPROCAL RESILIENCE (2019) *passim*.

when needed to give birth to the fetus because of the absence of informed consent is among the actions that are liable to cause irreversible harm.[14] Expanding the authority of the state to intervene in the woman's rights over her body is justified exactly for this reason, sometimes even on paternalistic grounds. A person's autonomy is not unlimited, and certainly not where another potential human life is concerned.

A viable fetus is a beginning-of-a-person, and even a beginning-of-a-person is entitled to rights similar in essence to those of a human being.[15] This is the central message of this book, which should guide us in meeting the continuing moral, ethical, and legal challenges intrinsic in the issue of balancing the rights of the woman and of the fetus she is carrying.

---

[14] Note that these are cases where there is no risk to the woman.

[15] For a recent landmark verdict supporting my contention, *see, for example,* Family Law, *Alabama Court Recognizes Aborted Fetus as Person with Rights,* FAM. LAW PROF. BLOG 11.03.19, https://lawprofessors.typepad.com/family law/2019/03/alabama-court-recognizes-aborted-fetus-as-person-with-rights.html. *See also* Timothy Williams & Alan Blinder, *Mississippi Bans Abortions If Heartbeat Can Be Heard. Expect a Legal Fight,* N.Y. TIMES, Mar. 21, 2019, https://www.nytimes.com/2019/03/21/us/abortion-laws-states.html; Brie Shea, Legislative Lowlights: *Total Abortion Bans Proposed in Colorado, Indiana, and Texas Last Week,* REWIRE. NEWS, Jan. 22, 2019, https://rewire.news/article/2019/01/22/legislative-lowlights-total-abortion-bans-proposed-in-colorado-indiana-and-texas-last-week/; Debra Cassens Weiss, *There's No Due Process Right to Perform Abortions, Says en Banc 6th Circuit in Funding Case,* ABA J., Mar. 13, 2019, http://www.abajournal.com/news/article/there-is-no-due-process-right-to-perform-abortions-en-banc-6th-circuit-says-in-funding-case.

www.ingramcontent.com/pod-product-compliance
Lightning Source LLC
LaVergne TN
LVHW101504200926
848483LV00001B/221